James R. (James Roberts) Gilmore

Among the Pines

James R. (James Roberts) Gilmore

Among the Pines

ISBN/EAN: 9783744653015

Printed in Europe, USA, Canada, Australia, Japan

Cover: Foto ©ninafisch / pixelio.de

More available books at **www.hansebooks.com**

AMONG THE PINES.

A NEW WORK,

Descriptive of Southern Social Life,

BY THE AUTHOR OF

AMONG THE PINES,

Is now in course of publication in

THE "CONTINENTAL MONTHLY,"

PUBLISHED BY

J. R. GILMORE,

532 Broadway, NEW YORK.

AMONG THE PINES:

OR,

SOUTH IN SECESSION-TIME.

BY

EDMUND KIRKE.

TWENTIETH THOUSAND.

NEW YORK:
J. R. GILMORE, 532 BROADWAY.

CHARLES T. EVANS.
1862.

Entered according to Act of Congress, in the year 1862,
BY J. R. GILMORE,
In the Clerk's Office of the District Court of the United States, for the
Southern District of New York.

M'CREA & MILLER, STEREOTYPERS.   C. A. ALVORD, PRINTER

TO

RICHARD B. KIMBALL,

THE ACCOMPLISHED AUTHOR, THE POLISHED GENTLEMAN,

AND

MY OLD AND EVER-VALUED FRIEND,

THESE SKETCHES ARE DEDICATED

BY THE

AUTHOR.

CONTENTS.

                                                                          PAGE

CHAPTER I.—ON THE ROAD.—Arrival at Georgetown.—The Village Inn.—Nocturnal Adventures.—My African Driver.—His Strange History.—Genuine Negro Songs.—Arrival at Bucksville.. 10

CHAPTER II.—WAYSIDE HOSPITALITY.—A Strange Meeting.—A Well Ordered Plantation.—A Thunder-storm.—A New Guest.—The Hidden Springs of Secession Exposed.—On the Way Again.—Intelligence of the Negro.—Renconter with a Secessionist.. 30

CHAPTER III.—CROSSING THE RUNS.—The Black Declines His Freedom.—His Reasons for so Doing.—A "native" Abolitionist.—Swimming the Run.—Black Spirits and White.—Shelter.. 55

CHAPTER IV.—POOR WHITES.—The Mills House.—South Carolina Clay-Eaters.—Political Discussion.—President Lincoln a Negro.—"Three in a Bed and one in the Middle."—$250 reward.—A Secret League.. 69

CHAPTER V.—ON THE PLANTATION.—The Planter's Dwelling.—His House-Keeper.—The Process of Turpentine Making.—Loss to Carolina by Secession.—The Dying Boy.—The Story of Jim.—A Northern Man with Southern Principles.—Sam Murdered.—Pursuit of the Overseer.. 94

CHAPTER VI.—THE PLANTER'S FAMILY.—The old Nurse.—Her Story.—A White Slave-Woman's Opinion of Slavery.—The Stables.—The Negro-Quarters.—Sunday Exercises.—The Taking of Moye.. 127

CHAPTER VII.—PLANTATION DISCIPLINE.—The "Ole Cabin."—The Mode of Negro Punishment.—The "Thumb-Screw."—A Ministering Angel.—A Negro Trial.—A Rebellion.—A Turpentine Dealer.—A Boston Dray on its Travels............. 150

CHAPTER VIII.—THE NEGRO HUNTER.—Young Democrats.—Political Discussion.—Startling Statistics.—A Freed Negro... 169

CHAPTER IX.—THE COUNTRY CHURCH.—Its Description.—
The "Corn-Cracker."—The News.—Strange Disclosure..... 180
CHAPTER X.—THE NEGRO FUNERAL.—The Burial Ground.—
A Negro Sermon.—The Appearance of Juley.—The Colonel's
Heartlessness.—The Octoroon's Explanation of it.—The Escape of Moye... 196
CHAPTER XI.—THE PURSUIT.—The Start.—"Carolina Race-Horses."—A Race.—We Lose the Trail. — A Tornado.—A Narrow Escape.—..................................... 207
CHAPTER XII.—THE YANKEE SCHOOLMISTRESS. — Our New Apparel.—"Kissing Goes by Favor."—Schools at the South... 222
CHAPTER XIII.—THE RAILWAY STATION.—The Village.—A Drunken Yankee.—A Narrow Escape. — Andy Jones.—A Light-Wood Fire.—The Colonel's Departure................ 227
CHAPTER XIV.—THE BARBACUE.—The Camp-Ground.—The Stump-Speaker.—A Stump Speech.—Almost a Fight.—The Manner of Roasting the Ox............................. 239
CHAPTER XV.—THE RETURN.—Arrival at the Plantation.—Disappearance of Juley and her child.—The Old Preacher's Story.—Scene Between the Master and the Slave.......... 253
CHAPTER XVI. — "ONE MORE UNFORTUNATE."—Attempted Whipping of Jim. — Appearance of the "Corn-Cracker." — "Drowned.—Drowned.".............................. 260
CHAPTER XVII.—THE SMALL PLANTER.—His House.—His Wife. — His Negroes. — A Juvenile Darky. — Lazarus in "Ab'ram's Buzzum."—White and Black Labor Compared.—The Mysteries of "Rosum" manufacture.................. 277
CHAPTER XVIII.—THE BURIAL OF JULE.—"He Tempers the Wind to the Shorn Lamb."—The Funeral.................. 295
CHAPTER XIX. — HOMEWARD BOUND. — Colonel A———Again.—Parting with Scipio.—Why this Book was Written. 298
CHAPTER XX.—CONCLUSION.—The Author's Explanations.—Last News from Moye and Scipio.—Affecting Letter from Andy Jones.—The End........................... 303

AMONG THE PINES.

CHAPTER I.

ON THE ROAD.

SOME winters ago I passed several weeks at Tallahassee, Florida, and while there made the acquaintance of Colonel J——, a South Carolina planter. Accident, some little time later, threw us together again at Charleston, when I was gratified to learn that he would be my *compagnon du voyage* as far north as New York.

He was accompanied by his body-servant, "Jim," a fine specimen of the genus darky, about thirty years of age, and born and reared in his master's family. As far as possible we made the journey by day, stopping at some convenient resting-place by night; on which occasions the Colonel, Jim, and myself would occupy the same or adjoining apartments, "we white folks" sleeping on four posts, while the more democratic negro spread his blanket on the floor. Thrown together thus intimately, it was but natural that we should learn much of each other.

The "Colonel" was a highly cultivated and intelligent gentleman, and during this journey a friendship sprung up between us—afterward kept alive by a regular correspondence—which led him, with his wife and daughter, and the man Jim, to my house on his next visit at the North, one year later. I then promised—if I should ever again travel in South Carolina—to visit him on his plantation in the extreme north-eastern part of the state.

In December last, about the time of the passage of the ordinance of secession, I had occasion to visit Charleston, and, previous to setting out, dispatched a letter to the Colonel with the information that I was ready to be led of him "into the wilderness." On arriving at the head-quarters of secession, I found a missive awaiting me, in which my friend cordially renewed his previous tender of hospitality, gave me particular directions how to proceed, and stated that his "man Jim" would meet me with a carriage at Georgetown, and convey me thence, seventy miles, to "the plantation."

Having performed the business which led me to Charleston, I set out for the rendezvous five days before the date fixed for the meeting, intending to occupy the intervening time in an exploration of the ancient town and its surroundings.

The little steamer Nina (a cross between a full-grown nautilus and a half-grown tub), which a few weeks later was enrolled as the first man-of-war of the Confederate navy, then performed the carrying trade between the two principal cities of South Carolina. On her, together with sundry boxes and bales, and certain human merchandise, I embarked at Charleston, and on a delicious morning, late in December, landed at Georgetown.

As the embryo war-steamer rounded up to the long, low, rickety dock, lumbered breast-high with cotton, turpentine, and rosin, not a white face was to be seen. A few half-clad, shiftless-looking negroes, lounging idly about, were the only portion of the population in waiting to witness our landing.

"Are all the people dead?" I inquired of one of them, thinking it strange that an event so important as the arrival of the Charleston packet should excite no greater interest in so quiet a town. "Not dead, massa," replied the black, with a knowing chuckle, "but dey'm gettin' ready for a fun'ral." "What funeral?" I asked. "Why, dey'm gwine to shoot all de boblition darkies at de Norf, and hab a brack burying; he! he!" and the sable gentleman expanded the opening in his countenance to an enormous extent, doubtless at the brilliancy of his wit.

I asked him to take my portmanteau, and conduct me to the best hotel. He readily assented, "Yas, yas, massa, I show you whar de *big-bugs* stop;" but at once turning to another darky standing near, he accosted him with, "Here, Jim, you lazy nigga, tote de gemman's tings."

"Why don't you take them yourself?" I asked; "you will then get all the pay." "No, no, massa; dat nigga and me in partenship; he do de work, and I keeps de change," was the grinning reply, and it admirably illustrates a peculiarity I have observed to be universal with the negro. When left to his own direction, he invariably "goes into partenship" with some one poorer than himself, and no matter how trivial the task, shirks all the labor he can.

The silent darky and my portmanteau in the van, and the garrulous old negro guarding my flank, I wended my way through the principal street to the hotel. On the route I resumed the conversation:

"So, uncle, you say the people here are getting ready for a black burying?"

"Yas, massa, gwine to bury all dem mis'able free niggas at de Norf."

"Why? What will you do that for?"

"Why for, massa! you ax why for!" he exclaimed in surprise.

"I don't know," I rejoined; "I'm a stranger here."

"Well, you see, massa, dem boblition niggas up dar hab gone and 'lected a ole darky, dey call Uncle Abe; and Old Abe he'se gwine to come down Souf, and cut de decent niggas' troats. He'll hab a good time—*he will!* My young massa's captin ob de sogers, and he'll cotch de ole coon, and string him up so high de crows

ON THE ROAD.

won't scent him; yas, he will;" and again the old darky's face opened till it looked like the entrance to the Mammoth Cave. He, evidently, had read the Southern papers.

Depositing my luggage at the hotel, which I found on a side street—a dilapidated, unpainted wooden building, with a female landlord—I started out to explore the town, till the hour for dinner. Retracing my steps in the direction of the steamboat landing, I found the streets nearly deserted, although it was the hour when the business of the day is usually transacted. Soon I discovered the cause. The militia of the place were out on parade. Preceded by a colored band, playing national airs—in doleful keeping with the occasion—and followed by a motley collection of negroes of all sexes and ages, the company was entering the principal thoroughfare. As it passed me, I could judge of the prowess of the redoubtable captain, who, according to Pompey, will hang the President "so high de crows won't scent him." He was a harmless-looking young man, with long, spindle legs, admirably adapted to running. Though not formidable in other respects, there *was* a certain martial air about an enormous sabre which hung at his side, and occasionally got entangled in his nether integuments, and a fiery, warlike look to the heavy tuft of reddish hair which sprouted in bristling defiance from his upper lip.

The company numbered about seventy, some with uniforms and some without, and bearing all sorts of arms, from the old flint-lock musket to the modern revolving rifle. They were, however, sturdy fellows, and looked as if they might do service at "the imminent deadly breach." Their full ranks, taken from a population of less than five hundred whites, told unmistakably the intense war feeling of the community.

Georgetown is one of the oldest towns in South Carolina, and it has a decidedly *finished* appearance. Not a single building, I was informed, had been erected there in five years. Turpentine is one of the chief productions of the district; yet the cost of white lead and chrome yellow has made paint a scarce commodity, and the houses, consequently, all wear a dingy, decayed look. Though situated on a magnificent bay, a little below the confluence of three noble rivers, which drain a country of surpassing richness, and though the centre of the finest rice-growing district in the world, the town is dead. Every thing about it wears an air of dilapidation. The few white men you meet in its streets, or see lounging lazily around its stores and warehouses, appear to lack all purpose and energy. Long contact with the negro seems to have given them his shiftless, aimless character.

The ordinance of secession passed the legislature shortly prior to my arrival, and, as might be expected, the political situation was the all-engrossing topic of thought and conversation. In the estimation of the whites a glorious future was about to open on the little state. Whether she stood alone, or supported by the other slave states, she would assume a high rank among the nations of the earth; her cotton and rice would draw trade and wealth from every land, and when she spoke, creation would tremble. Such overweening state pride in *such* a people—shiftless, indolent, and enervated as they are—strikes a stranger as in the last degree ludicrous; but when they tell you, in the presence of the black, whose strong brawny arm and sinewy frame show that in him lies the real strength of the state, that this great empire is to be built on the shoulders of the slave, your smile of incredulity gives way to an expression of pity, and you are tempted to ask if those sinewy machines may not THINK, and some day rise, and topple down the mighty fabric which is to be reared on their backs!

Among the "peculiar institutions" of the South are its inns. I do not refer to the pinchbeck, imitation St. Nicholas establishments, which flourish in the larger cities, but to those home-made affairs, noted for hog and hominy, corn-cake and waffles, which crop out here and there in the smaller towns, the natural growth of Southern life and institutions. A model of this class is the one at Georgetown. Hog, hominy, and corn-cake for breakfast; waffles, hog, and hominy for dinner; and hog, hominy, and corn-cake for supper—and such corn-cake, baked in the ashes of the hearth, a plentiful supply of the grayish condiment still clinging to it!—is its never-varying bill of fare. I endured this fare for a day, *how*, has ever since been a mystery to me, but when night came my experiences were indescribable. Retiring early, to get the rest needed to fit me for a long ride on the morrow, I soon realized that "there is no rest for the wicked," none, at least, for sinners at the South. Scarcely had my head touched the pillow when I was besieged by an army of red-coated secessionists, who set upon me without mercy. I withstood the assault manfully, till "bleeding at every pore," and then slowly and sorrowfully beat a retreat. Ten thousand to one is greater odds than the gallant Anderson encountered at Sumter. Yet I determined not to fully abandon the field. Placing three chairs in a row, I mounted upon them, and in that seemingly impregnable position hurled defiance at the enemy, in the words of Scott (slightly altered to suit the occasion):

"Come one, come all, these chairs shall fly
From their firm base as soon as I."

My exultation, however, was of short duration. The persistent foe, scaling my intrenchments, soon returned to the assault with redoubled vigor, and in utter despair I finally fled. Groping my way through the hall, and out of the street-door, I departed. The Sable Brother—alias the Son of Ham—alias the Image of GOD carved in Ebony—alias the Oppressed Type—alias the Contraband—alias the Irrepressible Nigger—alias the Chattel—alias the Darky—alias the Cullud Pusson—had informed me that I should find the Big Bugs at that hotel. I had found them.

Staying longer in such a place was out of the question, and I determined to make my way to the up-country without longer waiting for Jim. With the first streak of day I sallied out to find the means of locomotion.

The ancient town boasts no public conveyance, except a one-horse gig that carries the mail in tri-weekly trips to Charleston. That vehicle, originally used by some New England doctor, in the early part of the past century, had but one seat, and besides, was not going the way I intended to take, so I was forced to seek a conveyance at a livery-stable. At the only livery establishment in the place, kept by a "cullud pusson," who, though a slave, owns a stud of horses that might, among a people more *movingly* inclined, yield a respectable income, I found what I wanted—a light Newark buggy, and a spanking gray. Provided with these, and a darky driver, who was to accompany me to my destination, and return alone, I started. A trip of seventy miles is something of an undertaking in that region, and quite a crowd gathered around to witness our departure, not a soul of whom, I will wager, will ever hear the rumble of a stage-coach, or the whistle of a steam-car, in those sandy, deserted streets.

We soon left the village, and struck a broad avenue, lined on either side by fine old trees, and extending in an air-line for several miles. The road is skirted by broad rice-fields, and these are dotted here and there by large antiquated houses, and little collections of negro huts.

It was Christmas week; no hands were busy in the fields, and every thing wore the aspect of Sunday. We had ridden a few miles when suddenly the road sunk into a deep, broad stream, called, as the driver told me, the Black River. No appliance for crossing being at hand, or in sight, I was about concluding that some modern Moses accommodated travellers by passing them over its bed dry-shod, when a flat-boat shot out from the jungle on the opposite bank, and pulled toward us. It was built of two-inch plank, and manned by two infirm darkies, with frosted wool, who seemed to need all their strength to sit upright. In that leaky craft, kept afloat by incessant baling, we succeeded, at the end of an hour, in crossing the river. And this, be it understood, is travelling in one of the richest districts of South Carolina!

We soon left the region of the rice-fields, and plunged into dense forests of the long-leafed pine, where for miles not a house, or any other evidence of human occupation, is to be seen. Nothing could well be more dreary than a ride through such a region, and to while away the tedium of the journey I opened a conversation with the driver, who up to that time had maintained a respectful silence.

He was a genuine native African, and a most original and interesting specimen of his race. His thin, close-cut lips, straight nose and European features contrasted strangely with a skin of ebon blackness, and the quiet, simple dignity of his manner betokened superior intelligence. His story was a strange one. When a boy, he was with his mother, kidnapped by a hostile tribe, and sold to the traders at Cape Lopez, on the western coast of Africa. There, in the slave-pen, the mother died, and he, a child of seven years, was sent in the slave-ship to Cuba. At Havana, when sixteen, he attracted the notice of a gentleman residing in Charleston, who bought him and took him to "the States." He lived as house-servant in the family of this gentleman till 1855, when his master died, leaving him a legacy to a daughter. This lady, a kind, indulgent mistress, had since allowed him to "hire his time," and he then carried on an "independent business," as porter, and doer of all work around the wharves and streets of Georgetown. He thus gained a comfortable living, besides paying to his mistress one hundred and fifty dollars yearly for the privilege of earning his own support. In every way he was a remarkable negro, and my three days' acquaintance with him banished from my mind all doubt as to the capacity of the black for freedom, and all question as to the disposition of the slave to strike off his chains when the favorable moment arrives. From him I learned that the blacks, though pretending ignorance, are fully acquainted with the questions at issue in the pending contest. He expressed the opinion, that war would come in consequence of the stand South Carolina had taken; and when I said to him: "But if it comes you will be no better off. It will end in a compromise, and leave you where you are." He answered:

"No, massa, 't wont do dat. De Souf will fight hard, and de Norf will get de blood up, and come down har, and do 'way wid de *cause* ob all de trubble—and dat am de nigga."

"But," I said, "perhaps the South will drive the North back; as you say, they will fight hard."

"Dat dey will, massa, dey'm de fightin' sort, but dey can't whip de Norf, 'cause you see dey'll fight wid only one hand. When dey fight de Norf wid de right hand, dey'll hev to hold de nigga wid de leff."

"But," I replied, "the blacks wont rise; most of you have kind masters and fare well."

"Dat's true, massa, but dat an't freedom, and de black lub freedom as much as de white. De same blessed LORD made dem both, and HE made dem all 'like, 'cep de skin. De blacks hab strong hands, and when de day come you'll see dey hab heads, too!"

Much other conversation, showing him possessed of a high degree of intelligence, passed between us. In answer to my question if he had a family, he said: "No, sar. My blood shall neber be slaves! Ole massa flog me and threaten to kill me 'cause I wouldn't take to de wimmin; but I tole him to kill, dat 't would be more his loss dan mine."

I asked if the negroes generally felt as he did, and he told me that many did; that nearly all would fight for their freedom if they had the opportunity, though some preferred slavery because they were sure of being cared for when old and infirm, not considering that if their labor, while they were strong, made their masters rich, the same labor would afford *them* provision against old age. He told me that there are in the *district* of Georgetown twenty thousand blacks, and not more than two thousand whites, and "Suppose," he added, " dat one-quarter ob dese niggas rise—de rest keep still—whar den would de white folks be?"

"Of course," I replied, "they would be taken at a disadvantage; but it would not be long before aid came from Charleston, and you would be overpowered."

"No, massa, de chivarly, as you call dem, would be 'way in Virginny, and 'fore dey hard of it Massa Seward would hab troops 'nough in Georgetown to chaw up de hull state in less dan no time."

"But you have no leaders," I said, "no one to direct the movement. Your race is not a match for the white in generalship, and without generals, whatever your numbers, you would fare hardly."

To this he replied, an elevated enthusiasm lighting up his face, "De LORD, massa, made generals ob Gideon and David, and de brack man know as much 'bout war as dey did; p'raps," he added, with a quiet humor, " de brack aint equal to de white. I knows most ob de great men, like Washington and John and James and Paul, and dem ole fellers war white, but dar war Two Sand (Tousaint L'Overture), de Brack Douglass, and de Nigga Demus (Nicodemus), dey war brack."

The argument was unanswerable, and I said nothing. If the day which sees the rising of the Southern blacks comes to this generation, that negro will be among the leaders. He sang to me several of the songs current among the negroes of the district, and though of little poetic value, they interested me, as indicating the feelings of the slaves. The blacks are a musical race, and the readiness with which many of them improvise words and melody is wonderful; but I had met none who possessed the readiness of my new acquaintance. Several of the tunes he repeated several times, and each time with a new accompaniment of words. I will try to render the sentiment of a few of these songs into as good negro dialect as I am master of, but I cannot hope to repeat the precise words, or to convey the indescribable humor and pathos which my darky friend threw into them, and which made our long, solitary ride through those dreary pine-barrens pass rapidly and pleasantly away. The first referred to an old darky who was transplanted from the cotton-fields of "ole Virginny" to the rice-swamps of Carolina, and who did not like the change, but found consolation in the fact that rice is not grown on "the other side of Jordan."

"Come listen, all you darkies, come listen to my song,
It am about ole Massa, who use me bery wrong:
In de cole, frosty mornin', it an't so bery nice,
Wid de water to de middle to hoe among de rice;
  When I neber hab forgotten
  How I used to hoe de cotton,
  How I used to hoe de cotton,
    On de ole Virginny shore;

But I'll neber hoe de cotton,
Oh! neber hoe de cotton
    Any more.

"If I feel de drefful hunger, he tink it am a vice,
And he gib me for my dinner a little broken rice,
A little broken rice and a bery little fat—
And he grumble like de debil if I eat too much of dat;
    When I neber hab forgotten, etc.

"He tore me from my DINAH; I tought my heart would burst-
He made me lub anoder when my lub was wid de first,
He sole my picanninnies becase he got dar price,
And shut me in de marsh-field to hoe among de rice;
    When I neber had forgotten, etc.

"And all de day I hoe dar, in all de heat and rain,
And as I hoe away dar, my heart go back again,
·Back to de little cabin dat stood among de corn,
And to de ole plantation where she and I war born!
    Oh! I wish I had forgotten, etc.

"Den DINAH am beside me, de chil'ren on my knee,
And dough I am a slave dar, it 'pears to me I'm free,
Till I wake up from my dreaming, and wife and chil'ren gone,
I hoe away and weep dar, and weep dar all alone!
    Oh! I wish I had forgotten, etc.

'But soon a day am comin, a day I long to see,
When dis darky in de cole ground, foreber will be free,
When wife and chil'ren wid me, I'll sing in Paradise,
How HE, de blessed JESUS, hab bought me wid a price.
    How de LORD hab not forgotten
    How well I hoed de cotton,
    How well I hoed de cotton
    On de ole Virginny shore;

Dar I'll neber hoe de cotton,
Oh! neber hoe de cotton
Any more."

The politics of the following are not exactly those of the rulers at Washington, but we all may come to this complexion at last :

"Hark! darkies, hark! it am de drum
Dat calls ole Massa 'way from hum,
Wid powder-pouch and loaded gun,
To drive ole ABE from Washington;
Oh! Massa's gwine to Washington.
So clar de way to Washington—
Oh! wont dis darky hab sum fun
When Massa's gwine to Washington!

"Dis darky know what Massa do;
He take him long to brack him shoe,
To brack him shoe and tote him gun,
When he am 'way to Washington.
Oh! Massa's gwine to Washington,
So clar de way to Washington,
Oh! long afore de mornin' sun
Ole Massa's gwine to Washington!

"Ole Massa say ole ABE will eat
De niggas all excep' de feet—
De feet, may be, will cut and run,
When Massa gets to Washington,
When Massa gets to Washington;
So clar de way to Washington—
Oh! wont dis darky cut and run
When Massa gets to Washington!

"Dis nigga know ole ABE will save
His brudder man, de darky slave,
And dat he'll let him cut and run
When Massa gets to Washington,
  When Massa gets to Washington;
  So clar de way to Washington,
  Ole ABE will let the darkies run
  When Massa gets to Washington."

The next is in a similar vein:

"A storm am brewin' in de Souf,
A storm am brewin' now,
Oh! hearken den and shut your mouf,
And I will tell you how:
And I will tell you how, ole boy,
  De storm of fire will pour,
And make de darkies dance for joy,
  As dey neber danced afore:
So shut your mouf as close as deafh,
And all you niggas hole your breafh,
And I will tell you how.

"De darkies at de Norf am ris,
  And dey am comin' down—
Am comin' down, I know dey is,
  To do de white folks brown!
Dey'll turn ole Massa out to grass,
  And set de niggas free,
And when dat day am come to pass
  We'll all be dar to see!
So shut your mouf as close as death,
And all you niggas hole your breafh,
And do de white folks brown!

"Den all de week will be as gay
   As am de Chris'mas time;
We'll dance all night and all de day,
   And make de banjo chime—
And make de banjo chime, I tink,
   And pass de time away,
Wid 'nuf to eat and 'nuf to drink,
   And not a bit to pay!
So shut your mouf as close as deafh,
   And all you niggas hole your breaf,
   And make de banjo chime.

"Oh! make de banjo chime, you nigs,
   And sound de tamborin,
And shuffle now de merry jigs,
   For Massa's 'gwine in'—
For Massa's 'gwine in,' I know,
   And won't he hab de shakes,
When Yankee darkies show him how
   Dey cotch de rattle-snakes!*
So shut your mouf as close as deafh,
   And all you niggas hole your breaf,
   For Massa's 'gwine in'—
For Massa's 'gwine in,' I know,
   And won't he hab de shakes
When Yankee darkies show him how
   Dey cotch de rattle-snakes!"

    The reader must not conclude that my darky acquaintance is an average specimen of his class. Far from it. Such instances of intelligence are very rare, and are

---

* The emblem of South Carolina.

never found except in the cities. There, constant intercourse with the white renders the black shrewd and intelligent, but on the plantations, the case is different. And besides, my musical friend, as I have said, is a native African. Fifteen years of observation have convinced me that the imported negro, after being brought in contact with the white, is far more intelligent than the ordinary Southern-born black. Slavery cramps the intellect and dwarfs the nature of a man, and where the dwarfing process has gone on, in father and son, for two centuries, it must surely be the case—as surely as that the qualities of the parent are transmitted to the child—that the later generations are below the first. This deterioration in the better nature of the slave is the saddest result of slavery. His moral and intellectual degradation, which is essential to its very existence, constitutes the true argument against it. It feeds the body but starves the soul. It blinds the reason, and shuts the mind to truth. It degrades and brutalizes the whole being, and does it purposely. In that lies its strength, and in that, too, lurks the weakness which will one day topple it down with a crash that will shake the Continent. Let us hope the direful upheaving, which is now felt throughout the Union, is the earthquake that will bury it forever.

The sun was wheeling below the trees which skirted the western horizon, when we halted in the main road, abreast of one of those by-paths, which every traveller at the South recognizes as leading to a planter's house. Turning our horse's head, we pursued this path for a short distance, when emerging from the pine-forest, over whose sandy barrens we had ridden all the day, a broad plantation lay spread out before us. On one side was a row of perhaps forty small but neat cabins; and on the other, at the distance of about a third of a mile, a huge building, which, from the piles of timber near it, I saw was a lumber-mill. Before us was a smooth causeway, extending on for a quarter of a mile, and shaded by large live-oaks and pines, whose moss fell in graceful drapery from the gnarled branches. This led to the mansion of the proprietor, a large, antique structure, exhibiting the dingy appearance which all houses near the lowlands of the South derive from the climate, but with a generous, hospitable air about its wide doors and bulky windows, that seemed to invite the traveller to the rest and shelter within. I had stopped my horse, and was absorbed in contemplation of a scene as beautiful as it was new to me, when an old negro approached, and touching his hat, said: "Massa send his complimens to de gemman, and happy to hab him pass de night at Bucksville."

"Bucks*ville!*" I exclaimed, "and where is the village?"

"Dis am it, massa; and it am eight mile and a hard road to de 'Boro" (meaning Conwayboro, a one-horse village at which I had designed to spend the night). "Will de gemman please ride up to de piazza?" continued the old negro.

"Yes, uncle, and thank you," and in a moment I had received the cordial welcome of the host, an elderly gentleman, whose easy and polished manners reminded me of the times of our grandfathers in glorious New England. A few minutes put me on a footing of friendly familiarity with him and his family, and I soon found myself in a circle of daughters and grandchildren, and as much at home as if I had been a long-expected guest.

CHAPTER II.

WAYSIDE HOSPITALITY.

YEARS ago—how many it would not interest the reader to know, and might embarrass me to mention—accompanied by a young woman—a blue-eyed, golden-haired daughter of New-England—I set out on a long journey; a journey so long that it will not end till one or the other of us has laid off forever the habiliments of travel.

One of the first stations on our route was—Paris. While there, strolling out one morning alone, accident directed my steps to the *Arc d'Etoile*, that magnificent memorial of the greatness of a great man. Ascending its gloomy staircase to the roof, I seated myself, to enjoy the fine view it affords of the city and its environs.

I was shortly joined by a lady and gentleman, whose appearance indicated that they were Americans. Some casual remark led us into a conversation, and soon, to our mutual surprise and gratification, we learned that the lady was a dear and long-time friend of my travelling-companion. The acquaintance thus begun, has since grown into a close and abiding friendship.

The reader, with this preamble, can readily imagine my pleasure on learning, as we were seated after our evening meal, around that pleasant fireside in far-off

Carolina, that my Paris acquaintance was a favorite niece, or, as he warmly expressed it, "almost a daughter" of my host. This discovery dispelled any lingering feeling of "strangeness" that had not vanished with the first cordial greeting of my new-found friends, and made me perfectly "at home."

The evening wore rapidly away in a free interchange of "news," opinions, and "small-talk," and I soon gathered somewhat of the history of my host. He was born at the North, and his career affords a striking illustration of the marvellous enterprise of our Northern character. A native of the State of Maine, he emigrated thence when a young man, and settled down, amid the pine-forest in that sequestered part of Cottondom. Erecting a small saw-mill, and a log shanty to shelter himself and a few "hired" negroes, he attacked, with his own hands, the mighty pines, whose brothers still tower in gloomy magnificence around his dwelling.

From such beginnings he had risen to be one of the wealthiest land and slave owners of his district, with vessels trading to nearly every quarter of the globe, to the Northern and Eastern ports, Cadiz, the West Indies, South America, and if I remember aright, California. It seemed to me a marvel that this man, alone, and unaided by the usual appliances of commerce, had created a business, rivalling in extent the transactions of many a princely merchant of New York and Boston.

His "family" of slaves numbered about three hundred, and a more healthy, and to all appearance, happy set of laboring people, I had never seen. Well fed, comfortably and almost neatly clad, with tidy and well-ordered homes, exempt from labor in childhood and advanced age, and cared for in sickness by a kind and considerate mistress, who is the physician and good Samaritan of the village, they seemed to share as much physical enjoyment as ordinarily falls to the lot of the "hewer of wood and drawer of water." Looking at them, I began to question if Slavery is, in reality, the damnable thing that some untravelled philanthropists have pictured it. If —and in that "*if*" my good Abolition friend, is the only unanswerable argument against the institution—if they were taught, if they knew their nature and their destiny, the slaves of such an owner might unprofitably exchange situations with many a white man, who, with nothing in the present or the future, is desperately struggling for a miserable hand-to-mouth existence in our Northern cities. I say "of such an owner," for in the Southern Arcadia such masters are "few and far between"—rather fewer and farther between than "spots upon the sun."

But they are *not* taught. Public sentiment, as well as State law, prevents the enlightened master, who would fit the slave by knowledge for greater usefulness, from letting a ray of light in upon his darkened mind. The black knows his task, his name, and his dinner-hour. He knows there is a something within him—he does not understand precisely what—that the white man calls his soul, which he is told will not rest in the ground when his body is laid away in the grave, but will—if he is a "good nigger," obeys his master, and does the task allotted him—travel off to some unknown region, and sing hallelujahs to the LORD, forever. He rather sensibly imagines that such everlasting singing may in time produce hoarseness, so he prepares his vocal organs for the long concert by a vigorous discipline while here, and at the same time cultivates instrumental music, having a dim idea that the LORD has an ear for melody, and will let him, when he is tired of singing, vary the exercise " wid de banjo and de bones." This is all he knows; and his owner, however well-disposed he may be, cannot teach him more. Noble, Christian masters whom I have met—have told me that they did not *dare* instruct their slaves. Some of their negroes were born in their houses, nursed in their families, and have grown up the playmates of their children, and yet they are forced to see them live and die like the brutes. One need not be accused of fanatical abolitionism if he deems such a system a *little* in conflict with the spirit of the nineteenth century!

The sun had scarcely turned his back upon the world, when a few drops of rain, sounding on the piazza-roof over our heads, announced a coming storm. Soon it burst upon us in magnificent fury—a real, old-fashioned thunderstorm, such as I used to lie awake and listen to when a boy, wondering all the while if the angels were keeping a Fourth of July in heaven. In the midst of it, when the earth and the sky appeared to have met in true Waterloo fashion, and the dark branches of the pines seemed writhing and tossing in a sea of flame, a loud knock came at the hall-door (bells are not the fashion in Dixie), and a servant soon ushered into the room a middle-aged, unassuming gentleman, whom my host received with a respect and cordiality which indicated that he was no ordinary guest. There was in his appearance and manner that indefinable something which denotes the man of mark; but my curiosity was soon gratified by an introduction. It was "Colonel" A——. This title, I afterward learned, was merely honorary: and I may as well remark here, that nearly every one at the South who has risen to the ownership of a negro, is eithe a captain, a major, or a colonel, or, as my ebony driver expressed it: "Dey 'm all captins and mates, wid none to row de boat but de darkies." On hearing the name, I recognized it as that of one of the oldest and most aristocratic South Carolina families, and the new guest as a near relative to the gentleman who married the beautiful and ill-fated Theodosia Burr.

In answer to an inquiry of my host, the new-comer explained that he had left Colonel J——'s (the planta tion toward which I was journeying), shortly before noon, and being overtaken by the storm after leaving Conwayboro, had, at the solicitation of his "boys" (a familiar term for slaves), who were afraid to proceed, called to ask shelter for the night.

Shortly after his entrance, the lady members of the family retired; and then the "Colonel," the "Captain," and myself, drawing our chairs near the fire, and each lighting a fragrant Havana, placed on the table by our host, fell into a long conversation, of which the following was a part:

"It must have been urgent business, Colonel, that took you so far into the woods at this season," remarked our host.

"These are urgent times, Captain B——," replied the guest. "All who have any thing at stake, should be *doing.*"

"These *are* unhappy times, truly," said my friend; "has any thing new occurred?"

"Nothing of moment, sir; but we are satisfied Buchanan is playing us false, and are preparing for the worst."

"I should be sorry to know that a President of the United States had resorted to underhand measures! Has he really given you pledges?"

"He promised to preserve the *statu quo* in Charleston harbor, and we have direct information that he intends to send out reinforcements," rejoined Colonel A——.

"Can that be true? You know, Colonel, I never admired your friend, Mr. Buchanan, but I cannot see how, if he does his duty, he can avoid enforcing the laws in Charleston, as well as in the other cities of the Union."

"The 'Union,' sir, does not exist. Buchanan has now no more right to quarter a soldier in South Carolina than I have to march an armed force on to Boston Common.

If he persists in keeping troops near Charleston, we shall dislodge them."

"But that would make war! and war, Colonel," replied our host, "would be a terrible thing. Do you realize what it would bring upon us? And what could our little State do in a conflict with nearly thirty millions?"

"We should not fight with thirty millions. The other Cotton States are with us, and the leaders in the Border States are pledged to Secession. They will wheel into line when we give the word. But the North will not fight. The Democratic party sympathizes with us, and some of its influential leaders are pledged to our side. They will sow division there, and paralyze the Free States; besides, the trading and manufacturing classes will never consent to a war that will work their ruin. With the Yankees, sir, the dollar is almighty."

"That may be true," replied our host; "but I think if we go too far, they will fight. What think you, Mr. K——?" he continued, appealing to me, and adding: "This gentleman, Colonel, is very recently from the North."

Up to that moment, I had avoided taking part in the conversation. Enough had been said to satisfy me that while my host was a staunch Unionist,* his visitor was

---

* I very much regret to learn, that since my meeting with this most excellent gentleman, being obnoxious to the Secession leaders for his well-known Union sentiments, he has been very onerously assessed by them for contributions for carrying on the war. The sum he has been forced to pay, is stated as high as forty thousand dollars, but that may be, and I trust is, an exaggeration. In ad-

not only a rank Secessionist, but one of the leaders of the movement, and even then preparing for desperate measures. Discretion, therefore, counselled silence. To this direct appeal, however, I was forced to reply, and answered: "I think, sir, the North does not yet realize that the South is in earnest. When it wakes up to that fact, its course will be decisive."

"Will the Yankees *fight*, sir?" rather impatiently and imperiously asked the Colonel, who evidently thought I intended to avoid a direct answer to the question.

Rather nettled by his manner, I quickly responded: "Undoubtedly they will, sir. They have fought before, and it would not be wise to count them cowards."

A true gentleman, he at once saw that his manner had given offence, and instantly moderating his tone, rather apologetically replied: "Not cowards, sir, but too much absorbed in the 'occupations of peace,' to go to war for an idea."

"But what you call an 'idea,'" said our host, "*they* may think a great fact on which their existence depends. *I* can see that we will lose vastly by even a peaceful separation. Tell me, Colonel, what we will gain?"

"Gain!" warmly responded the guest. "Every thing! Security, freedom, room for the development of our in-

dition—and this fact is within my own knowledge—five of his vessels have been seized in the Northern ports by our Government. This exposure of true Union men to a double fire, is one of the most unhappy circumstances attendant upon this most unhappy war.

stitutions, and such progress in wealth as the world has never seen."

"All that is very fine," rejoined the "Captain," "but where there is wealth, there must be work; and who will do the work in your new Empire—I do not mean the agricultural labor; you will depend for that, of course, on the blacks—but who will run your manufactories and do your mechanical labor? The Southern gentleman would feel degraded by such occupation; and if you put the black to any work requiring intelligence, you must let him *think*, and when he THINKS, *he is free!*"

"All that is easily provided for," replied the Secessionist. "We shall form intimate relations with England. She must have our cotton, and we in return will take her manufactures."

"That would be all very well at present, and so long as you should keep on good terms with her; but suppose, some fine morning, Exeter Hall got control of the English Government, and hinted to you, in John Bull fashion, that cotton produced by free labor would be more acceptable, what could three, or even eight millions, cut off from the sympathy and support of the North, do in opposition to the power of the British empire?"

"Nothing, perhaps, if we *were* three or even eight millions, but we shall be neither one nor the other. Mexico and Cuba are ready, now, to fall into our hands, and before two years have passed, with or without the Border States, we shall count twenty millions. Long before England is abolitionized, our population will outnumber hers, and our territory extend from the Atlantic to the Pacific, and as far south as the Isthmus. We are founding, sir, an empire that will be able to defy all Europe—one grander than the world has seen since the age of Pericles!"

"You say, with or without the Border States," remarked our host. "I thought you counted on their support."

"We do if the North makes war upon us, but if allowed to go in peace, we can do better without them. They will be a wall between us and the abolitionized North."

"You mistake," I said, "in thinking the North is abolitionized. The Abolitionists are but a handful there. The great mass of our people are willing the South should have undisturbed control of its domestic concerns."

"Why, then, do you send such men as Seward, Sumner, Wilson, and Grow to Congress? Why have you elected a President who approves of nigger-stealing? and why do you tolerate such incendiaries as Greeley, Garrison, and Phillips?"

"Seward, and the others you name," I replied, "are not Abolitionists; neither does Lincoln approve of nigger-stealing. He is an honest man, and I doubt not, when inaugurated, will do exact justice by the South. As to incendiaries, you find them in both sections. Phillips and Garrison are only the opposite poles of Yancey and Wise."

"Not so, sir; they are more. Phillips, Greeley, and Garrison create and control your public opinion. They are mighty powers, while Yancey and Wise have no influence whatever. Yancey is a mere bag-pipe; we play upon him, and like the music, but smile when he attempts to lead us. Wise is a harlequin; we let him dance because he is good at it, and it amuses us. Lincoln may be honest, but if made President he will be controlled by Seward, who hates the South. Seward will whine, and wheedle, and attempt to cajole us back, but mark what I say, sir, I *know* him; he is physically, morally, and constitutionally a COWARD, and will never strike a blow for the UNION. If hard pressed by public sentiment, he may, to save appearances, bluster a little, and make a show of getting ready for a fight; but he will find some excuse at the last moment, and avoid coming to blows. For our purposes, we had rather have the North under his control than under that of the old renegade, Buchanan!"

"All this may be very true," I replied, "but perhaps you attach too much weight to what Mr. Seward or Mr. Lincoln may or may not do. You seem to forget that there are twenty intelligent millions at the North, who will have something to say on this subject, and who may not consent to be driven into disunion by the South, or wheedled into it by Mr. Seward."

"I do not forget," replied the Secessionist, "that you have four millions of brave, able-bodied men, while we have not, perhaps, more than two millions; but bear in mind that you are divided, and therefore weak; we united, and therefore strong!"

"But," I inquired, "*have* you two millions without counting your blacks; and are *they* not as likely to fight on the wrong as on the right side?"

"They will fight on the right side, sir. We can trust them. You have travelled somewhat here. Have you not been struck with the contentment and cheerful subjection of the slaves?"

"No, sir, I have not been! On the contrary, their discontent is evident. You are smoking a cigar on a powder-barrel."

An explosion of derisive laughter from the Colonel followed this remark, and turning to the Captain, he good-humoredly exclaimed: "Hasn't the gentleman used his eyes and ears industriously!"

"I am afraid he is more than half right," was the reply. "If this thing should go on, I would not trust my own slaves, and I think they are truly attached to me. If the fire once breaks out, the negroes will rush into it, like horses into a burning barn."

"Think you so!" exclaimed the Colonel in an excited manner. "By Heaven, if I believed it, I would cut the throat of every slave in Christendom! What," addressing me, "have you seen or heard, sir, that gives you that opinion?"

"Nothing but a sullen discontent and an eagerness for news, which show they feel intense interest in what is going on, and know it concerns *them*."

"I haven't remarked that," he said rather musingly "but it *may* be so. Does the North believe it? If w came to blows, would they try to excite servile insur rection among us?"

"The North, beyond a doubt, believes it," I replied "yet I think even the Abolitionists would aid you i putting down an insurrection; but war, in my opinion would not leave you a slave between the Rio Grand and the Potomac."

The Colonel at this rose, remarking: "You ar mistaken. You are mistaken, sir!" then turnin to our host, said: "Captain, it is late: had we no better retire?" Bidding me "good-night," he wa gone.

Our host soon returned from showing the guest t his apartment, and with a quiet but deliberate manne said to me: "You touched him, Mr. K——, on a poir where he knows we are weakest; but allow me to cau tion you about expressing your opinions so freely. Th Colonel is a gentleman, and what you have said will d no harm, but, long as I have lived here, *I* dare not sa to many what you have said to him to-night."

Thanking the worthy gentleman for the caution, followed him up stairs, and soon lost, in a sweet ol livion, all thoughts of Abolitionists, niggers, and th "grand empire."

I was awakened in the morning by music under m window, and looking out discovered about a dozen da kies gathered around my ebony driver, who was claw ing away with all his might at a dilapidated banjo, while his auditory kept time to his singing, by striking the hand on the knee, and by other gesticulations too numerous to mention. The songs were not much to boast of, but the music was the genuine, dyed-in-the-wool, darky article. The following was the refrain of one of the songs, which the reader will perceive was an exhortation to early rising:

> "So up, good massa, let's be gwoin',
> Let's be scratchin' ob de grabble;
> For soon de wind may be a blowin',
> An' we'se a sorry road to trabble."

The storm of the previous night had ceased, but the sky was overcast, and looked as if "soon de wind might be a-blowin'." Prudence counselled an early start, for, doubtless, the runs, or small creeks, had become swollen by the heavy rain, and would be unsafe to cross after dark. Besides, beyond Conwayboro, our route lay for thirty miles through a country without a solitary house where we could get decent shelter, were we overtaken by a storm.

Hurriedly performing my toilet, I descended to the drawing-room, where I found the family assembled. After the usual morning salutations were exchanged, a signal from the mistress caused the sounding of a bell in the hall, and some ten or twelve men and women house-servants, of remarkably neat and tidy appearance, among whom was my darky driver, entered the apartment. They took a stand at the remote end of the room, and our host, opening a large, well-worn family BIBLE, read the fifty-fourth chapter of Isaiah. Then, all kneeling, he made a short extemporaneous petition, closing with the LORD's Prayer; all present, black as well as white, joining in it. Then Heber's beautiful hymn, "From Greenland's icy mountains," was sung; the negroes, to my ear, making much better music than the whites.

The services over, we adjourned to the dining-room, and after we were seated, the "Colonel" remarked to me: "Did you notice how finely that negro 'boy' (he was fully forty years old) sung?"

"Yes," I replied, "I did. Do you know him, sir?"

"Oh! yes, very well. His mistress wishes to sell him, but finds difficulty in doing so. Though a likely negro, people will not buy him. He's too smart."

"That strikes me as a singular objection," I remarked.

"Oh! no, not at all! These *knowing* niggers frequently make a world of trouble on a plantation."

It was after ten o'clock before we were ready to start. The mills, the negro-quarters, and various other parts of the plantation, and then several vessels moored at the wharf, had to be seen before I could get away. Finally, I bade my excellent host and his family farewell, and with nearly as much regret as I ever felt at leaving my own home. I had experienced the much-heard-of Southern hospitality, and had found the report far below the reality.

The other guest had taken his leave some time before, but not till he had given me a cordial invitation to return by the way I came, and spend a day or two with him, at his plantation on the river, some twenty miles below.

The sky was lowery, and the sandy road heavy with the recent rain, when we started. The gloomy weather seemed to have infected the driver as well as myself. He had lost the mirthfulness and loquacity of the previous day, and we rode on for a full hour in silence. Tiring at last of my own thoughts, I said to him: "Scip, what is the matter with you? what makes you so gloomy?"

"Nuffin, massa; I war only tinkin'," he abstractedly replied.

"And what are you thinking about?"

"I's wond'rin', massa, if de LORD mean de darkies in dose words of HIS dat Massa B—— read dis mornin'."

"What words do you mean?"

"Dese, massa: 'O dou 'fflicted! tossed wid de tempest, and habin no comfort, behold, I will make you hous'n ob de fair colors, and lay dar foundations wid safomires. All dy chil'ren shill be taught ob de LORD, and great shill be dar peace. In de right shill dey be 'stablished; dey shill hab no fear, no terror; it shan't come nigh 'em, and who come against dem shill fall. Behold! I hab make de blacksmif dat blow de coals, and make de weapons; and I hab make de waster dat shill destroy de oppressors.'"

If he had repeated one of Webster's orations I could not have been more astonished. I did not remember the exact words of the passage, but I knew he had caught its spirit. Was this his recollection of the reading heard in the morning? or had he previously committed it to memory? These questions I asked myself; but, restraining my curiosity, I answered: "Undoubtedly they are meant for both the black and the white."

"Do dey mean, massa, dat we shall be like de wite folks—wid our own hous'n, our chil'ren taught in de schools, and wid weapons to strike back when dey strike us?"

"No, Scipio, they don't mean that. They refer principally to spiritual matters. They were a promise to *all the world* that when the SAVIOUR came, all, even the greatly oppressed and afflicted, should hear the great truths of the BIBLE about GOD, REDEMPTION, and the FUTURE."

"But de SAVIOUR hab come, massa; and dose tings an't taught to de black chil'ren. We hab no peace, no rights; nuffin buf fear, 'pression, and terror."

"That is true, Scipio. The LORD takes HIS own time, but HIS time will *surely* come."

"De LORD bless you, massa, for saying dat; and de LORD bless you for telling dat big Cunnel, dat if dey gwo to war de brack man will be FREE!"

"Did you hear what we said?" I inquired, greatly surprised, for I remembered remarking, during the interview of the previous evening, that our host carefully kept the doors closed.

"Ebery word, massa."

"But how *could* you hear? The doors and windows were shut. Where were you?"

"On de piazzer; and when I seed fru de winder dat de ladies war gwine, I know'd you'd talk 'bout politics and de darkies—gemmen allers do. So I opened de winder bery softly—you didn't har 'cause it rained and blowed bery hard, and made a mighty noise. Den I stuffed my coat in de crack, so de wind could'nt blow in and lef you know I was dar, but I lef a hole big 'nough to har. My ear froze to dat hole, massa, bery tight, I 'shore you."

"But you must have got very wet and very cold."

"Wet, massa! wetter dan a 'gator dat's been in de riber all de week, but I didn't keer for de rain or de cold. What I hard made me warm all de way fru."

To my mind there was a rough picture of true heroism in that poor darky standing for hours in his shirt-sleeves, in the cold, stormy night, the lightning playing about him, and the rain drenching him to the skin—that he might hear something he thought would benefit his down-trodden race.

I noticed his clothing though bearing evident marks of a drenching, was then dry, and I inquired: "How did you dry your clothes?"

"I staid wid some ob de cullud folks, and arter you gwoes up stars, I went to dar cabin, and dey gabe me some dry cloes. We made up a big fire, and hung mine up to dry, and de ole man and woman and me sot up all night and talked ober what you and de oder gemmen said."

"Will not those folks tell what you did, and thus get you into trouble?"

"Tell! LORD bless you, massa, *de bracks am all freemasons;* dat ar ole man and woman wud die 'fore dey'd tell."

"But are not Captain B——'s negroes contented?" I asked; "they seem to be well treated."

"Oh! yas, dey am. All de brack folks 'bout har want de Captin to buy 'em. He bery nice man—one ob de LORD's own people. He better man dan David, 'cause David did wrong, and I don't b'lieve de Captin eber did."

"I should think he was a very good man," I replied.

"Bery good man, massa, but de white folks don't like him, 'cause dey say he treats him darkies so well, all dairn am uncontented."

"Tell me, Scipio," I resumed after a while, "how it is you can repeat that passage from Isaiah so well?"

"Why, bless you, massa, I know Aziar and Job and de Psalms 'most all by heart. Good many years ago, when I lib'd in Charles'on, the gub'ness learned me to read, and I hab read dat BOOK fru good many times."

"Have you read any others?" I asked.

"None but dat and Doctor Watts. I hab *dem*, but wite folks wont sell books to de bracks, and I wont steal 'em. I read de papers sometimes."

I opened my portmanteau, that lay on the floor of the wagon, and handed him a copy of Whittier's poems. It happened to be the only book, excepting the BIBLE, that I had with me.

"Read that, Scipio," I said. "It is a book of poetry, but written by a good man at the North, who greatly pities the slave."

He took the book, and the big tears rolled down his cheeks, as he said: "Tank you, massa, tank you. Nobody war neber so good to me afore."

During our conversation, the sky, which had looked threatening all the morning, began to let fall the big drops of rain; and before we reached Conwayboro, it poured down much after the fashion of the previous night. It being cruelty to both man and beast to remain out in such a deluge, we pulled up at the village hotel (kept, like the one at Georgetown, by a lady), and determined to remain overnight, unless the rain should abate in time to allow us to reach our destination before dark.

Dinner being ready soon after our arrival (the people of Conwayboro, like the "common folks" that Davy Crockett told about, dine at twelve), I sat down to it, first hanging my outer garments, which were somewhat wet, before the fire in the sitting-room. The house seemed to be a sort of public boarding-house, as well as hotel, for quite a number of persons, evidently town's-people were at the dinner-table. My appearance attracted some attention, though not more, I thought, than would be naturally excited in so quiet a place by the arrival of a stranger; but "as nobody said nothing to me, I said nothing to nobody."

Dinner over, I adjourned to the "sitting-room," and seating myself by the fire, watched the drying of my "outer habiliments." While thus engaged, the door opened, and three men—whom I should have taken for South Carolina gentlemen, had not a further acquaintance convinced me to the contrary—entered the room. Walking directly up to where I was sitting, the foremost one accosted me something after this manner:

"I see you are from the North, sir."

Taken a little aback by the abruptness of the "salute," but guessing his object, I answered: "No, sir; I am from the South."

"From what part of the South?"

"I left Georgetown yesterday, and Charleston two days before that," I replied, endeavoring to seem entirely oblivious to his meaning.

"We don't want to know whar you war yesterday; we want to know whar you *belong*," he said, with a little impatience.

"Oh! that's it. Well, sir, I belong *here* just at present, or rather I shall, when I have paid the landlady for my dinner."

Annoyed by my coolness, and getting somewhat excited, he replied quickly: "You mustn't trifle with us, sir. We know you. You're from the North. We've seen it on your valise, and we can't allow a man who carries the New York *Independent* to travel in South Carolina."

The scoundrels had either broken into my portmanteau, or else a copy of that paper had dropped from it on to the floor of the wagon when I gave the book to Scipio. At any rate, they had seen it, and it was evident "Brother Beecher" was getting me into a scrape. I felt indignant at the impudence of the fellow, but determined to keep cool, and, a little sarcastically, replied to the latter part of his remark:

"That's a pity, sir. South Carolina will lose by it."

"This game wont work, sir. We don't want such people as you har, and the sooner you make tracks the better."

"I intend to leave, sir, as soon as the rain is over, and shall travel thirty miles on your sandy roads to-day, if you don't coax me to stay here by your hospitality," I quietly replied.

The last remark was just the one drop needed to make his wrath "bile over," and he savagely exclaimed: "I tell you, sir, we will not be trifled with. You must be off to Georgetown at once. You can have just half an hour to leave the Boro', not a second more."

His tone and manner aroused what little combativeness there is in me. Rising from my chair, and taking up my outside-coat, in which was one of Colt's six-shooters, I said to him: "Sir, I am here, a peaceable man, on peaceable, private business. I have started to go up the country, and go there I shall; and I shall leave this place at my convenience—not before. I have endured your impertinence long enough, and shall have no more of it. If you attempt to interfere with my movements, you will do so at your peril."

My blood was up, and I was fast losing that better part of valor called discretion; and *he* evidently understood my movement, and did not dislike the turn affairs were taking. There is no telling what might have followed had not Scip just at that instant inserted his woolly head between us, excitedly exclaiming: "Lord bless you, Massa B——ll; what *am* you 'bout? Why, dis gemman am a 'ticlar friend of Cunnel A——. He'm a reg'lar sesherner. He hates de ablisherners worser dan de debble. I hard him swar a clar, blue streak 'bout dem only yesterday."

"Massa B——ll" was evidently taken aback by the announcement of the negro, but did not seem inclined to "give it up so" at once, for he asked: "How do you know he's the Colonel's friend, Scip? Who told you so?"

"Who told me so?" exclaimed the excited negro, "why, didn't he stay at Captin B——'s, wid de Cunnel, all night last night; and didn't dey set up dar doin' politic business togedder till arter midnight? Didn't de Cunnel come dar in all de storm 'pressly to see dis gemman?"

The ready wit and rude eloquence of the darky amused me, and the idea of the "Cunnel" travelling twenty miles through the terrible storm of the previous night to meet a man who had the New York *Independent* about him, was so perfectly ludicrous, that I could not restrain my laughter. That laugh did the business for "Massa B——ll." What the negro had said staggered, but did not convince him; but my returning good-humor brought him completely round. Extending his hand to me, he said: "I see, sir, I've woke up the wrong passenger. Hope you'll take no offence. In these times we need to know who come among us."

"No offence whatever, sir," I replied. "It is easy to be mistaken; but," I added smilingly, "I hope, for the sake of the next traveller, you'll be less precipitate another time."

"I *am* rather hasty; that's a fact," he said. "But no harm is done. So let's take a drink, and say no more about it. The old lady har keeps nary a thing, but we can get the *raal stuff* close by."

Though not a member of a "Total Abstinence Society," I have always avoided indulging in the quality of fluid that is the staple beverage at the South. I therefore hesitated a moment before accepting the gentleman's invitation; but the alternative seemed to be squarely presented, pistols or drinks; cold lead or poor whiskey, and—I am ashamed to confess it—I took the whiskey.

Returning to the hotel, I found Scip awaiting me. "Massa," he said, "we better be gwine. Dat dar sesherner am ugly as de bery ole debble; and soon as he knows I cum de possum ober him 'bout de Cunnel; he'll be down on you *shore*."

The rain had dwindled to a drizzle, which the sun was vigorously struggling to get through with a tolerable prospect of success, and I concluded to take the African's advice. Wrapping myself in an India-rubber overcoat, and giving the darky a blanket of the same material, I started.

CHAPTER III.

CROSSING THE "RUNS."

THE long, tumble-down bridge which spans the Waccamaw at Conwayboro, trembled beneath our horse's tread, as with lengthened stride he shook the secession mud from his feet, and whirled us along into the dark, deep forest. It may have been the exhilaration of a hearty dinner of oats, or it may have been sympathy with the impatience of his fellow-travellers that spurred him on; whichever it was, away he went as if Lucifer—that first Secessionist—were following close at his heels.

The sun, which for a time had been industriously wedging his way into the dark masses of cloud, finally slunk out of sight and left us enveloped in a thick fog, which shut from view all of Cottondom, except a narrow belting of rough pines, and a few rods of sandy road that stretched out in dim perspective before us. There being nothing in the outside creation to attract my attention, I drew the apron of the carriage about me, and settling myself well back on the seat to avoid the thick-falling mist, fell into a train of dreamy reflection.

Niggers, slave-auctions, cotton-fields, rice-swamps, and King Cotton himself, that blustering old despot, with his swarthy arms and "under-pinning," his face of brass, and body of "raw material," passed through my mind, like Georgia trains through the Oconee Swamp, till finally my darky friend came into view. He seemed at first a little child, amid the blazing ruins of his wilderness home, gazing in stupid horror on the burning bodies of his father and his kindred. Then he was kneeling at the side of his dying mother in the slave-pen at Cape Lopez, and—still a child—cooped in the "Blackhole" of the accursed slave-ship, his little frame burning with the fever-fire, and his child-heart longing for death. Then he seemed mounting the Cuban slave-block, and as the "going! going! gone!" rung in my ear, he was hurried away, and driven to the cruel task— still a child—on the hot, unhealthy sugar-field. Again he appeared, stealing away at night to a lonely hut, and by the light of a pine-knot, wearily poring over the BOOK of BOOKS, slowly putting letters into words, and words into sentences, that he might know "*What God says to the black man.*" Then he seemed a man—splendid of frame, noble of soul—suspended in the whipping-rack, his arms bound above his head, his body resting on the tips of his toes, and the merciless lash falling on his bare back, till the red stream ran from it like a river —scourged because he would not aid in creating beings as wretched as himself, and make merchandise of his own blood to gorge the pocket of an incarnate white devil.

As these things passed before me, and I thought of his rare intelligence, of his fine traits of character, and of the true heroism he had shown in risking, perhaps, his own life to get me—a stranger—out of an ugly hobble, I felt a certain spot in my left side warming toward him, very much as it might have done had his blood been as pure as my own. It seemed to me a pity—anti-Abolitionist and Southern-sympathizer though I was—that a man of such rare natural talent, such character and energy, should have his large nature dwarfed, be tethered for life to a cotton-stalk, and made to wear his soul out in a tread-mill, merely because his skin had a darker tinge and his shoe a longer heel than mine.

As I mused over his "strange, eventful history," and thought of the handy way nature has of putting the *right* man in the *wrong* place, it occurred to me how "Brother Beecher" one evening, not a long time before, had charmed the last dollar from my waistcoat pocket by exhibiting, *à la* Barnum, a remarkably ugly " cullud pusson" on his pulpit stairs, and by picturing the awful doom which awaited her—that of being reduced from baby-tending to some less useful employment—if his audience did not at once "do the needful." Then it occurred to me how much finer a spectacle my ebony friend would make; how well his six feet of manly sinew would grace those pulpit stairs; how eloquently the reverend gentleman might expatiate on the burning sin of shrouding the light of such an intellect in the mists of niggerdom, only to see it snuffed out in darkness; how he might enlarge on what the black could do in elevating his race, either as " cullud" assistant to "Brother

3*

Pease" at the Five-Points, or as co-laborer with Fred Douglass at abolition conventions, or, if that did'nt *pay*, how, put into the minstrel business, he might run the white "troupes" off the track, and yield a liberal revenue to the "Cause of Freedom." As I thought of the probable effect of this last appeal, it seemed to me that the thing was already done, and that SCIP was FREE.

I got back from dreamland by the simple act of opening my eyes, and found myself still riding along in that Jersey wagon, over that heavy, sandy road, and drenched with the mists of that dreary December day. The reverie made, however, a deep impression on me, and I gave vent to it somewhat as follows:

"Colonel A—— tells me, Scip, that your mistress wants to sell you. Do you know what she asks?"

"She ax fifteen hundred dollar, massa, but I an't worth dat now. Nigger property's mighty low."

"What is your value now?"

"P'raps eight hundred, p'raps a thousand dollar, massa."

"Would your mistress take a thousand for you?"

"Don't know, sar, but reckon she would. She'd be glad to get shut of me. She don't like me on de plantation, 'cause she say de oder darkies tink too much ob me; and she don't like me in de city, 'cause she 'fraid I run away."

"Why afraid you'll run away? Did you ever try to?"

"Try to! LOR bless you, massa, I neber taught ob such a ting—wouldn't gwo ef I could."

"But wouldn't you?" I asked, thinking he had conscientious scruples about running away; "wouldn't you if you could buy yourself, and go honestly, as a *free* man?"

"Buy myself, sar!" he exclaimed in surprise; "buy *my own* flesh and blood dat de LORD hisself gabe me! No, no! massa; I'd likes to be free, but I'd neber do dat!"

"Why not do that?" I asked.

"'Cause 't would be owning dat de white folks hab a right to de brack; and 'cause, sar, if I war free I couldn't stay har."

"Why should you stay here? You have no wife nor child; why not go where the black man is respected and useful?"

"I'se 'spected and useful har, massa. I hab no wife nor child, and dat make me feel, I s'pose, like as ef all de brack people war my chil'ren."

"But they are not your children; and you can be of no service to them. At the North you might learn, and put your talents to some use."

"Sar," he replied, a singular enthusiasm lighting up his face, "de LORD, dat make me what I ar, put me har, and I must stay. Sometimes when tings look bery brack, and I feel a'most 'scouraged, I goes to HIM, and I say, 'LORD, I's ob no use, take me 'way; let me get fru wid dis; let me no more see de suffrin' and 'pression ob de pore cullud race;' den HE say to me, just so plain as I say it to you, 'Keep up good courage, Scipio, de time will come;* and now, bless de LORD, de time am coming!"

"*What* time is coming, Scipio?"

He gave me a quick, suspicious glance, but his face in a moment resumed its usual expression, as he replied: "I'se sure, massa, dat I could trust you. I feel you am my friend, but I can't say no more."

"You need not, Scip—I can guess. What you have said is safe with me. But let me counsel you—wait for the white man. Do not let your freedom come in blood!"

"It will come, massa, as de LORD will. When HE war freed *de earth shook, and de vail ob de temple war rent in twain!*"

We said no more, but rode on in silence; the darky absorbed in his own reflections, I musing over the black volcano, whose muffled echoes I then heard "away down South in Dixie."

We had ridden on for about an hour, when an opening in the trees disclosed a by-path, leading to a plantation. Following it for a short distance, we came upon a small clearing, in the midst of which, flanked by a ragged corn and potato patch, squatted a dilapidated, unpainted wooden building, a sort of "half-way house"

---

* The Southern blacks, like all ignorant people, are intensely fanatical on religious subjects. The most trifling occurrences have to their minds a hidden significance, and they believe the LORD speaks to them in signs and dreams, and in almost every event of nature. This superstition, which has been handed down from their savage ancestry, has absolute sway over them, and one readily sees what immense power it would give to some leading, adroit mind, that knew how to use it. By means of it they might be led to the most desperate deeds, fully believing all the while that they were "led ob de LORD."

between a hut and a shanty. In its door-way, seated on a chair which wanted one leg and a back, was a suit of linsey-woolsey, adorned by enormous metal buttons, and surmounted by a queer-looking headpiece that might have passed for either a hat or an umbrella. I was at a loss to determine whether the object were a human being or a scarecrow, when, at the sound of our approach, the umbrella-like article lifted, and a pair of sunken eyes, a nose, and an enormous beard, disclosed themselves. Addressing myself to the singular figure, I inquired how far we were from our destination, and the most direct route to it.

"Wal, stranger," was the reply, "it's a right smart twenty mile to the Cunnel's, but I reckon ye'll get thar, if ye follow yer critter's nose, and ar good at swimming."

"Why good at swimming?" I inquired.

"'Cause the 'runs' have ris, and ar considerable deep by this time."

"That's comforting news."

"Yas, to a man as seems in a hurry," he replied, looking at my horse, which was covered with foam.

"How far is it to the nearest run?" I asked.

"Wal, it mought be six mile; it mought be seven, but you've one or two all-fired ones to cross arter that."

Here was a pleasant predicament. It was nearly five o'clock, and our horse, though a noble animal, could not make the distance on an unobstructed route, in the then heavy state of the roads, in less than three hours. Long before that time it would be dark, and no doubt stormy, for the sky, which had lowered all the afternoon, every now and then uttered an ominous growl, and seemed ready to fall down upon us. But turning back was out of the question, so, thanking the "native," I was about to proceed, when he hailed me as follows:

"I say, stranger, what's the talk in the city?"

"Nothing, sir," I replied, "but fight and Secession."

"D—n Secession!" was the decidedly energetic answer.

"Why so, my friend? That doctrine seems to be popular hereabouts."

"Yas, pop'lar with them South Car'lina chaps. They'd be oneasy in heaven if Gabriel was cook, and the LORD head-waiter."

"They must be hard to suit," I said; "I 'kalkerlate' *you're* not a South Carolinian."

"No, sir-ee! not by several mile. My mother moved over the line to born me a decent individual."

"But why are you for the Union, when your neighbors go the other way?"

"'Cause it's allers carried us 'long as slick as a cart with new-greased wheels; and 'cause, stranger, my grand'ther was one of Marion's boys, and spilt a lettle claret at Yewtaw for the old consarn, and I reckon he'd be oneasy in his grave if I turned my back on it now."

"But, my friend," I said, "they say Lincoln is an Abolitionist, and if inaugurated, he will free every darky you've got."

"He can't do that, stranger, 'cordin' to the Constetution, and grand'ther used to say that ar dokermunt would hold the d—l himself; but, for my part, I'd like to see the niggers free."

"See the niggers free!" I replied in undisguised astonishment; "why, my good sir, that is rank treason and abolition."

"Call it what yer a mind to, them's my sentiments; but I say, stranger, if thar's ony thing on airth that I uttarly dispise it ar a Northern dough-face, and it's clar yer one on 'em."

"There, my friend, you're mistaken. I'm neither an Abolitionist nor a dough-face. But *why* do you go for freeing the niggers?"

"'Cause the white folks would be better off. You see, I have to feed and clothe my niggers, and pay a hundred and twenty and a hundred and fifty a year for 'em, and if the niggers war free, they'd work for 'bout half that."

Continuing the conversation, I learned that the umbrella-hatted gentleman worked twenty hired negroes in the gathering of turpentine; and that the district we were entering was occupied by persons in the same pursuit, who nearly all employed "hired hands," and entertained similar sentiments; Colonel J———, whom I was about to visit, and who was a large slave-*owner*, being about the only exception. This, the reader will please remember, was the state of things at the date of which I am writing, in the *very heart* of Secessiondom.

Bidding the turpentine-getter a rather reluctant "good-by," I rode on into the rain.

It was nearly dark when we reached the first "run," but, fortunately, it was less swollen than our way-side acquaintance had represented, and we succeeded in crossing without difficulty. Hoping that the others might be equally as fordable, we pushed rapidly on, the darkness meanwhile gathering thickly about us, and the rain continuing to fall. Our way lay through an unbroken forest, and as the wind swept fiercely through it, the tall dark pines which towered on either side, moaned and sighed like a legion of unhappy spirits let loose from the dark abodes below. Occasionally we came upon a patch of woods where the turpentine-gatherer had been at work, and the white faces of the "tapped" trees, gleaming through the darkness, seemed an army of "sheeted ghosts" closing steadily around us. The darkness, the rain, and the hideous noises in the forest, called up unpleasant associations, and I inwardly determined to ask hospitality from the first human being, black or white, whom we should meet.

We had ridden on for about an hour after dark, when suddenly our horse's feet plashed in the water, and he sank to his middle in a stream. My first thought was that we were in the second "run," but as he pushed slowly on, the water momentarily growing deeper, and spreading on either side as far as we could see, it flashed upon me that we had missed the road in the darkness, and were fairly launched into the Waccamaw river!

Turning to the darky, who was then driving, I said quickly:

"Scip, stop the horse. Where are we?"

"Don't know, massa; reckon we'se in de riber."

"A comfortable situation this. We can't turn round. The horse can't swim such a stream in harness. What shall we do?"

"Can you swim, massa?" he quietly asked.

"Yes, like an eel."

"Wal, den, we'd better gwo on. De hoss 'll swim. But, massa, you might take off your boots and overcoat, and be ready for a spring ef he gwo down."

I did as he directed, while he let down the apron and top of the wagon, and fastened the reins loosely to the dash-board, saying as he did so, "You must allers gib a hoss his head when he swim, massa; if you rein him, he gwo down, shore." Then, undoing a portion of the harness, to give the horse the free use of his legs, he shouted, "Gee up, ole Gray," and we started.

The noble animal stepped off slowly and cautiously, as if fully aware of the danger of the passage, but had proceeded only about fifty yards when he lost his footing, and plunged us into an entirely new and decidedly cold hip-bath. "Now's de time, ole Gray," "show your broughten up, ole boy," "let de gemman see you swim, ole feller," and similar remarks proceeded rapidly from the darky, who all the time avoided touching the reins.

It may have been one minute, it may have been five minutes—I took "no note of *time*"—before the horse again struck bottom, and halted from sheer exhaustion, the water still almost level with his back, and the opposite bank too far-off to be seen through the darkness. After a short rest, he again "breasted the waters," and in a few moments landed us on the shore; not, unfortunately, in the road, but in the midst of the pine-trees, there so entangled with under-growth, that not even a man, much less a horse, could make his way through them. Wet to the skin, and shivering with the cold, we had no time to lose "in gittin' out of dat," if we would avoid greater dangers than those we had escaped. So, springing from the wagon, the darky waded up the stream, near its bank, to reconnoitre. Returning in a few minutes, he reported that we were about a hundred yards below the road. We had been carried that far down stream by the strength of the current. Our only course was to follow the "run" up along its bank; this we did, and in a short time had the satisfaction of striking the high road. Arranging the harness, we were soon under way again, the horse bounding along as if he felt the necessity of vigorous exercise to restore his chilled circulation. We afterward learned that it was not the Waccamaw we had crossed, but the second "run" our native friend had told us of, and that the water in the middle of its stream was fifteen feet deep!

Half-dead with cold and wet, we hurried on, but still no welcome light beckoned us to a human habitation. The darkness grew denser till we could not even distinguish the road, much less our horse's nose, which we had been directed to follow. Inwardly cursing the folly which brought me into such a wilderness, I said to the darky:

"Scip, I'm sorry I took you on such a trip as this."

"Oh! neber mind me, massa; I ruther like de dark night and de storm."

"Like the night and the storm! why so?"

"'Cause den de wild spirits come out, and talk in de trees. Dey make me feel bery strong *har*," he replied, striking his hand on his breast.

"The night and the storm, Scip, make *me* feel like cultivating another sort of *spirits*. There are some in the wagon-box; suppose we stop and see what they are."

We stopped, and I took out a small willow-flask, which held the "spirits of Otard," and offered it to the darky.

"No, massa," he said, laughing, "I neber touch dem sort ob spirits; dey raise de bery ole deble."

Not heeding the darky's example, I took "a long and a strong pull," and—felt the better for it.

Again we rode on, and again and again I "communed with the spirits," till a sudden exclamation from Scip aroused me from the half-stupor into which I was falling.

"What's the matter?" I asked.

"A light, massa, a light!"

"Where?"

"Dar, way off in de trees—"

"Sure enough, glory, hallelujah, there it is! We're all right now, Scip."

We rode on till we came to the inevitable opening in the trees, and were soon at the door of what I saw, by the light which came through the crevices in the logs, was a one-story shanty, about twenty feet square. "Will you let us come in out of de rain?" asked Scip of a wretched-looking, half-clad, dirt-bedraggled woman, who thrust her head from the doorway.

"Who ar ye?" was the reply.

"Only massa and me, and de hoss, and we'm half dead wid de cold," replied Scip; "can we cum in out ob de rain?"

"Wal, strangers," replied the woman, eyeing us as closely as the darkness would permit, "you'll find mighty poor fixins har, but I reckon ye can come in."

CHAPTER IV.

POOR WHITES.

ENTERING the house, we saw, by the light of a blazing pile of pine-knots, which roared and crackled on the hearth, that it contained only a single apartment. In front of the fire-place, which occupied the better half of one side of this room, the floor was of the bare earth, littered over with pine chips, dead cinders, live coals, broken pots, and a lazy spaniel dog. Opposite to this, at the other end of the room, were two low beds, which looked as if they had been "slept in forever, and never made up." Against the wall, between the beds and the fire-place, stood a small pine table, and on it was a large wooden bowl, from whose mouth protruded the handles of several unwashed pewter spoons. On the right of the fire was a razeed rocking-chair, evidently the peculiar property of the mistress of the mansion, and three blocks of pine log, sawn off smoothly, and made to serve for seats. Over against these towered a high-backed settle, something like that on which

> "sot Huldy all alone,
> When Zeke peeked thru the winder;"

and on it, her head resting partly on her arm, partly on the end of the settle, one small, bare foot pressing the ground, the other, with the part of the person which is supposed to require stockings, extended in a horizontal direction—reclined, not Huldy, but her Southern cousin, who, I will wager, was decidedly the prettier and dirtier of the two. Our entrance did not seem to disconcert her in the least, for she lay there as unmoved as a marble statue, her large black eyes riveted on my face, as if seeing some nondescript animal for the first time. I stood for a moment transfixed with admiration. In a somewhat extensive observation of her sex in both hemispheres, I had never witnessed such a form, such eyes, such faultless features, and such wavy, black, luxuriant hair. A glance at her dress—a soiled, greasy, grayish linsey-woolsey gown, apparently her only garment—and a second look at her face, which, on closer inspection, had precisely the hue of a tallow candle, recalled me to myself, and allowed me to complete the survey of the premises.

The house was built of unhewn logs, separated by wide interstices, through which the cold air came, in decidedly fresh if not health-giving currents, while a large rent in the roof, that let in the rain, gave the inmates an excellent opportunity for indulging in a shower-bath, of which they seemed greatly in need. The chimney, which had intruded a couple of feet into the room, as if to keep out of the cold, and threatened momentarily to tumble down, was of sticks, built up in clay, while the windows were of thick, unplaned boards.

Two pretty girls, one of perhaps ten and the other of

fourteen years, evidently sisters of the unadorned beauty, the middle-aged woman who had admitted us, and the dog—the only male member of the household—composed the family. I had seen negro cabins, but these people were whites, and these whites were *South Carolinians.* When such counterparts of the feudal serfs still exist, who will say that the days of chivalry are over!

After I had seated myself by the fire, and the driver had gone out to stow the horse away under the tumble-down shed at the back of the house, the elder woman said to me—

"Reckon yer wet. Ben in the rain!"

"Yes, madam, we've been out most of the day, and got in the river below here."

"Did ye? Ye mean the 'run.' I reckon it's right deep now."

"Yes, our horse had to swim," I replied.

"Ye orter strip and put on dry cloes to onst."

"Thank you, madam, I will."

Going to my portmanteau, which the darky had placed near the door, I found it dripping with wet, and opening it I discovered that every article had undergone the rite of immersion.

"Every thing is thoroughly soaked, madam. I shall have to dry myself by your fire. Can you get me a cup of tea?"

"Right sorry, stranger, but I can't. Haint a morsel to eat or drink in the house."

Remembering that our excellent hostess of the night before had insisted on filling the wagon-box with a quantity of "clficken fixins," to serve us in an emergency, and that my brandy flask was in my India-rubber coat, I sent Scip out for them.

The stores disclosed boiled chicken, bacon, sandwiches, sweet potatoes, short cake, corn-bread, buttered waffles, and 'common doin's' too numerous to mention, enough to last a family of one for a fortnight, but all completely saturated with water. Wet or dry, however, the provisions were a godsend to the half-starved family, and their hearts seemed to open to me with amazing rapidity. The dog got up and wagged his tail, and even the marble-like beauty rose from her reclining posture and invited me to a seat with her on the bench.

The kettle was soon steaming over the fire, and the boiling water, mixed with a little brandy, served as a capital substitute for tea. After the chicken was re-cooked, and the other edibles "warmed up," the little pine table was brought out, and I learned—what I had before suspected—that the big wooden bowl and the half dozen pewter spoons were the only "crockery" the family possessed.

I declined the proffered seat at the table, the cooking utensils being any thing but inviting, and contented myself with the brandy and water; but, forgetting for a moment his color, I motioned to the darky—who was as wet and jaded, and much more hungry than I was— to take the place offered to me. The negro did not seem inclined to do so, but the woman, observing my gesture, yelled out, her eyes flashing with anger:

"No, sar! No darkies eats with us. Hope you don't reckon *yerself* no better than a good-for-nothin', no account nigger!"

"I beg your pardon, madam; I intended no offence. Scipio has served me very faithfully for two days, and is very tired and hungry. I forgot myself."

This mollified the lady, and she replied:

"Niggers is good enuff in thar place, but warn't meant to 'sociate with white folks."

There may have been some ground for a distinction in that case; there certainly was a difference between the specimens of the two races then before me; but, not being one of the chivalry, it struck me that the odds were on the side of the black man. The whites were shiftless, ragged, and starving; the black well clad, cleanly, energetic, and as much above the others in intellect as Jupiter is above a church steeple. To be sure, color was against him, and he was, after all, a servant in the land of chivalry and of servant-owners. Of course the woman was right.

She soon resumed the conversation with this remark:

"Reckon yer a stranger in these parts; whar d'ye come from?"

"From New York, madam."

"New York! whar's that?"

"It's a city at the North."

4

"Oh! yas; I've heern tell on it: that's whar the Cunnel sells his turpentime. Quite a place, arnt it?"

"Yes, quite a place. Something larger than all South Carolina."

"What d'ye say? Larger nor South Carolina. Kinder reckon tain't, is't?"

"Yes, madam, it is."

"Du tell! 'Taint so large as Charles'n, is't?"

"Yes, twenty times larger than Charleston."

"Lord o'massy! How does all the folks live thar?"

"Live quite as well as they do here."

"Ye don't have no niggers thar, does ye?"

"Yes, but none that are slaves."

"Have Ablisherners thar, don't ye? them people that go agin the South?"

"Yes, some of them."

"What do they go agin the South for?"

"They go for freeing the slaves. Some of them think a black man as good as a white one."

"Quar, that; yer an Ablisherner, arnt ye?"

"No, I'm an old-fashioned Whig."

"What's that? Never heerd on them afore."

"An old-fashioned Whig, madam, is a man whose political principles are perfect, and who is as perfect as his principles."

That was a "stumper" for the poor woman, who evidently did not understand one-half of the sentence.

"Right sort of folks, them," she said, in a half inquiring tone.

"Yes, but they're all dead now."

"Dead?"

"Yes, dead, beyond the hope of resurrection."

"Iv'e heern all the dead war to be resurrected. Didn't ye say ye war one on 'em? *Ye* aint dead yet," said the woman, chuckling at having cornered me.

"But I'm more than *half* dead just now."

"Ah," replied the woman, still laughing, "yer a chicken."

"A chicken! what's that?"

"A thing that goes on tu legs, and karkles," was the ready reply.

"Ah, my dear madam, you can out-talk me."

"Yas, I reckon I kin outrun ye, tu. Ye arnt over rugged." Then, after a pause, she added—"What d'ye 'lect that darky, Linkum, President for?"

"I didn't elect him. *I* voted for Douglas. But Lincoln is not a darky."

"He's a mullater, then; I've heern he war," she replied.

"No, he's not a mulatto; he's a rail-splitter."

"Rail-splitter? *Then he's a nigger, shore.*"

"No, madam; white men at the North split rails."

"An' white wimmin tu, p'raps," said the woman, with a contemptuous toss of the head.

"No, they don't," I replied, "but white women *work* there."

"White wimmin work thar!" chimed in the hitherto speechless beauty, showing a set of teeth of the exact color of her skin—*yaller*. "What du the' du?"

"Some of them attend in stores, some set type, some teach school, and some work in factories."

"Du tell! Dress nice, and make money?"

"Yes," I replied, "they make money, and dress like fine ladies; in fact, *are* fine ladies. I know one young woman, of about your age, that had to get her own education, who earns a thousand dollars a year by teaching, and I've heard of many factory-girls who support their parents, and lay by a great deal of money, by working in the mills."

"Wal!" replied the young woman, with a contemptuous curl of her matchless upper lip; "schule-marms arn't fine ladies; fine ladies don't work; only niggers works *har*. I reckon I'd ruther be 'spectable than work for a livin'."

I could but think how magnificently the lips of some of our glorious Yankee girls would have curled had they have heard that remark, and have seen the poor girl that made it, with her torn, worn, greasy dress; her bare, dirty legs and feet, and her arms, neck, and face so thickly encrusted with a layer of clayey mud that there was danger of hydrophobia if she went near a wash-tub. Restraining my involuntary disgust, I replied:

"We at the North think work is respectable. We do not look down on a man or a woman for earning their daily bread. We all work."

"Yas, and that's the why ye'r all sech cowards," said the old woman.

"Cowards!" I said; "who tells you that?"

"My old man; he says one on our *boys* can lick five of your Yankee *men*."

"Perhaps so. Is your husband away from home?"

"Yas, him and our Cal. ar down to Charles'n."

"Cal. is your son, is he?"

"Yas, he's my oldest, and a likely lad he ar tu—he's twenty-one, and his name are JOHN CAL'OUN MILLS. He's gone a troopin' it with his fader."

"What, both gone and left you ladies here alone?"

"Yas, the Cunnel sed every man orter go, and they warn't to be ahind the rest. The Cunnel—Cunnel J.—looks arter us while they is away."

"But I should think the Colonel looked after you poorly—giving you nothing to eat."

"Oh! it's ben sech a storm to-day, the gals couldn't go for the vittles, though 'tain't a great way. We'r on his plantation; this house is his'n."

This last was agreeable news, and it occurred to me that if we were so near the Colonel's we might push on, in spite of the storm, and get there that night; so I said:

"Indeed; I'm going to the Colonel's. How far is his house from here?"

"A right smart six mile; it's at the Cross roads. Ye know the Cunnel, du ye?"

"Oh, yes, I know him well. If his house is not more than six miles off, I think we had better go on to-night. What do you say, Scip?"

"I reckon we'd better gwo, massa," replied the darky,

who had spread my travelling-shawl in the chimney-corner, and was seated on it, drying his clothes.

"Ye'd better not," said the woman; "ye'd better stay har; thar's a right smart run twixt har and the Cunnel's, and 'tain't safe to cross arter dark."

"If that is so we'd better stay, Scip; don't you think so?" I said to the darky.

"Jess as you say, massa. We got fru wid de oder one, and I reckon taint no wuss nor dat."

"The bridge ar carried away, and ye'll hev to swim *shore*," said the woman. "Ye'd better stay."

"Thank you, madam, I think we will," I replied, after a moment's thought; "our horse has swum one of your creeks to-night, and I dare not try another."

Having taken off my coat, I had been standing, during the greater part of this conversation, in my shirt-sleeves before the fire, turning round occasionally to facilitate the drying process, and taking every now and then a sip from the gourd containing our brandy and water; aided in the latter exercise by the old woman and the eldest girl, who indulged quite as freely as I did

"Mighty good brandy that," at last said the woman. "Ye like brandy, don't ye?"

"Not very much, madam. I take it to-night because I've been exposed to the storm, and it stimulates the circulation. But Scip, here, don't like spirits. He'll get the rheumatism because he don't."

"Don't like dem sort of sperits, massa; but rumatics neber trubble me."

"But I've got it mighty bad," said the woman, "*and I take 'em whenever I kin get 'em.*"

I rather thought she did, but I "reckoned" her principal beverage was whiskey.

"You have the rheumatism, madam, because your house is so open; a draught of air is always unhealthy."

"I allers reckoned 'twar *healthy*," she replied. "Ye Yankee folks have quar notions."

I looked at my watch, and found it was nearly ten o'clock, and, feeling very tired, said to the hostess:

"Where do you mean we shall sleep?"

"Ye can take that ar bed," pointing to the one nearer the wall, "the darky can sleep har;" motioning to the settle on which she was seated.

"But where will you and your daughters sleep? I don't wish to turn you out of your beds."

"Oh! don't ye keer for us; we kin all bunk together; dun it afore. Like to turn in now?"

"Yes, thank you, I would;" and without more ceremony I adjourned to the further part of the room, and commenced disrobing. Doffing my boots, waistcoat, and cravat, and placing my watch and purse under the pillow, I gave a moment's thought to what a certain not very old lady, whom I had left at home, might say when she heard of my lodging with a grass-widow and three young girls, and sprang into bed. There I removed my under-mentionables, which were still too damp to sleep in, and in about two minutes and thirty seconds sunk into oblivion.

A few streaks of grayish light were beginning to creep through the crevices in the logs, when a movement at the foot of the bed awakened me, and glancing downward I beheld the youngest girl emerging from under the clothes at my feet. She had slept there, "cross-wise," all night. A stir in the adjoining bed soon warned me that the other feminines were preparing to follow her example; so, turning my face to the wall, I feigned to be sleeping. Their toilet was soon made, when they quietly left Scip and myself in possession of the premises.

The darky rose as soon as they were gone, and, coming to me, said:

"Massa, we'd better be gwine. I'se got your cloes all dry, and you can rig up and breakfust at de Cunnel's."

The storm had cleared away, and the sun was struggling to get through the distant pines, when Scip brought the horse to the door, and we prepared to start. Turning to the old woman, I said:

"I feel greatly obliged to you, madam, for the shelter you have given us, and would like to make you some recompense for your trouble. Please to tell me what I shall pay you."

"Wal, stranger, we don't gin'rally take in lodgers, but seein' as how as thar ar tu on ye, and ye've had a good night on it, I don't keer if ye pay me tu dollars."

That struck me as "rather steep" for "common doin's," particularly as we had furnished the food and "the drinks;" yet, saying nothing, I handed her a two-dollar bank-note. She took it, and held it up curiously to the sun for a moment, then handed it back, saying, "I don't know nuthin' 'bout that ar sort o' money; haint you got no silver?"

I fumbled in my pocket a moment, and found a quarter-eagle, which I gave her.

"Haint got nary a fip o' change," she said, as she took it.

"Oh! never mind the change, madam; I shall want to stop and *look* at you when I return," I replied, good-humoredly.

"Ha! ha! yer a chicken," said the woman, at the same time giving me a gentle poke in the ribs. Fearing she might, in the exuberance of her joy at the sight of the money, proceed to some more decided demonstration of affection, I hastily stepped into the wagon, bade her good-by, and was off.

We were still among the pines, which towered gigantically all around us, but were no longer alone. Every tree was scarified for turpentine, and the forest was alive with negro men and women gathering the "last dipping," or clearing away the stumps and underbrush preparatory to the spring work. It was Christmas week; but, as I afterward learned, the Colonel's negroes were accustomed to doing "half tasks" at that season, being paid for their labor as if they were free. They stopped their work as we rode by, and stared at us with a stupid, half-frightened curiosity, very much like the look of a cow when a railway train is passing. It needed but little observation to convince me that their *status* was but one step above the level of the brutes.

As we rode along I said to the driver, "Scip, what did you think of our lodgings?"

"Mighty pore, massa. Niggas lib better'n dat."

"Yes," I replied, "but these folks despise you blacks; they seem to be both poor and proud."

"Yas, massa, dey'm pore 'cause dey wont work, and dey'm proud 'cause dey'r white. Dey wont work 'cause dey see de darky slaves doin' it, and tink it am beneaf white folks to do as de darkies do. Dis habin' slaves keeps dis hull country pore."

"Who told you that?" I asked, astonished at hearing a remark showing so much reflection from a negro.

"Nobody, massa; I see it myself."

"Are there many of these poor whites around Georgetown?"

"Not many 'round Georgetown, sar, but great many in de up-country har, and dey'm all 'like—pore and no account; none ob 'em kin read, and dey all eat clay."

"Eat clay!" I said; "what do you mean by that?"

"Didn't you see, massa, how yaller all dem wimmin war? Dat's 'cause dey eat clay. De little children begin 'fore dey kin walk, and dey eat it till dey die; dey chaw it like 'backer. It makes all dar stumacs big, like as you seed 'em, and spiles dar 'gestion. It 'm mighty onhealfy."

"Can it be possible that human beings do such things! The brutes wouldn't do that."

"No, massa, but *dey* do it; dey'm pore trash. Dat's what de big folks call 'em, and it am true; dey'm long way lower down dan de darkies."

By this time we had arrived at the "run." We found the bridge carried away, as the woman had told us; but its abutments were still standing, and over these planks had been laid, which afforded a safe crossing for foot-passengers. To reach these planks, however, it was necessary to wade into the stream for full fifty yards, the "run" having overflowed its banks for that distance on either side of the bridge. The water was evidently receding, but, as we could not well wait, like the man in the fable, for it all to run by, we alighted, and counselled as to the best mode of making the passage.

Scip proposed that he should wade in to the first abutment, ascertain the depth of the stream, and then, if it was not too deep for the horse to ford to that point, drive that far, get out, and walk to the end of the planking, leading the horse, and then again mount the wagon at the further end of the bridge. We were sure the horse would have to swim in the middle of the current, and perhaps for a considerable distance beyond; but, having witnessed his proficiency in aquatic performances, we had no doubt he would get safely across.

The darky's plan was decided on, and divesting himself of his trowsers, he waded into the "run" to take the soundings.

While he was in the water my attention was attracted to a printed paper, posted on one of the pines near the roadside. Going up to it, I read as follows:

"$250 REWARD.

"RAN away from the subscriber, on Monday, November 12th, his mulatto man, SAM. Said boy is stout-built, five feet nine inches high, 31 years old, weighs 170 lbs., and walks very erect, and with a quick, rapid gait. The American flag is tattooed on his right arm above the elbow. There is a knife-cut over the bridge of his nose, a fresh bullet-wound in his left thigh, and his back bears marks of a recent whipping. He is supposed to have made his way back to Dinwiddie County, Va., where he was raised, or to be lurking in the swamps in this vicinity.

"The above reward will be paid for his confinement in any jail in North or South Carolina, or Virginia, or for his delivery to the subscriber on his plantation at ——.

"——, December 2, 1860."

The name signed to this hand-bill was that of the planter I was about to visit.

Scip having returned, and reported the stream fordable to the bridge, I said to him, pointing to the "notice:"

"Read that, Scip."

He read it, but made no remark.

"What does it mean—that fresh bullet wound, and the marks of a recent whipping?" I asked.

"It mean, massa, dat de darky hab run away, and ben took; and dat when dey took him dey shot him, and flogged him arter dat. Now, he hab run away agin. De Cunnel's mighty hard on his niggas!"

"Is he? I can scarcely believe that."

"He am, massa; but he arnt so much to blame, nuther; dey'm awful bad, most ob 'em—so dey say."

Our conversation was here interrupted by our reaching the bridge. After safely "walking the plank," and making our way to the opposite bank, I resumed it by asking:

"Why are the Colonel's negroes so particularly bad?"

"'Cause, you see, massa, de turpentime business hab made great profits for sum yars now, and de Cunnel hab been gettin' rich bery fass. He put all his money, jes so fass as he make it, into darkies, so to make more; for he's got bery big plantation, and need nuffin' but darkies to work it to make money jess like a gold mine. He goes up to Virginny to buy niggas; and up dar *now* dey don't sell none less dey'm bad uns, 'cep when sum massa die or git pore. Virginny darkies dat cum down har aint gin'rally ob much account. Dey'm either kinder good-for-nuffin, or dey'm ugly; and de Cunnel 'd ruther hab de ugly dan de no-account niggas."

"How many negroes has he?"

"'Bout two hundred, men and wimmin, I b'lieve, massa."

"It can't be pleasant for his family to remain in such an out-of-the-way place, with so bad a gang of negroes about them, and no white people near."

"No, massa, not in dese times; but de missus and de young lady arnt dar now."

"Not there now? The Colonel said nothing to me about that. Are you sure?"

"Oh yas, massa; I seed 'em gwo off on de boat to Charles'n most two weeks ago. Dey don't mean to cum back till tings am more settled; dey'm 'fraid to stay dar."

"Would it be safe for the Colonel there, if a disturbance broke out among the slaves."

"'T wouldn't be safe den anywhar, sar; but de Cunnel am a bery brave man. He'm better dan twenty of *his* niggas."

"Why better than twenty of *his* niggers?"

"'Cause dem ugly niggas am gin'rally cowards. De darky dat is quiet, 'spectful, and does his duty, am de brave sort; *dey'll* fight, massa, till dey'm cut down."

We had here reached a turn in the road, and passing it, came suddenly upon a coach, attached to which were a pair of magnificent grays, driven by a darky in livery.

"Hallo, dar!" said Scip to the driver, as we came nearly abreast of the carriage. "Am you Cunnel J——'s man?"

"Yas, I is dat," replied the darky.

At this moment a woolly head, which I recognized at once as that of the Colonel's man "Jim," was thrust from the window of the vehicle.

"Hallo, Jim," I said. "How do you do? I'm glad to see you."

"Lor bress me, Massa K——, am dat you?" exclaimed the astonished negro, hastily opening the door, and coming to me. "Whar *did* you cum from? I'se mighty glad to see you;" at the same time giving my hand a hearty shaking. I must here say, in justice to the reputation of South Carolina, that no respectable Carolinian refuses to shake hands with a black man, unless—the black happens to be free.

"I thought I would'nt wait for you," I replied. "But how did you expect to get on? the 'runs' have swollen into rivers."

"We got a 'flat' made for dis one—it's down by dis time—de oders we tought we'd get ober sumhow."

"Jim, this is Scip," I said, seeing the darkies took no notice of each other.

"How d'ye do, Scip*io*?" said Jim, extending his hand to him. A look of singular intelligence passed over the faces of the two negroes as their hands met; it vanished in an instant, and was so slight that none but a close observer would have detected it, but some words that Scip had previously let drop had put me on the alert, and I felt sure it had a hidden significance.

"Wont you get into de carriage, massa?" inquired Jim.

"No, thank you, Jim. I'll ride on with Scip. Our horse is jaded, and you had better go ahead."

Jim mounted the driver's seat, turned the carriage, and drove off at a brisk pace to announce our coming at the plantation, while Scip and I rode on at a slower gait.

"Scip, did you know Jim before?" I asked.

"Hab seed him afore, massa, but neber know'd him."

"How is it that you have lived in Georgetown five years, and have not known him?"

"I cud hab know'd him, massa, good many time, ef I'd liked, but darkies hab to be careful."

"Careful of what?"

"Careful ob who dey knows; good many bad niggas 'bout."

"Pshaw, Scip, you're 'coming de possum;' there isn't a better nigger than Jim in all South Carolina. I know him well."

"P'raps he am; reckon he *am* a good 'nuff nigga."

"Good enough nigga, Scip! Why, I tell you he's a splendid fellow; just as true as steel. He's been North with the Colonel, often, and the Abolitionists have tried to get him away; he knew he could go, but wouldn't budge an inch."

"I knew he wouldn't," said the darky, a pleasurable gleam passing through his eyes; "dat sort don't run; dey face de music!"

"Why don't they run? What do you mean by facing the music?"

"Nuffin' massa—only dey'd ruther stay har."

"Come, Scip, you've played this game long enough. Tell me, now, what that look you gave each other when you shook hands meant."

"What look, massa? Oh! I s'pose 'twar 'cause we'd both *heerd* ob each oder afore."

"'Twas more than that, Scip. Be frank; you know you can trust *me*."

"Wal, den, massa," he replied hesitatingly, adding, after a short pause, " de ole woman called you a Yankee, sar—you can guess."

"If I should guess, 't would be that it meant *mischief*."

"It don't mean mischief, sar," said the darky, with a tone and air that would not have disgraced a Cabinet officer; "it mean only RIGHT and JUSTICE."

"It means that there is some secret understanding between you."

"I toled you, massa," he replied, relapsing into his usual manner, "dat de blacks am all Freemasons. I gabe Jim de grip, and he knowd me. He'd ha knowd my name ef you hadn't toled him."

"Why would he have known your name?"

"'Cause I gabe de grip, dat tole him."

"Why did he call you Scip*io*? I called you *Scip*."

"Oh! de darkies all do dat. Nobody but de white folks call me *Scip*. I can't say no more, massa; I SHUD BREAK DE OATH EF I DID!"

"You have said enough to satisfy me that there is a secret league among the blacks, and that you are a leader in it. Now, I tell you, you'll get yourself into a scrape. I've taken a liking to you, Scip, and I should be *very sorry* to see you run yourself into danger."

"I tank you, massa, from de bottom ob my soul I tank you," he said, as the tears moistened his eyes. "You bery kind, massa; it do me good to talk wid you. But what am my life wuth? What am any *slave's* life wuth? *Ef you war me you'd do like me!*"

I could not deny it, and I made no reply.

The writer is aware that he is here making an important statement, and one that may be called in question by those persons who are accustomed to regard the Southern blacks as only reasoning brutes. The great mass of them *are* but a little above the brutes in their habits and instincts, but a large body are fully on a par, except in mere book-education, with their white masters.

The conversation above recorded is, *verbatim et literatim*, TRUE. It took place at the time indicated, and was taken down, as were other conversations recorded in this book, within twenty-four hours after its occurrence. The name and the locality, only, I have, for very evident reasons, disguised.

From this conversation, together with others, held with the same negro, and from after developments made to me at various places, and at different times, extending over a period of six weeks, I became acquainted with the fact that there exists among the blacks a secret and wide-spread organization of a Masonic character, having its grip, pass-word, and oath. It has various grades of leaders, who are competent and *earnest* men, and its ultimate object is FREEDOM. It is quite as secret and wide-spread as the order of the "Knights of the Golden Circle," the kindred league among the whites.

This latter organization, which was instituted by John C. Calhoun, William L. Porcher, and others, as far back as 1835, has for its sole object the dissolution of the Union, and the establishment of a Southern Empire—Empire is the word, not Confederacy, or Republic; and it was solely by means of its secret but powerful machinery that the Southern States were plunged into revolution, in defiance of the will of a majority of their voting population.

Nearly every man of influence at the South (and many a pretended Union man at the North) is a member of this organization, and sworn, under the penalty of assassination, to labor " in season and out of season, by fair means and by foul, at all times, and all occasions," for the accomplishment of its object. The blacks are bound together by a similar oath, and only *bide their time.*

The knowledge of the real state of political affairs which the negroes have acquired through this organization is astonishingly accurate; their leaders possess every essential of leadership—except, it may be, military skill —and they are fully able to cope with the whites.

The negro whom I call Scipio, on the day when Major Anderson evacuated Fort Moultrie, and before he or I knew of that event, which set all South Carolina in a blaze, foretold to me the breaking out of this war in Charleston harbor, and as confidently predicted that it would result in the freedom of the slaves!

The fact of this organization existing is not positively known (for the black is more subtle and crafty than any thing human), but it is suspected by many of the whites, the more moderate of whom are disposed to ward off the impending blow by some system of gradual emancipation—declaring all black children born after a certain date free—or by some other action that will pacify and keep down the slaves. These persons, however, are but a small minority, and possess no political power, and the South is rushing blindly on to a catastrophe, which, if not averted by the action of our government, will make the horrors of San Domingo and the French Revolution grow pale in history.

I say the action of our government, for with it rests the responsibility. What the black wants is freedom. Give him that, and he will have no incentive to insurrection. If emancipation is proclaimed at the head of our armies—emancipation for *all*—confiscation for the slaves of rebels, compensation for the slaves of loyal citizens—the blacks will rush to the aid of our troops, the avenging angel will pass over the homes of the many true and loyal men who are still left at the South, and the thunderbolts of this war will fall only—where they should fall—on the heads of its blood-stained authors. If this is not done, after we have put down the whites we shall have to meet the blacks, and after we have waded knee-deep in the blood of both, we shall end the war where it began, but with the South desolated by fire and sword, the North impoverished and loaded down with an everlasting debt, and our once proud, happy, and glorious country the by-word and scorn of the civilized world.

Slavery is the very bones, marrow, and life-blood of this rebellion, and it cannot be crushed till we have destroyed that accursed institution. If a miserable peace is patched up before a death-stroke is given to slavery, it will gather new strength, and drive freedom from this country forever. In the nature of things it cannot exist in the same hemisphere with liberty. Then let every man who loves his country determine that if this war must needs last for twenty years, it shall not end until this root of all our political evils is weeded out forever.

A short half-hour took us to the plantation, where I found the Colonel on the piazza awaiting me. After our greeting was over, noticing my soiled and rather dilapidated condition, he inquired where I had passed the night. I told him, when he burst into a hearty fit of laughter, and for several days good-naturedly bantered me about "putting up" at the most aristocratic hotel in South Carolina—the "Mills House."

We soon entered the mansion, and the reader will, I trust, pardon me, if I leave him standing in its door-way till another chapter.

CHAPTER V.

ON THE PLANTATION.

The last chapter left the reader in the door-way of the Colonel's mansion. Before entering, we will linger there awhile and survey the outside of the premises.

The house stands where two roads meet, and, unlike most planters' dwellings, is located in full view of the highway. It is a rambling, disjointed structure, thrown together with no regard to architectural rules, and yet there is a rude harmony in its very irregularities that has a pleasing effect. The main edifice, with a frontage of nearly eighty feet, is only one and a half stories high, and is overshadowed by a broad projecting roof, which somehow, though in a very natural way, drops down at the eaves, and forms the covering of a piazza, twenty feet wide, and extending across the entire front of the house. At its south-easterly angle, the roof is truncated, and made again to form a covering for the piazza, which there extends along a line of irregular buildings for sixty yards. A portion of the verandah on this side being enclosed, forms a bowling-alley and smoking-room, two essential appendages to a planter's residence. The whole structure is covered with yellow-pine weather boarding, which in some former age was covered with paint of a grayish brown color. This, in many places, has peeled off and allowed the sap to ooze from the pine, leaving every here and there large blotches on the surface, somewhat resembling the "warts" I have seen on the trunks of old trees.

The house is encircled by grand old pines, whose tall, upright stems, soaring eighty and ninety feet in the air, make the low hamlet seem lower by the contrast. They have stood there for centuries, their rough, shaggy coats buttoned close to their chins, and their long green locks waving in the wind; but the long knife has been thrust into their veins, and their life-blood is now fast oozing away.

With the exception of the negro huts, which are scattered at irregular intervals through the woods in the rear of the mansion, there is not a human habitation within an hour's ride; but such a cosy, inviting, hospitable atmosphere surrounds the whole place, that a stranger does not realize he has happened upon it in a wilderness.

The interior of the dwelling is in keeping with the exterior, though in the drawing-rooms, where rich furniture and fine paintings actually lumber the apartments, there is evident the lack of a nice perception of the "fitness of things," and over the whole hangs a "dusty air," which reminds one that the Milesian Bridget does not "flourish" in South Carolina.

I was met in the entrance-way by a tall, fine-looking woman, to whom the Colonel introduced me as follows:

"Mr. K——, this is Madam P——, my housekeeper; she will try to make you forget that Mrs. J—— is absent."

After a few customary courtesies were exchanged, I was shown to a dressing-room, and with the aid of Jim, a razor, and one of the Colonel's shirts—all of mine having undergone a drenching—soon made a tolerably presentable appearance. The negro then conducted me to the breakfast-room, where I found the family assembled.

It consisted, besides the housekeeper, of a tall, raw-boned, sandy-haired personage, with a low brow, a blear eye, and a sneaking look—the overseer of the plantation; and of a well-mannered, intelligent lad—with the peculiarly erect carriage and uncommon blending of good-natured ease and dignity which distinguished my host—who was introduced to me as the housekeeper's son.

Madam P——, who presided over the "tea-things," was a person of perhaps thirty-five, but a rich olive complexion, enlivened by a delicate red tint, and relieved by thick masses of black hair, made her appear to a casual observer several years younger. Her face bore vestiges of great beauty, which time, and, perhaps, care, had mellowed but not obliterated, and her conversation indicated high cultivation. She had evidently mingled in refined society in this country and in Europe, and it was a strange freak of fortune that had reduced her to a menial condition in the family of a backwoods planter.

After some general conversation, the Colonel remarked that his wife and daughter would pass the winter in Charleston.

"And do *you* remain on the plantation?" I inquired.

"Oh yes, I am needed here," he replied; "but Madam's son is with my family."

"Madam's son!" I exclaimed in astonishment, forgetting in my surprise that the lady was present.

"Yes, sir," she remarked, "my oldest boy is twenty."

"Excuse me, Madam; I forgot that in your climate one never grows old."

"There you are wrong, sir; I'm sure I *feel* old when I think how soon my boys will be men."

"Not old yet, Alice," said the Colonel, in a singularly familiar tone; "you seem to me no older than when you were fifteen."

"You have been long acquainted," I remarked, not knowing exactly what to say.

"Oh, yes," replied my host, "we were children together."

"Your Southern country, Madam, affords a fine field for young men of enterprise."

"My eldest son resides in Germany," replied the lady. "He expects to make that country his home. He would have passed his examination at Heidelberg this autumn had not circumstances called him here."

"You are widely separated," I replied.

"Yes, sir; his father thinks it best, and I suppose it

is. Thomas, here, is to return with his brother, and I may live to see neither of them again."

My curiosity was naturally much excited to learn more, but nothing further being volunteered, and the conversation soon turning to other topics, I left the table with it unsatisfied.

After enjoying a quiet hour with the Colonel in the smoking-room, he invited me to join him in a ride over the plantation. I gladly assented, and Jim shortly announced the horses were in waiting. That darky, who invariably attended his master when the latter proceeded from home, accompanied us. As we were mounting I bethought me of Scip, and asked where he was.

"He'm gwine to gwo, massa, and want to say good-by to you."

It seemed madness for Scip to start on a journey of seventy miles without rest, so I requested the Colonel to let him remain till the next day. He cheerfully assented, and sent Jim to find him. While waiting for the darky, I spoke of how faithfully he had served me during my journey.

"He's a splendid nigger," replied the Colonel; "worth his weight in gold. If affairs were more settled I would buy him."

"But Colonel A—— tells me he is too intelligent. He objects to 'knowing' niggers."

"*I* do not," replied my host, "if they are honest, and I would trust Scip with uncounted gold. Look at him," he continued, as the negro approached; "were flesh and bones ever better put together?"

The darky *was* a fine specimen of sable humanity, and I readily understood why the practiced eye of the Colonel appreciated his physical developments.

"Scip," I said, "you must not think of going to-day; the Colonel will be glad to let you remain until you are fully rested."

"Tank you, massa, tank you bery much, but de ole man will spec' me, and I orter gwo."

"Oh, never mind old ——," said the Colonel, "I'll take care of him."

"Tank you, Cunnel, den I'll stay har till de mornin'."

Taking a by-path which led through the forest in the rear of the mansion, we soon reached a small stream, and, following its course for a short distance, came upon a turpentine distillery, which the Colonel explained to me was one of three that prepared the product of his plantation for market, and provided for his family of nearly three hundred souls.

It was enclosed, or rather roofed, by a rude structure of rough boards, which was open at the sides, and sustained on a number of pine poles about thirty feet in height, and bore a strong resemblance to the usual covering of a New England haystack.

Three stout negro men, divested of all clothing excepting a pair of coarse gray trowsers and a red shirt—it was a raw, cold, wintry day—and with cotton bandannas bound about their heads, were "tending the still." The foreman stood on a raised platform level with its top, but as we approached very quietly seated himself on a turpentine barrel which a moment before he had rolled over the mouth of the boiler. Another negro was below, feeding the fire with "light wood," and a third was tending the trough by which the liquid rosin found its way into the semicircle of rough barrels intended for its reception.

"Hello, Junius, what in creation are you doing there?" asked the Colonel, as we approached, of the negro on the turpentine barrel.

"Holein' her down, Cunnel; de ole ting got a mine to blow up dis mornin'; I'se got dis barrl up har to hole her down."

"Why, you everlasting nigger, if the top leaks you'll be blown to eternity in half a second."

"Reckon not, massa; be barrl and me kin hole her. We'll take de risk."

"Perhaps *you* will," said the Colonel, laughing, "but I wont. Nigger property isn't of much account, but you're too good a darky, June, to be sent to the devil for a charge of turpentine."

"Tank you, massa, but you dun kno' dis ole ting like I do. You cudn't blow her up nohow; I'se tried her afore dis way."

"Don't you do it again; now mind; if you do I'll make a white man of you." (This I suppose referred to a process of flaying with a whip; though the whip is generally thought to *redden*, not *whiten*, the negro.)

The black did not seem at all alarmed, for he showed his ivories in a broad grin as he replied, "Jess as you say, massa; you'se de boss in dis shanty."

Directing the fire to be raked out, and the still to stand unused until it was repaired, the Colonel turned his horse to go, when he observed that the third negro was shoeless, and his feet chapped and swollen with the cold. "Jake," he said, "where are your shoes?"

"Wored out, massa."

"Worn out! Why haven't you been to me?"

"'Cause, massa, I know'd you'd jaw; you tole me I wears 'em out mighty fass."

"Well, you do, that's a fact; but go to Madam and get a pair; and you, June, you've been a decent nigger, you can ask for a dress for Rosy. How is little June?"

"Mighty pore, massa; de ma'am war dar lass night and dis mornin', and she reckun he'm gwine to gwo, sartain."

"Sorry to hear that," said the Colonel. "I'll go and see him. Don't feel badly, June," he continued, for the tears welled up to the eyes of the black man as he spoke of his child; "we all must die."

"I knows dat, massa, but it am hard to hab 'em gwo."

"Yes, it is, June, but we may save him."

"Ef you cud, massa! Oh, ef you cud!" and the poor darky covered his face with his great hands and sobbed like a child.

We rode on to another "still," and there dismounting, the Colonel explained to me the process of gathering and manufacturing turpentine. The trees are "boxed" and "tapped" early in the year, while the frost is still in the ground. "Boxing" is the process of scooping a cavity in the trunk of the tree by means of a peculiarly shaped axe, made for the purpose; "tapping" is scarifying the rind of the wood above the boxes. This is never done until the trees have been worked one season, but it is then repeated year after year, till on many plantations they present the marks of twenty and frequently thirty annual "tappings," and are often denuded of bark for a distance of thirty feet from the ground. The necessity for this annual tapping arises from the fact that the scar on the trunk heals at the end of a season, and the sap will no longer run from it; a fresh wound is therefore made each spring. The sap flows down the scarified surface and collects in the boxes, which are emptied six or eight times in a year, according to the length of the season. This is the process of "dipping," and it is done with a tin or iron vessel constructed to fit the cavity in the tree.

The turpentine gathered from the newly boxed or virgin tree is very valuable, on account of its producing a peculiarly clear and white rosin, which is used in the manufacture of the finer kinds of soap, and by "Rosin the Bow." It commands, ordinarily, nearly five times the price of the common article. When barrelled, the turpentine is frequently sent to market in its crude state, but more often is distilled on the plantation, the gatherers generally possessing means sufficient to own a still.

In the process of distilling, the crude turpentine is "dumped" into the boiler through an opening in the top—the same as that on which we saw Junius composedly seated—water is then poured upon it, the aperture made tight by screwing down the cover and packing it with clay, a fire built underneath, and when the heat reaches several hundred degrees Fahrenheit, the process of manufacture begins. The volatile and more valuable part of the turpentine, by the action of the heat, rises as vapor, then condensing flows off through a pipe in the top of the still, and comes out spirits of turpentine, while the heavier portion finds vent at a lower aperture, and comes out rosin.

No article of commerce is so liable to waste and leakage as turpentine. The spirits can only be preserved in tin cans, or in thoroughly seasoned oak barrels, made tight by a coating of glue on the inner side. Though the material for these barrels exists at the South in luxuriant abundance, they are all procured from the North, and the closing of the Southern ports has now entirely cut off the supply; for while the turpentine farmer may improvise coopers, he can by no process give the oak timber the seasoning which is needed to render the barrel spirit-tight. Hence it is certain that a large portion of the last crop of turpentine must have gone to waste. When it is remembered that the one State of North Carolina exports annually nearly twenty millions in value of this product, and employs fully two-thirds of its negroes in its production, it will be seen how dearly the South is paying for the mad freak of secession. Putting out of view his actual loss of produce, how does the turpentine farmer feed and employ his negroes? and pressed as these blacks inevitably are by both hunger and idleness, those prolific breeders of sedition, what will keep them quiet?

"What effect will secession have on your business?" I asked the Colonel, after a while.

"A favorable one. I shall ship my crop direct to Liverpool and London, instead of selling it to New York middle-men."

"But is not the larger portion of the turpentine crop consumed at the North?"

"Oh, yes. We shall have to deal with the Yankees anyhow, but we shall do as little with them as possible."

"Suppose the Yankees object to your setting up by yourselves, and put your ports under lock and key?"

"They wont do that, and if they do, England will break the blockade."

"We may rap John Bull over the knuckles in that event," I replied.

"Well, suppose you do; what then?"

"Merely, England would not have a ship in six months to carry your cotton. A war with her would ruin the shipping trade of the North. Our marine would seek employment at privateering, and soon sweep every

British merchant ship from the ocean. We could afford to give up ten years' trade with you, and to put secession down by force, for the sake of a year's brush with John Bull."

"But, my good friend, where would the British navy be all this while?"

"Asleep. The English haven't a steamer that can catch a Brookhaven schooner. The last war proved that government vessels are no match for privateers."

"Well, well! but the Yankees wont fight."

"Suppose they do. Suppose they shut up your ports, and leave you with your cotton and turpentine unsold? You raise scarcely any thing else—what would you eat?"

"We would turn our cotton fields into corn and wheat. Turpentine-makers, of course, would suffer."

"Then why are not *you* a Union man?"

"My friend, I have nearly three hundred mouths to feed. I depend on the sale of my crop to give them food. If our ports are closed, I cannot do it—they will starve, and I be ruined. But sooner than submit to the domination of the cursed Yankees, I will see my negroes starving, and my child a beggar!"

At this point in the conversation we arrived at the negro shanty where the sick child was. Dismounting, the Colonel and I entered.

The cabin was almost a counterpart of the "Mills House," described in the previous chapter, but it had a plank flooring, and was scrupulously neat and clean.

The logs were stripped of bark, and whitewashed. A bright, cheerful fire was blazing on the hearth, and an air of rude comfort pervaded the whole interior. On a low bed in the farther corner of the room lay the sick child. He was a boy of about twelve years, and evidently in the last stages of consumption. By his side, bending over him as if to catch his almost inaudible words, sat a tidy, youthful-looking colored woman, his mother, and the wife of the negro we had met at the "still." Playing on the floor, was a younger child, perhaps five years old, but while the faces of the mother and the sick lad were of the hue of charcoal, *his* skin by a process well understood at the South, had been bleached to a bright yellow.

The woman took no notice of our entrance, but the little fellow ran to the Colonel and caught hold of the skirts of his coat in a free-and-easy way, saying, "Ole massa, you got suffin' for Dicky?"

"No, you little nig," replied the Colonel, patting his woolly head as I might have done a white child's, "Dicky isn't a good boy."

"Yas, I is," said the little darky; "you'se ugly ole massa to gib nuffin' to Dick."

Aroused by the Colonel's voice, the woman turned toward us. Her eyes were swollen, and her face bore traces of deep emotion.

"Oh massa!" she said, "de chile am dyin'! It'm all along ob his workin' in de swamp—no *man* orter work dar, let alone a chile like dis."

"Do you think he is dying, Rosy?" asked the Colonel, approaching the bed-side.

"Shore, massa, he'm gwine fass. Look at 'im."

The boy had dwindled to a skeleton, and the skin lay on his face in crimpled folds, like a mask of black crape. His eyes were fixed, and he was evidently going.

"Don't you know massa, my boy?" said the Colonel, taking his hand tenderly in his.

The child's lips slightly moved, but I could hear no sound. The Colonel put his ear down to him for a moment, then, turning to me, said:

"He *is* dying. Will you be so good as to step to the house and ask Madam P—— here, and please tell Jim to go for Junius and the old man."

I returned in a short while with the lady, but found the boy's father and "the old man"—the darky preacher of the plantation—there before us. The preacher was a venerable old negro, much bowed by years, and with thin wool as white as snow. When we entered, he was bending over the dying boy, but shortly turning to my host, said:

"Massa, de blessed Lord am callin' for de chile— shall we pray?"

The Colonel nodded assent, and we all, blacks and whites, knelt down on the floor, while the old preacher made a short, heart-touching prayer. It was a simple, humble acknowledgment of the dependence of the creature on the Creator—of His right to give and to take away, and was uttered in a free, conversational tone, as if long communion with his Maker had placed the old negro on a footing of friendly familiarity with Him, and given the black slave the right to talk with the Deity as one man talks with another.

As we rose from our knees my host said to me, "It is *my* duty to stay here, but I will not detain *you*. Jim will show you over the plantation. I will join you at the house when this is over." The scene was a painful one, and I gladly availed myself of the Colonel's suggestion.

Mounting our horses, Jim and I rode off to the negro house where Scip was staying.

Scip was not at the cabin, and the old negro woman told us he had been away for several hours.

"Reckon he'll be 'way all day, sar," said Jim, as we turned our horses to go.

"He ought to be resting against the ride of to-morrow. Where has he gone?"

"Dunno, sar, but reckon he'm gwine to fine Sam."

"Sam? Oh, he's the runaway the Colonel has advertised."

"Yas, sar, he'm 'way now more'n a monfh."

"How can Scip find him?"

"Dunno, sar. Scipio know most ebery ting—reckon he'll track him. He know him well, and Sam'll cum back ef he say he orter."

"Where do you think Sam is?"

"P'raps in de swamp."

"Where is the swamp?"

" 'Bout ten mile from har."

" Oh, yes! the shingles are cut there. I should think a runaway would be discovered where so many men are at work."

" No, massa, dar'm places dar whar de ole debble cudn't fine him, nor de dogs nudder."

" I thought the bloodhounds would track a man anywhere."

" Not fru de. water, massa; dey lose de scent in de swamp."

" But how can a man live there—how get food?"

" De darkies dat work dar take 'em nuff."

" Then the other negroes know where the runaways are; don't they sometimes betray them?"

" Neber, massa; a darky neber tells on anoder. De Cunnel had a boy in dat swamp once good many years."

" Is it possible! Did he come back?"

" No, he died dar. Sum ob de hands found him dead one mornin' in de hut whar he lib'd, and buried him dar."

" Why did Sam run away?"

" 'Cause de oberseer flog him. He use him bery hard, massa."

" What had Sam done?"

" Nuffin, massa."

" Then why was he flogged? Did the Colonel know it?"

" Oh, yas; Moye cum de possum ober de Cunnel, and

make him b'lieve Sam war bad. De Cunnel dunno de hull ob dat story."

"Why didn't *you* tell him? The Colonel trusts *you*."

"'T wudn't hab dun no good; de Cunnel wud hab flogged me for tellin' on a wite man. Nigga's word aint ob no account."

"What is the story about, Sam?"

"You wont tell dat *I* tole you, massa?"

"No, but I'll tell the Colonel the truth."

"Wal den, sar, you see Sam's wife am bery good-lookin', her skin's most wite—her mudder war a mulatter, her fader a wite man—she lub'd Sam 'bout as well as de wimmin ginrally lub dar husbands" (Jim was a bachelor, and his observation of plantation morals had given him but little faith in the sex), "but most ob 'em, ef dey'm married or no, tink dey must smile on de wite men, so Jule she smiled on de oberseer—so Sam tought—and it made him bery jealous. He war sort o' sassy, and de oberseer strung him up, and flog him bery hard. Den Sam took to de swamp, but he didn't know whar to gwo, and de dogs tracked him; he'd ha' got 'way dough ef ole Moye hadn't a shot him; den he cudn't run. Den Moye flogged him till he war 'most dead, and arter dat chained him down in de ole cabin, and gave him 'most nuflin' to eat. De Cunnel war gwine to take Sam to Charles'on and sell him, but somehow he got a file and sawed fru de chain and got 'way in de night to de 'still.' Den when de oberseer come dar in de mornin', Sam jump on him and 'most kill him. He'd hab sent him whar dar aint no niggas, ef Junius hadn't a holed him. *I'd* a let de ole debble gwo."

"Junius, then, is a friend of the overseer."

"No, sar; *he* haint no friends, 'cep de debble; but June am a good nigga, and he said 'twarn't right to kill ole Moye so sudden, for den dar'd be no chance for de Lord to forgib him."

"Then Sam got away again?"

"Oh yas; nary one but darkies war round, and dey wouldn't hole him. Ef dey'd cotched him den, dey'd hung him, shore."

"Why hung him?"

"'Cause he'd struck a wite man; it 'm shore death to do dat."

"Do you think Scip will bring him back?"

"Yas; 'cause he'm gwine to tell massa de hull story. De Cunnel will b'lieve Scipio ef he *am* brack. Sam'll know dat, so he'll come back. De Cunnel'll make de State too hot to hole ole Moye, when he fine him out."

"Does Sam's wife 'smile' on the overseer now?"

"No; she see de trubble she bring on Sam, and she bery sorry. She wont look at a wite man now."

During the foregoing conversation, we had ridden for several miles over the western half of the plantation, and were again near the house. My limbs being decidedly stiff and sore from the effect of the previous day's journey, I decided to alight and rest until the hour for dinner.

I mentioned my jaded condition to Jim, who said:

"Dat's right, massa; come in de house. I'll cure de rumatics; I knows how to fix dem."

Fastening the horses at the door, Jim accompanied me to my sleeping-room, where he lighted a fire of pine knots, which in a moment blazed up on the hearth and sent a cheerful glow through the apartment; then, saying he would return after stabling the horses, the darky left me.

I took off my boots, drew the sofa near the fire, and stretched myself at full length upon it. If ever mortal was tired, "I reckon" I was. It seemed as though every joint and bone in my body had lost the power of motion, and sharp, acute pains danced along my nerves, as I have seen the lightning play along the telegraph wires. My entire system had the toothache.

Jim soon returned, bearing in one hand a decanter of "Otard," and in the other a mug of hot water and a crash towel.

"I'se got de stuff dat'll fix de rumatics, massa."

"Thank you, Jim; a glass will do me good. Where did you get it?" I asked, thinking it strange the Colonel should leave his brandy-bottle within reach of the negroes, who have an universal weakness for spirits.

"Oh, I keeps de keys; de Cunnel hissef hab to come to me when he want suffin' to warm hissef."

It was the fact; Jim had exclusive charge of the wine-cellar; in short, was butler, barber, porter, footman, and body-servant, all combined.

"Now, massa, you lay right whar you is, and I'll make you ober new in less dan no time."

And he did; but I emptied the brandy-bottle. Lest my temperance friends should be horror-stricken, I will mention, however, that I took the fluid by external absorption. For all rheumatic sufferers, I would prescribe hot brandy, in plentiful doses, a coarse towel, and an active Southern darky, and if on the first application the patient is not cured, the fault will not be the negro's. Out of mercy to the chivalry, I hope our government, in saving the Union, will not annihilate the order of body-servants. They are the only perfect institution in the Southern country, and, so far as I have seen, about the only one worth saving.

The dinner-bell sounded a short while after Jim had finished the scrubbing operation, and I went to the table with an appetite I had not felt for a week. My whole system was rejuvenated, and I am not sure that I should, at that moment, have declined a wrestling match with Heenan himself.

I found at dinner only the overseer and the young son of Madam P——, the Colonel and the lady being still at the cabin of the dying boy. The dinner, though a queer mixture of viands, would not have disgraced, except, perhaps, in the cooking, the best of our Northern hotels. Venison, bacon, wild fowl, hominy, poultry, corn bread, French "made-dishes," and Southern "common doin's," with wines and brandies of the choicest brands, were placed on the table together.

"Dis, massa," said Jim, "am de raal juice; it hab been in de cellar eber since de house war built. Massa tole me to gib you some, wid him complimen's."

Passing it to my companions, I drank the Colonel's health in as fine wine as I ever tasted.

I had taken an instinctive dislike to the overseer at the breakfast-table, and my aversion was not lessened by learning his treatment of Sam; curiosity to know what manner of man he was, however, led me, toward the close of our meal, to "draw him out," as follows:

"What is the political sentiment, sir, of this section of the State?"

"Wal, I reckon most of the folks 'bout har' is Union; they'm from the 'old North,' and gin'rally pore trash."

"I have heard that the majority of the turpentine farmers are enterprising men and good citizens—more enterprising, even, than the cotton and rice planters."

"Wal, they is enterprisin', 'cause they don't keer for nuthin' 'cep' money."

"The man who is absorbed in money-getting is generally a quiet citizen."

"P'raps that's so. But I think a man sh'u'd hev a soul suthin' 'bove dollars. Them folks will take any sort o' sarce from the Yankees, ef they'll only buy thar truck."

"What do you suffer from the Yankees?"

"Suffer from the Yankees? Don't they steal our niggers, and haint they 'lected an ab'lishener for President?"

"I've been at the North lately, but I am not aware that is so."

"So! it's damnably so, sir. I knows it. We don't mean to stand it eny longer."

"What will you do?"

"We'll give 'em h—l, ef they want it!"

"Will it not be necessary to agree among yourselves before you do that? I met a turpentine farmer below here who openly declared that he is friendly to abolishing slavery. He thinks the masters can make more money by hiring than by owning the negroes."

"Yes, that's the talk of them North County* fellers, who've squatted round har. We'll hang every mother's son on 'em, by ——."

"I wouldn't do that: in a free country every man has a right to his opinions."

"Not to sech opinions as them. A man may think, but he mustn't think onraasonable."

"I don't know, but it seems to me reasonable, that if

---

* The "North Counties" are the north-eastern portion of North Carolina, and include the towns of Washington and Newbern. They are an old turpentine region, and the trees are nearly exhausted. The finer virgin forests of South Carolina, and other cotton States, have tempted many of the North County farmers to emigrate thither, within the past ten years, and they now own nearly all the trees that are worked in South Carolina, Georgia, and Florida. They generally have few slaves of their own, their hands being hired of wealthier men in their native districts. The "hiring" is an annual operation, and is done at Christmas time, when the negroes are frequently allowed to go home. They treat the slaves well, give them an allowance of meat (salt pork or beef), as much corn as they can eat, and a gill of whiskey daily. No class of men at the South are so industrious, energetic, and enterprising. Though not so well informed, they have many of the traits of our New England farmers; in fact, are frequently called "North Carolina Yankees." It was these people the overseer proposed to hang. The reader will doubtless think that "hanging was not good enough for them."

the negroes cost these farmers now one hundred and fifty dollars a year, and they could hire them, if free, for seventy-five or a hundred, that they would make by abolition."

"Ab'lish'n! By—, sir, ye aint an ab'lishener, is ye?" exclaimed the fellow, in an excited manner, bringing his hand down on the table in a way that set the crockery a-dancing.

"Come, come, my friend," I replied, in a mild tone, and as unruffled as a pool of water that has been out of a December night; "you'll knock off the dinner things, and I'm not quite through."

"Wal, sir, I've heerd yer from the North, and I'd like to know if yer an ab'lishener."

"My dear sir, you surprise me. You certainly can't expect a modest man like me to speak of himself."

"Ye can speak of what ye d—please, but ye can't talk ab'lish'n har, by —," he said, again applying his hand to the table, till the plates and saucers jumped up, performed several jigs, then several reels, and then rolled over in graceful somersaults to the floor.

At this juncture, the Colonel and Madam P—— entered.

Observing the fall in his crockery, and the general confusion of things, my host quietly asked, "What's to pay?"

I said nothing, but burst into a fit of laughter at the awkward predicament of the overseer. That gentleman also said nothing, but looked as if he would like to find vent through a rat-hole or a window-pane. Jim, however, who stood at the back of my chair, gave *his* eloquent thoughts utterance, very much as follows :

"Moye hab 'sulted Massa K——, Cunnel, awful bad. He hab swore a blue streak at him, and called him a d— ab'lishener, jess 'cause Massa K—— wudn't get mad and sass him back. He hab disgrace your hosspital, Cunnel, wuss dan a nigga."

The Colonel turned white with rage, and striding up to Moye, seized him by the throat, yelling, rather than speaking, these words: "You d—— —— —— —— —— ——, have you dared to insult a guest in my house?"

"I did'nt mean to 'sult him," faltered out the overseer, his voice running through an entire octave, and changing with the varying pressure of the Colonel's fingers on his throat; "but he said he war an ab'lishener."

"No matter what he said, he is my guest, and in my house he shall say what he pleases, by —. Apologize to him, or I'll send you to h— in a second."

The fellow turned cringingly to me, and ground out something like this, every word seeming to give him the face-ache:

"I meant no offence, sar; I hope ye'll excuse me."

This satisfied me, but, before I could reply, the Colonel again seized him by the throat and yelled:

"None of your sulkiness; you d— white-livered hound, ask the gentleman's pardon like a man."

The fellow then got out, with less effort than before:

"I 'umbly ax yer pardon, sar, very 'umbly, indeed."

"I am satisfied, sir," I replied. "I bear you no ill-will."

"Now go," said the Colonel; "and in future take your meals in your cabin. I have none but gentlemen at my table."

The fellow went. As soon as he closed the door, the Colonel said to me:

"Now, my dear friend, I hope you will pardon *me* for this occurrence. I sincerely regret you have been insulted in my house."

"Don't speak of it, my dear sir; the fellow is ignorant, and really thinks I am an abolitionist. His zeal in politics led to his warmth. I blame him very little," I replied.

"But he lied, Massa K——," chimed in Jim, very warmly; "you neber said you war an ab'lishener."

"You know what *they* are, Jim, don't you?" said the Colonel, laughing, and taking no notice of his breach of decorum in wedging black ideas into a white conversation.

"Yas, I does dat," said the darky, grinning.

"Jim," said his master, "you're a prince of a nigger, but you talk too much; ask me for something to-day, and I reckon you'll get it; but go now, and tell Chloe (the cook) to get us some dinner."

The negro left, and, excusing myself, I soon followed suit.

I went to my room, laid down on the lounge, and soon fell asleep. It was nearly five o'clock when a slight noise in the apartment awoke me, and, looking up, I saw the Colonel quietly seated by the fire, smoking a cigar. His feet were elevated above his head, and he appeared absorbed in no very pleasant reflections.

"How is the sick boy, Colonel?" I asked.

"It's all over with him, my friend. He died easy; but 'twas very painful to me; I feel I have done him wrong."

"How so?"

"I was away all summer, and that cursed Moye sent him to the swamp to tote for the shinglers. It killed him."

"Then you are not to blame," I replied.

"I wish I could feel so."

The Colonel remained with me till supper-time, evidently much depressed by the events of the morning, which had affected him more than I should have thought possible. I endeavored, by directing his mind to other topics, to cheer him, and in a measure succeeded.

While we were seated at the supper table, the black cook entered from the kitchen—a one-story shanty, detached from, and in the rear of the house—and, with a face expressive of every conceivable emotion a negro can feel—joy, sorrow, wonder, and fear all combined—exclaimed, " O massa, massa! dear massa! Sam, O Sam!"

"Sam!" said the Colonel; " what about Sam?"

"Why, he hab—dear, dear massa, don't yer, don't yer hurt him—he hab come back!"

If a bombshell had fallen in the room, a greater sensation could not have been produced. Every individual arose from the table, and the Colonel, striding up and down the apartment, exclaimed:

"Is he mad? The everlasting fool! Why in h— has he come back?"

"Oh, don't ye hurt him massa," said the black cook, wringing her hands. "Sam hab been bad, bery bad, but he won't be so no more."

"Stop your noise, aunty," said the Colonel, but with no harshness in his tone. "I shall do what I think right."

"Send for him, David," said Madame P——; "let us hear what he has to say. He would not come back if he meant to be ugly."

"*Send* for him, Alice!" replied my host. "He's prouder than Lucifer, and would send me word to come to *him*. I will go. Will you accompany me, Mr. K——? You'll hear what a runaway nigger thinks of slavery: Sam has the gift of speech, and uses it regardless of persons."

"Yes, sir, I'll go with pleasure."

It was about an hour after nightfall when we emerged from the door of the mansion and took our way to the negro quarters. The full moon had risen half way above the horizon, and the dark pines cast their shadows around the little collection of negro huts, which straggled about through the woods for the distance of a third of a mile. It was dark, but I could distinguish the figure of a man striding along at a rapid pace a few hundred yards in advance of us.

"Is'nt that Moye?" I asked the Colonel, directing his attention to the receding figure.

"I reckon so; that's his gait. He's had a lesson to-day that'll do him good."

"I don't like that man's looks," I replied, carelessly; "but I've heard of singed cats."

"He *is* a sneaking d—l," said the Colonel; "but he's very valuable to me. I never had an overseer who got so much work out of the hands."

"Is he severe with them?"

"Well, I reckon he is; but a nigger is like a dog— you must flog him to make him like you."

"I judge your niggers haven't been flogged into liking Moye."

"Why, have you heard any of them speak of him?"

"Yes; though, of course, I've made no effort to draw gossip from them. I had to hear."

"O yes; I know; there's no end to their gabble; niggers will talk. But what have you heard?"

"That Moye is to blame in this affair of Sam, and that you don't know the whole story."

"What *is* the whole story?" he asked, stopping short in the road; "tell me before I see Sam."

I then told him what Jim had recounted to me. He heard me through attentively, then laughingly exclaimed:

"Is that all! Lord bless you, he didn't seduce her. There's no seducing these women; with them it's a thing of course. It was Sam's d— high blood that made the trouble. His father was the proudest man in Virginia, and Sam is as like him as a nigger can be like a white man."

"No matter what the blood is, it seems to me such an injury justifies revenge."

"Pshaw, my good fellow, you don't know these people. I'll stake my plantation against a glass of whiskey there's not a virtuous woman with a drop of black blood in her veins in all South Carolina. They prefer the white men; their husbands know it, and take it as a matter of course."

We had here reached the negro cabin. It was one of the more remote of the collection, and stood deep in the woods, an enormous pine growing up directly beside the doorway. In all respects it was like the other huts on the plantation. A bright fire lit up its interior, and through the crevices in the logs we saw, as we approached, a scene that made us pause involuntarily, when within a few rods of the house. The mulatto man, whose clothes were torn and smeared with swamp mud, stood near the fire. On a small pine table near him lay a large carving-knife, which glittered in the blaze, as if recently sharpened. His wife was seated on the side of the low bed at his back, weeping. She was two or three shades lighter than the man, and had the peculiar brown, kinky hair, straight, flat nose, and speckled, gray eyes which mark the metif. Tottling on the floor at the feet of the man, and caressing his knees, was a child of perhaps two years.

As we neared the house, we heard the voice of the

overseer issuing from the doorway on the other side of the pine-tree.

"Come out, ye black rascal."

"Come in, you wite hound, ef you dar," responded the negro, laying his hand on the carving-knife.

"Come out, I till ye; I sha'n't ax ye agin."

"I'll hab nuffin' to do wid you. G'way and send your massa har," replied the mulatto man, turning his face away with a lordly, contemptuous gesture, that spoke him a true descendant of Pocahontas. This movement exposed his left side to the doorway, outside of which, hidden from us by the tree, stood the overseer.

"Come away, Moye," said the Colonel, advancing with me toward the door; "*I'll* speak to him."

Before all of the words had escaped the Colonel's lips, a streak of fire flashed from where the overseer stood, and took the direction of the negro. One long, wild shriek—one quick, convulsive bound in the air—and Sam fell lifeless to the floor, the dark life-stream pouring from his side. The little child also fell with him, and its greasy, grayish shirt was dyed with its father's blood. Moye, at the distance of ten feet, had discharged the two barrels of a heavily-loaded shot-gun directly through the negro's heart.

"You incarnate son of h—," yelled the Colonel, as he sprang on the overseer, bore him to the ground, and wrenched the shot-gun from his hand. Clubbing the weapon, he raised it to brain him. The movement occupied but a second; the gun was descending, and in another instant Moye would have met Sam in eternity, had not a brawny arm caught the Colonel's, and, winding itself around his body, pinned his limbs to his side so that motion was impossible. The woman, half frantic with excitement, thrust open the door when her husband fell, and the light which came through it revealed the face of the new-comer. But his voice, which rang out on the night air as clear as a bugle, had there been no light, would have betrayed him. It was Scip. Spurning the prostrate overseer with his foot, he shouted:

"Run, you wite debble run for your life!"

"Let me go, you black scoundrel," shrieked the Colonel, wild with rage.

"When he'm out ob reach, you'd kill him," replied the negro, as cool as if he was doing an ordinary thing.

"I'll kill you, you black — hound, if you don't let me go," again screamed the Colonel, struggling violently in the negro's grasp, and literally foaming at the mouth.

"I shan't lef you gwo, Cunnel, till you 'gree not to do dat."

The Colonel was a stout, athletic man, in the very prime of life, and his rage gave him more than his ordinary strength, but Scip held him as I might have held a child.

"Here, Jim," shouted the Colonel to his body-servant, who just then emerged from among the trees, "'rouse the plantation—shoot this d— nigger."

"Dar aint one on 'em wud touch him, massa. He'd send *me* to de debble wid one fist."

"You ungrateful dog," groaned his master. "Mr. K——, will you stand by and see me handcuffed by a miserable slave?"

"The black means well, my friend; he has saved you from murder. Say he is safe, and I'll answer for his being away in an hour."

The Colonel made one more ineffectual attempt to free himself from the vice-like grip of the negro, then relaxing his efforts, and, gathering his broken breath, he said, "You're safe *now*, but if you're found within ten miles of my plantation by sunrise, by — you're a dead man."

The negro relinquished his hold, and, without saying a word, walked slowly away.

"Jim, you — rascal," said the Colonel to that courageous darky, who was skulking off, "raise every nigger on the plantation, catch Moye, or I'll flog you within an inch of your life."

"I'll do dat, Cunnel; I'll kotch de ole debble, ef he's dis side de hot place."

His words were echoed by about twenty other darkies, who, attracted by the noise of the fracas, had gathered within a safe distance of the cabin. They went off with Jim, to raise the other plantation hands, and inaugurate the hunt.

"If that — nigger hadn't held me, I'd had Moye in — by this time," said the Colonel to me, still livid with excitement.

"The law will deal with him, my friend. The negro has saved you from murder."

"The law be d—; it's too good for such a — hound; and that the d— nigger should have dared to hold me— by — he'll rue it."

He then turned, exhausted with the recent struggle, and, with a weak, uncertain step, entered the cabin. Kneeling down by the dead body of the negro, he attempted to raise it; but his strength was gone. He motioned to me to aid him, and we placed the corpse on the bed. Tearing open the clothing, we wiped away the still flowing blood, and saw the terrible wound which had sent the negro to his account. It was sickening to look on, and I turned to go.

The negro woman, who was weeping and wringing her hands, now approached, and, in a voice nearly choked with sobs, said:

"Massa, oh massa, I done it! it's me dat killed him!"

"I know you did, you d— —. Get out of my sight."

"Oh, massa," sobbed the woman, falling on her knees, "I'se so sorry; oh, forgib me!"

"Go to —, you — —, that's the place for you," said the Colonel, striking the kneeling woman with his foot, and felling her to the floor.

Unwilling to see or hear more, I left the master with the slave.

CHAPTER VI.

THE PLANTER'S "FAMILY."

A QUARTER of a mile through the woods brought me to the cabin of the old negress where Scip lodged. I rapped at the door, and was admitted by the old woman. Scip, nearly asleep, was lying on a pile of blankets in the corner.

"Are you mad?" I said to him. "The Colonel is frantic with rage, and swears he will kill you. You must be off at once."

"No, no, massa; neber fear; I knows him. He'd keep his word, ef he loss his life by it. I'm gwine afore sunrise; till den I'm safe."

"Der ye tink Massa Davy wud broke his word, sar?" said the old negress, bridling up her bent form, and speaking in a tone in which indignation mingled with wounded dignity; "p'raps gemmen do dat at de Norf—dey neber does it har."

"Excuse me, Aunty; I know your master is a man of honor; but he's very much excited, and very angry with Scip."

"No matter for dat, sar; Massa Davy neber done a mean ting sense he war born."

"Massa K—— tinks a heap ob de Cunnel, Aunty; but

he reckon he'm sort o' crazy now; dat make him afeard," said Scip, in an apologetic tone.

"What ef he am crazy? You'se safe *har*," rejoined the old woman, dropping her aged limbs into a chair, and rocking away with much the air which ancient white ladies occasionally assume.

"Wont you ax Massa K—— to a cheer?" said Scip; "he hab ben bery kine to me."

The negress then offered me a seat; but it was some minutes before I rendered myself sufficiently agreeable to thaw out the icy dignity of her manner. Meanwhile I glanced around the apartment.

Though the exterior of the cabin was like the others on the plantation, the interior had a rude, grotesque elegance about it far in advance of any negro hut I had ever seen. The logs were chinked with clay, and the one window, though destitute of glass, and ornamented with the inevitable board-shutter, had a green moreen curtain, which kept out the wind and the rain. A worn but neat and well swept carpet partly covered the floor, and on the low bed was spread a patch-work counterpane. Against the side of the room opposite the door stood an antique, brass-handled bureau, and an old-fashioned table, covered with a faded woollen cloth, occupied the centre of the apartment. In the corner near the fire was a curiously-contrived sideboard, made of narrow strips of yellow pine, tongued and grooved together, and oiled so as to bring out the beautiful grain of the wood. On it were several broken and cracked glasses, and an array of irregular crockery. The rocking chair, in which the old negress passed the most of her time, was of mahogany, wadded and covered with chintz, and the arm-seat I occupied, though old and patched in many places, had evidently moved in good society.

The mistress of this second-hand furniture establishment was arrayed in a mass of cast-off finery, whose gay colors were in striking contrast with her jet-black skin and bent, decrepit form. Her gown, which was very short, was of flaming red and yellow worsted stuff, and the enormous turban that graced her head and hid all but a few tufts of her frizzled, "pepper-and-salt" locks, was evidently a contribution from the family stock of worn-out pillow-cases. She was very aged—upward of seventy—and so thin that, had she not been endowed with speech and motion, she might have passed for a bundle of whalebone thrown into human shape, and covered with a coating of gutta-percha. It was evident she had been a valued house-servant, whose few remaining years were being soothed and solaced by the kind and indulgent care of a grateful master.

Scip, I soon saw, was a favorite with the old negress, and the marked respect he showed me quickly dispelled the angry feeling my doubts of "Massa Davy" had excited, and opened her heart and her mouth at the same moment. She was terribly garrulous; her tongue, as soon as it got under way, ran on as if propelled by machinery and acquainted with the secret of perpetual motion; but she was an interesting study. The single-hearted attachment she showed for her master and his family gave me a new insight into the practical working of "the peculiar institution," and convinced me that even slavery, in some of its aspects, is not so black as it is painted.

When we were seated, I said to Scip, "What induced you to lay hands on the Colonel? It is death, you know, if he enforces the law."

"I knows dat, massa; I knows dat; but I had to do it. Dat Moye am de ole debble, but de folks round har wud hab turned on de Cunnel, shore, ef he'd killed him. Dey don't like de Cunnel; dey say he'm a stuck-up seshener."

"The Colonel, then, has befriended you at some time?"

"No, no, sar; 'twarn't dat; dough I'se know'd him a long w'ile—eber sense my ole massa fotched me from Habana—but 'twarn't dat."

"Then *why* did you do it?"

The black hesitated a moment, and glanced at the old negress, then said:

"You see, massa, w'en I fuss come to Charles'n, a pore little ting, wid no friend in all de worle, dis ole aunty war a mudder to me. She nussed de Cunnel; he am jess like her own chile, and I know'd 'twud kill her ef he got hissef enter trubble."

I noticed certain convulsive twitchings about the corners of the old woman's mouth as she rose from her seat, threw her arms around Scip, and, in words broken by sobs, faltered out:

"*You* am my chile; I loves you better dan Massa Davy—better dan all de worle."

The scene, had they not been black, would have been one for a painter.

"You were the Colonel's nurse, Aunty," I said, when she had regained her composure. "Have you always lived with him?"

"Yas, sar, allers; I nussed him, and den de chil'ren—all ob 'em."

"*All* the children? I thought the Colonel had but one—Miss Clara."

"Wal, he habn't, massa, only de boys."

"What boys? I never heard he had sons."

"Neber heerd of young Massa Davy, nor Massa Tommy! Haint you *seed* Massa Tommy, sar?"

"Tommy! I was told he was Madam P——'s son."

"So he am; Massa Davy had *her* long afore he had missus."

The truth flashed upon me; but could it be possible? Was I in South Carolina or in Utah?

"Who *is* Madam P——?" I asked.

The old woman hesitated a moment as if in doubt whether she had not said too much; but Scip quietly replied:

"She'm jess what aunty am—*de Cunnel's slave!*"

"His *slave!* it can't be possible; she is white!"

"No, massa; she am brack, and de Cunnel's slave!"

Not to weary the reader with a long repetition of negro-English, I will tell in brief what I gleaned from an hour's conversation with the two blacks.

Madam P—— was the daughter of Ex-Gov. ——, of Virginia, by a quarteron woman. She was born a slave, but was acknowledged as her father's child, and reared in his family with his legitimate children. When she was ten years old her father died, and his estate proving insolvent, the land and negroes were brought under the hammer. His daughter, never having been manumitted, was inventoried and sold with the other property. The Colonel, then just of age, and a young man of fortune, bought her and took her to the residence of his mother in Charleston. A governess was provided for her, and a year or two afterward she was taken to the North to be educated. There she was frequently visited by the Colonel; and when fifteen her condition became such that she was obliged to return home. He conveyed her to the plantation, where her elder son, David, was soon after born, "Aunt Lucy" officiating on the occasion. When the child was two years old, leaving it in charge of the aged negress, she accompanied the Colonel to Europe, where they remained for a year. Subsequently she passed another year at a Northern seminary; and then, returning to the homestead, was duly installed as its mistress, and had ever since presided over its domestic affairs. She was kind and good to the negroes, who were greatly

THE PLANTER'S "FAMILY." 133

attached to her, and much of the Colonel's wealth was due to her excellent management of the plantation.

Six years after the birth of "young Massa Davy," the Colonel married his present wife, that lady having full knowledge of his left-handed connection with Madam P——, and consenting that the "bond-woman" should remain on the plantation, as its mistress. The legitimate wife resided, during most of the year, in Charleston, and when at the homestead took little interest in domestic matters. On one of her visits to the plantation, twelve years before, her daughter, Miss Clara, was born, and within a week, under the same roof, Madam P—— presented the Colonel with a son—the lad Thomas, of whom I have spoken. As the mother was slave, the children were so also at birth, but *they* had been manumitted by their father. One of them was being educated in Germany; and it was intended that both should spend their lives in that country, the taint in their blood being an insuperable bar to their ever acquiring social position at the South.

As she finished the story, the old woman said, "Massa Davy am bery kind to the missus, sar, but he *love* de ma'am; an' he can't help it, 'cause she'm jess so good as de angels."*

---

* Instances are frequent where Southern gentlemen form these left-handed connections, and rear two sets of differently colored children; but it is not often that the two families occupy the same domicil. The only other case within my *personal* knowledge was that of the well-known President of the Bank of St. M——, at Columbus, Ga. That gentleman, whose note ranked in Wall Street, when the writer was acquainted with that locality, as "A No. 1," lived for fifteen years with two "wives" under one roof. One, an accomplished white woman,

I looked at my watch—it was nearly ten o'clock, and I rose to go. As I did so the old negress said:

"Don't yer gwo, massa, 'fore you hab sum ob aunty's wine; you'm good friends wid Scip, and I knows *you'se* not too proud to drink wid brack folks, ef you am from de Norf."

Being curious to know what quality of wine a plantation slave indulged in, I accepted the invitation. She went to the side-board, and brought out a cut-glass decanter, and three cracked tumblers, which she placed on the table. Filling the glasses to the brim, she passed one to Scip, and one to me; and, with the other in her hand, resumed her seat. Wishing her a good many happy years, and Scip a pleasant journey home, I emptied my glass. It was Scuppernong, and the pure juice of the grape!

"Aunty," I said, "this wine is as fine as I ever tasted."

"Oh, yas, massa, it am de raal stuff. I growed de grapes myseff."

"You grew them?"

"Yas, sar, an' Massa Davy make de wine. He do it ebery yar for de ole nuss."

and the mother of several children—did the honors of his table, and moved with him in "the best society;" the other—a beautiful quadroon, also the mother of several children—filled the humbler office of nurse to her own and the other's offspring.

In conversation with a well-known Southern gentleman, not long since, I mentioned these two cases, and commented on them as a man educated with New England ideas might be supposed to do. The gentleman admitted that he knew of twenty such instances, and gravely defended the practice as being infinitely more moral and respectable than *the more common relation* existing between masters and slaves.

"The Colonel is very good. Do you raise any thing else?"

"Yas, I hab collards and taters, a little corn, and most ebery ting."

"But who does your work? *You* certainly can't do it?"

"Oh, de ma'am looks arter dat, sar; she'm bery good to de ole aunty."

Shaking hands with both the negroes, I left the cabin, fully convinced that all the happiness in this world is not found within plastered apartments.

The door of the mansion was bolted and barred; but, rapping for admission, I soon heard the Colonel's voice asking, "Who is there?" Giving a satisfactory answer, I was admitted. Explaining that he supposed I had retired to my room, he led the way to the library.

That apartment was much more elegantly furnished than the drawing-rooms. Three of its sides were lined with books, and on the centre-table, papers, pamphlets, and manuscripts were scattered in promiscuous confusion. In an arm-chair near the fire, Madame P—— was seated, reading. The Colonel's manner was as composed as if nothing had disturbed the usual routine of the plantation; no trace of the recent terrible excitement was visible; in fact, had I not been a witness to the late tragedy, I should have thought it incredible that he, within two hours, had been an actor in a scene which had cost a human being his life.

"Where in creation have you been, my dear fellow?" he asked, as we took our seats.

"At old Lucy's cabin, with Scip," I replied.

"Indeed. I supposed the darky had gone."

"No, he doesn't go till the morning."

"I told you he wouldn't, David," said Madame P——; "now, send for him—make friends with him before he goes."

"No, Alice, it wont do. I bear him no ill-will, but it wont do. It would be all over the plantation in an hour."

"No matter for that; our people would like you the better for it."

"No, no. I can't do it. I mean him no harm, but I can't do that."

"He told me *why* he interfered between you and Moye," I remarked.

"Why did he?"

"He says old Lucy, years ago, was a mother to him; that she is greatly attached to you, and it would kill her if any harm happened to you; and that your neighbors bear you no good-will, and would have enforced the law had you killed Moye."

"It is true, David; you would have had to answer for it."

"Nonsense! what influence could this North County scum have against *me?*"

"Perhaps none. But that makes no difference; Scipio did right, and you should tell him you forgive him."

The Colonel then rang a small bell, and a negro wo-

THE PLANTER'S "FAMILY." 137

man soon appeared. "Sue," he said, "go to Aunt Lucy's, and ask Scip to come here. Bring him in at the front door, and, mind, let no one know he comes."

The woman in a short time returned with Scip. There was not a trace of fear or embarrassment in the negro's manner as he entered the room. Making a respectful bow, he bade us "good evening."

"Good evening, Scip," said the Colonel, rising and giving the black his hand; "let us be friends. Madam tells me I should forgive you, and I do."

"Aunt Lucy say ma'am am an angel, sar, and it am tru—*it am tru*, sar," replied the negro with considerable feeling.

The lady rose, also, and took Scip's hand, saying, "*I* not only forg've you, but I *thank* you for what you have done. I shall never forget it."

"You'se too good, ma'am; you'se too good to say dat," replied the darky, the moisture coming to his eyes; "but I meant nuffin' wrong—I meant nuffin' dis'specful to de Cunnel."

"I know you didn't, Scip; but we'll say no more about it;—good-by," said the Colonel.

Shaking hands with each one of us, the darky left the apartment.

One who does not know that the high-bred Southern gentleman considers the black as far below him as the horse he drives, or the dog he kicks, cannot realize the amazing sacrifice of pride which the Colonel made in seeking a reconciliation with Scip. It was the cutting off of his right hand. The circumstance showed the powerful influence held over him by the octoroon woman. Strange that she, his slave, cast out from society by her blood and her life, despised, no doubt, by all the world, save by him and a few ignorant blacks, should thus control a proud, self-willed, passionate man, and control him, too, only for good.

After the black had gone, I said to the Colonel, "I was much interested in old Lucy. A few more such instances of cheerful and contented old age, might lead me to think better of slavery."

"Such cases are not rare, sir. They show the paternal character of our 'institution.' We are *forced* to care for our servants in their old age."

"But have your other aged slaves the same comforts that Aunt Lucy has?"

"No; they don't need them. She has been accustomed to live in my house, and to fare better than the plantation hands; she therefore requires better treatment."

"Is not the support of that class a heavy tax upon you?"

"Yes, it *is* heavy. We have, of course, to deduct it from the labor of the able-bodied hands."

"What is the usual proportion of sick and infirm on your plantation?"

"Counting in the child-bearing women, I reckon about twenty per cent."

"And what does it cost you to support each hand?"

"Well, it costs *me*, for children and all, about seventy-five dollars a year. In some places it costs less. *I* have to buy all my provisions."

"What proportion of your slaves are able-bodied hands?"

"Somewhere about sixty per cent. I have, all told, old and young—men, women, and children—two hundred and seventy. Out of that number I have now equal to a hundred and fifty-four *full* hands. You understand that we classify them: some do only half tasks, some three-quarters. I have *more* than a hundred and fifty-four working-men and women, but they do only that number of full tasks."

"What does the labor of a *full* hand yield?"

"At the present price of turpentine, my calculation is about two hundred dollars a year."

"Then your crop brings you about thirty-one thousand dollars, and the support of your negroes costs you twenty thousand."

"Yes."

"If that's the case, my friend, let me advise you to sell your plantation, free your niggers, and go North."

"Why so, my dear fellow?" asked the Colonel laughing.

"Because you'd make money by the operation."

"I never was good at arithmetic; go into the figures," he replied, still laughing, while Madam P——, who had laid aside her book, listened very attentively.

"Well, you have two hundred and seventy negroes,

whom you value, we'll say, with your mules, 'stills,' and movable property, at two hundred thousand dollars; and twenty thousand acres of land, worth about three dollars and a half an acre; all told, two hundred and seventy thousand dollars. A hundred and fifty-four able-bodied hands produce you a yearly profit of eleven thousand dollars, which, saying nothing about the cost of keeping your live stock, the wear and tear of your mules and machinery, and the yearly loss of your slaves by death, is only four per cent. on your capital. Now, with only the price of your land, say seventy thousand dollars, invested in safe stocks at the North, you could realize eight per cent.—five thousand six hundred dollars—and live at ease; and that, I judge, if you have many runaways, or many die on your hands, is as much as you really *clear* now. Besides, if you should invest seventy thousand dollars in almost any legitimate business at the North, and should add to it, *as you now do*, your *time* and *labor*, you would realize far more than you do at present from your entire capital."

"I never looked at the matter in that light. But I have given you my profits as they *now* are; some years I make more; six years ago I made twenty-five thousand dollars."

"Yes; and six years hence you may make nothing."

"That's true. But it would cost me more to live at the North."

"There you are mistaken. What do you pay for your corn, your pork, and your hay, for instance?"

"Well, my corn I have to bring round by vessel from Washington (North Carolina), and it costs me high when it gets here—about ten bits (a dollar and twenty-five cents), I think."

"And in New York you could buy it now at sixty to seventy cents. What does your hay cost?"

"Thirty-five dollars. I pay twenty for it in New York—the balance is freight and hauling."

"Your pork costs you two or three dollars, I suppose, for freight and hauling."

"Yes; about that."

"Then in those items you might save nearly a hundred per cent.; and they are the principal articles you consume."

"Yes; there's no denying that. But another thing is just as certain: it costs less to support one of my niggers than one of your laboring men."

"That may be true. But it only shows that our laborers fare better than your slaves."

"I am not sure of that. I *am* sure, however, that our slaves are more contented than the run of laboring men at the North."

"That proves nothing. Your blacks have no hope, no chance to rise; and they submit—though I judge not cheerfully—to an iron necessity. The Northern laborer, if very poor, may be discontented; but discontent urges him to effort, and leads to the bettering of his condition. I tell you, my friend, slavery is an expensive luxury.

You Southern nabobs *will* have it; and you have to *pay for it.*"

"Well, we don't complain. But, seriously, my good fellow, I feel that I am carrying out the design of the Almighty in holding my niggers. I think he made the black to serve the white."

"*I* think," I replied, "that whatever He designs works perfectly. Your institution certainly does not. It keeps the producer, who, in every society, is the really valuable citizen, in the lowest poverty, while it allows those who do nothing to be 'clad in fine linen, and to fare sumptuously every day.'"

"It does more than that, sir," said Madam P——, with animation; "it brutalizes and degrades the *master* and the *slave;* it separates husband and wife, parent and child; it sacrifices virtuous women to the lust of brutal men; and it shuts millions out from the knowledge of their duty and their destiny. A good and just God could not have designed it; and it *must* come to an end."

If lightning had struck in the room I could not have been more startled than I was by the abrupt utterance of such language in a planter's house, in his very presence, and *by his slave.* The Colonel, however, expressed no surprise and no disapprobation. It was evidently no new thing to him.

"It is rare, madam," I said, "to hear such sentiments from a Southern lady—one reared among slaves."

Before she could reply, the Colonel laughingly said:

"Bless you, Mr. K——, madam is an out-and-out abolitionist, worse by fifty per cent. than Garrison or Wendell Phillips. If she were at the North she would take to pantaloons, and 'stump' the entire free States; wouldn't you, Alice?"

"I have no doubt of it," rejoined the lady, smiling. "But I fear I should have poor success. I've tried for ten years to convert *you*, and Mr. K—— can see the result."

It had grown late; and with my head full of working niggers and white slave-women, I went to my apartment.

The next day was Sunday. It was near the close of December, yet the air was as mild and the sun as warm as in our Northern October. It was arranged at the breakfast-table that we all should attend service at "the meeting-house," a church of the Methodist persuasion, located some eight miles away; but as it wanted some hours of the time for religious exercises to commence, I strolled out after breakfast, with the Colonel, to inspect the stables of the plantation. "Massa Tommy" accompanied us, without invitation; and in the Colonel's intercourse with him I observed as much freedom and familiarity as he would have shown to an acknowledged son. The youth's manners and conversation showed that great attention had been given to his education and training, and made it evident that the mother whose influence was forming his character, whatever a false system of society had made her life, possessed some of the best traits of her sex.

The stables, a collection of one-story framed buildings, about a hundred rods from the house, were well lighted and ventilated, and contained all "the modern improvements." They were better built, warmer, more commodious, and in every way more comfortable than the shanties occupied by the human cattle of the plantation. I remarked as much to the Colonel, adding that one who did not know would infer that he valued his horses more than his slaves.

"That may be true," he replied, laughing. "Two of my horses are worth more than any eight of my slaves;" at the same time calling my attention to two magnificent thorough-breds, one of which had made "2.32" on the Charleston course. The establishment of a Southern gentleman is not complete until it includes one or two of these useless appendages. I had an argument with my host as to their value compared with that of the steam-engine, in which I forced him to admit that the iron horse is the better of the two, because it performs more work, eats less, has greater speed, and is not liable to the spavin or the heaves; but he wound up by saying, "After all, I go for the thorough-breds. You Yankees have but one test of value—use."

A ramble through the negro-quarters, which followed our visit to the stables, gave me some further glimpses of plantation life. Many of the hands were still away in pursuit of Moye, but enough remained to make it evident that Sunday is the happiest day in the darky calendar. Groups of all ages and colors were gathered in front of several of the cabins, some singing, some dancing, and others chatting quietly together, but all enjoying themselves as heartily as so many young animals let loose in a pasture. They saluted the Colonel and me respectfully, but each one had a free, good-natured word for "Massa Tommy," who seemed an especial favorite with them. The lad took their greetings in good part, but preserved an easy, unconscious dignity of manner that plainly showed he did not know that *he* too was of their despised, degraded race.

The Colonel, in a rapid way, gave me the character and peculiarities of nearly every one we met. The titles of some of them amused me greatly. At every step we encountered individuals whose names have become household words in every civilized country.* Julius Cæsar, slightly stouter than when he swam the Tiber, and somewhat tanned from long exposure to a Southern sun, was seated on a wood-pile, quietly smoking a pipe; while near him, Washington, divested of regimentals, and clad in a modest suit of reddish-gray, his thin locks frosted by time, and his fleshless visage showing great age, was gazing, in rapt admiration, at a group of dancers in front of old Lucy's cabin.

In this group about thirty men and women were making the ground quake and the woods ring with their unrestrained jollity. Marc Antony was rattling away

---

* Among the things of which slavery has deprived the black is a *name*. A slave has no family designation. It may be for that reason that a high-sounding appellation is usually selected for the single one he is allowed to appropriate

at the bones, Nero fiddling as if Rome were burning, and Hannibal clawing at a banjo as if the fate of Carthage hung on its strings. Napoleon, as young and as lean as when he mounted the bridge of Lodi, with the battle-smoke still on his face, was moving his legs even faster than in the Russian retreat; and Wesley was using his heels in a way that showed *they* didn't belong to the Methodist church. But the central figures of the group were Cato and Victoria. The lady had a face like a thunder-cloud, and a form that, if whitewashed, would have outsold the "Greek Slave." She was built on springs, and "floated in the dance" like a feather in a high wind. Cato's mouth was like an alligator's, but when it opened, it issued notes that would draw the specie even in this time of general suspension. As we approached he was singing a song, but he paused on perceiving us, when the Colonel, tossing a handful of coin among them, called out, "Go on, boys; let the gentleman have some music; and you, Vic, show your heels like a beauty."

A general scramble followed, in which "Vic's" sense of decorum forbade her to join, and she consequently got nothing. Seeing that, I tossed her a silver piece, which she caught. Grinning her thanks, she shouted, "Now, clar de track, you nigs; start de music. I'se gwine to gib de gemman de breakdown."

And she did; and such a breakdown! "We w'ite folks," though it was no new thing to the Colonel or Tommy, almost burst with laughter.

In a few minutes nearly every negro on the plantation, attracted by the presence of the Colonel and myself, gathered around the performers; and a shrill voice at my elbow called out, "Look har, ye lazy, good-for-nuffin' niggers, carn't ye fotch a cheer for Massa Davy and de strange gemman?"

"Is that you, Aunty?" said the Colonel. "How d'ye do?"

"Sort o' smart, Massa Davy; sort o' smart; how is ye?"

"Pretty well, Aunty; pretty well. Have a seat." And the Colonel helped her to one of the chairs that were brought for us, with as much tenderness as he would have shown to an aged white lady.

The "exercises," which had been suspended for a moment, recommenced, and the old negress entered into them as heartily as the youngest present. A song from Cato followed the dance, and then about twenty "gentleman and lady" darkies joined, two at a time, in a half "walk-round" half breakdown, which the Colonel told me was the original of the well-known dance and song of Lucy Long. Other performances succeeded, and the whole formed a scene impossible to describe. Such uproarious jollity, such full and perfect enjoyment, I had never seen in humanity, black or white. The little nigs, only four or five years old, would rush into the ring and shuffle away at the breakdowns till I feared their short legs would come off; while all the darkies joined in the songs, till the branches of the old pines above shook as if they too had caught the spirit of the music. In the midst of it, the Colonel said to me, in an exultant tone:

"Well, my friend, what do you think of slavery now?"

"About the same that I thought yesterday. I see nothing to change my views."

"Why, are not these people happy? Is not this perfect enjoyment?"

"Yes; just the same enjoyment that aunty's pigs are having; don't you hear *them* singing to the music? I'll wager they are the happier of the two."

"No; you are wrong. The higher faculties of the darkies are being brought out here."

"I don't know that," I replied. "Within the sound of their voices, two of their fellows—victims to the inhumanity of slavery—are lying dead, and yet they make *Sunday* "hideous" with wild jollity, while Sam's fate may be theirs to-morrow."

Spite of his genuine courtesy and high breeding, a shade of displeasure passed over the Colonel's face as I made this remark. Rising to go, he said, a little impatiently, "Ah, I see how it is; that d— Garrison's sentiments have impregnated even you. How can the North and the South hold together when moderate men like you and me are so far apart?"

"But you," I rejoined, good-humoredly, "are not a moderate man. You and Garrison are of the same stripe, both extremists. *You* have mounted one hobby, *he* another; that is all the difference."

"I should be sorry," he replied, recovering his good-nature, "to think myself like Garrison. I consider him the —— scoundrel unhung."

"No; I think he means well. But you are both fanatics, both 'bricks' of the same material; we conservatives, like mortar, will hold you together and yet keep you apart."

"I, for one, *won't* be held. If I can't get out of this cursed Union in any other way, I'll emigrate to Cuba."

I laughed, and just then, looking up, caught a glimpse of Jim, who stood, hat in hand, waiting to speak to the Colonel, but not daring to interrupt a white conversation.

"Hallo, Jim," I said; 'have you got back?"

"Yas, sar," replied Jim, grinning all over as if he had some agreeable thing to communicate.

"Where is Moye?" asked the Colonel.

"Kotched, massa; I'se got de padlocks on him."

"Kotched," echoed half a dozen darkies, who stood near enough to hear; "Ole Moye is kotched," ran through the crowd, till the music ceased, and a shout went up from two hundred black throats that made the old trees tremble.

"Now gib him de lashes, Massa Davy," cried the old nurse. "Gib him what he gabe pore Sam; but mine dat you keeps widin de law."

"Never fear, Aunty," said the Colonel; "I'll give him —."

How the Colonel kept his word will be told in another chapter.

CHAPTER VII.

PLANTATION DISCIPLINE.

The "Ole Cabin" to which Jim had alluded as the scene of Sam's punishment by the overseer, was a one-story shanty in the vicinity of the stables. Though fast falling to decay, it had more the appearance of a human habitation than the other huts on the plantation. Its thick plank door was ornamented with a mouldy brass knocker, and its four windows contained sashes, to which here and there clung a broken pane, the surviving relic of its better days. It was built of large unhewn logs, notched at the ends and laid one upon the other, with the bark still on. The thick, rough coat which yet adhered in patches to the timber had opened in the sun, and let the rain and the worm burrow in its sides, till some parts had crumbled entirely away. . At one corner the process of decay had gone on till roof, superstructure, and foundation had rotted down and left an opening large enough to admit a coach and four horses. The huge chimneys which had graced the gable ends of the building were fallen in, leaving only a mass of sticks and clay to tell of their existence, and two wide openings to show how great a figure they had once made in the world. A small space in front of the cabin would have been a lawn, had the grass been willing to grow upon it; and a few acres of cleared land in its rear might have passed for a garden, had it not been entirely overgrown with young pines and stubble. This primitive structure was once the "mansion" of that broad plantation, and, before the production of turpentine came into fashion in that region, its rude owner drew his support from its few surrounding acres, more truly independent than the present aristocratic proprietor, who, raising only one article, and buying all his provisions, was forced to draw his support from the Yankee or the Englishman.

Only one room, about forty feet square, occupied the interior of the cabin. It once contained several apartments, vestiges of which still remained, but the partitions had been torn away to fit it for its present uses. What those uses were, a moment's observation showed me.

In the middle of the floor, a space about fifteen feet square was covered with thick pine planking, strongly nailed to the beams. In the centre of this planking, an oaken block was firmly bolted, and to it was fastened a strong iron staple that held a log-chain, to which was attached a pair of shackles. Above this, was a queer frame-work of oak, somewhat resembling the contrivance for drying fruit I have seen in Yankee farmhouses. Attached to the rafters by stout pieces of timber, were two hickory poles, placed horizontally, and about four feet apart, the lower one rather more than eight feet from the floor. This was the whipping-rack, and hanging to it were several stout whips with short hickory handles, and long triple lashes. I took one down for closer inspection, and found burned into the wood, in large letters, the words " Moral Suasion." I questioned the appropriateness of the label, but the Colonel insisted with great gravity, that the whip is the only " moral suasion" a darky is capable of understanding.

When punishment is inflicted on one of the Colonel's negroes, his feet are confined in the shackles, his arms tied above his head, and drawn by a stout cord up to one of the horizontal poles; then, his back bared to the waist, and standing on tip-toe, with every muscle stretched to its utmost tension, he takes "de lashes."

A more severe but more unusual punishment is the " thumb-screw." In this a noose is passed around the negro's thumb and fore-finger, while the cord is thrown over the upper cross-pole, and the culprit is drawn up till his toes barely touch the ground. In this position the whole weight of the body rests on the thumb and fore-finger. The torture is excruciating, and strong, able-bodied men can endure it but a few moments. The Colonel naively told me that he had discontinued its practice, as several of his *women* had nearly lost the use of their hands, and been incapacitated for field labor, by its too frequent repetition. "My —— drivers,"* he added, "have no discretion, and no humanity; if they have a pique against a nigger, they show him no mercy."

The old shanty I have described was now the place of the overseer's confinement. Open as it was at top, bot-

---

* The negro-whippers and field overseers.

tom, and sides, it seemed an unsafe prison-house; but Jim had secured its present occupant by placing "de padlocks on him."

"Where did you catch him?" asked the Colonel, as, followed by every darky on the plantation, we took our way to the old building.

"In de swamp, massa. We got Sandy and de dogs arter him—dey treed him, but he fit like de debble."

"Any one hurt?"

"Yas, Cunnel; he knifed Yaller Jake, and ef I hadn't a gibin him a wiper, you'd a had anudder nigger short dis mornin'—shore."

"How was it? tell me," said his master, while we paused, and the darkies gathered around.

"Wal, yer see, massa, we got de ole debble's hat dat he drapped wen you had him down; den we went to Sandy's fur de dogs—dey scented him to onst, and off dey put for de swamp. 'Bout twenty on us follored 'em. He'd a right smart start on us, and run like a deer, but de hounds kotched up wid him 'bout whar he shot pore Sam. He fit 'em and cut up de Lady awful, but ole Cæsar got a hole ob him, and sliced a breakfuss out ob his legs. Somehow, dough, he got 'way from de ole dog, and clum a tree. 'Twar more'n an hour afore we kotched up; but dar he war, and de houns baying 'way as ef dey know'd what an ole debble he am. I'd tuk one ob de guns—you warn't in de house, massa, so I cudn't ax you."

"Never mind that; go on," said the Colonel.

7*

"Wal, I up wid de gun, and tole him ef he didn't cum down I'd gib him suffin' dat 'ud sot hard on de stummuk. It tuk him a long w'ile, but—he *cum down.*" Here the darky showed a row of ivory that would have been a fair capital for a metropolitan dentist.

"When he war down," he resumed, "Jake war gwine to tie him, but de ole 'gator, quicker dan a flash, put a knife enter him."

"Is Jake much hurt?" interrupted the Colonel.

"Not bad, massa; de knife went fru his arm, and enter his ribs, but de ma'am hab fix him, and she say he'll be 'round bery sudden."

"Well, what then?" inquired the Colonel.

"Wen de ole debble seed he hadn't finished Jake, he war gwine to gib him anudder dig, but jus den I drap de gun on his cocoanut, and he neber trubble us no more. 'Twar mons'rous hard work to git him out ob de swamp, 'cause he war jess like a dead man, and had to be toted de hull way; but he'm dar now, massa (pointing to the old cabin), and de bracelets am on him."

"Where is Jake?" asked the Colonel.

"Dunno, massa, but reckon he'm to hum."

"One of you boys go and bring him to the cabin," said the Colonel.

A negro man went off on the errand, while we and the darkies resumed our way to the overseer's quarters. Arrived there, I witnessed a scene that words cannot picture.

Stretched at full length on the floor, his clothes torn

to shreds, his coarse carroty hair matted with blood, and his thin, ugly visage pale as death, lay the overseer. Bending over him, wiping away the blood from his face, and swathing a ghastly wound on his forehead, was the negress Sue; while at his shackled feet, binding up his still bleeding legs, knelt the octoroon woman!

"Is *she* here?" I said, involuntarily, as I caught sight of the group.

"It's her nature," said the Colonel, with a pleasant smile; "if Moye were the devil himself, she'd do him good if she could; another such woman never lived."

And yet this woman, with all the instincts that make her sex angel-ministers to man, lived in daily violation of the most sacred of all laws—because she was a slave. Can Mr. Caleb Cushing or Charles O'Conor tell us why the Almighty invented a system which forces his creatures to break laws of His own making?

"Don't waste your time on him, Alice," said the Colonel, kindly; "he isn't worth the rope that'll hang him."

"He was bleeding to death; unless he has care he'll die," said the octoroon woman.

"Then let him die, d—— him," replied the Colonel, advancing to where the overseer lay, and bending down to satisfy himself of his condition.

Meanwhile more than two hundred dusky forms crowded around and filled every opening of the old building. Every conceivable emotion, except pity, was depicted on their dark faces. The same individuals whose cloudy visages a half hour before I had seen distended with a wild mirth and careless jollity, that made me think them really the docile, good-natured animals they are said to be, now glared on the prostrate overseer with the infuriated rage of aroused beasts when springing on their prey.

"You can't come the possum here. Get up, you —— hound," said the Colonel, rising and striking the bleeding man with his foot.

The fellow raised himself on one elbow and gazed around with a stupid, vacant look. His eye wandered unsteadily for a moment from the Colonel to the throng of cloudy faces in the doorway; then, his recent experience flashing upon him, he shrieked out, clinging wildly to the skirts of the octoroon woman, who was standing near, "Keep off them cursed hounds—keep them off, I say—they'll kill me! they'll kill me!"

One glance satisfied me that his mind was wandering. The blow on the head had shattered his reason, and made the strong man less than a child.

"You wont be killed yet," said the Colonel. "You've a small account to settle with me before you reckon with the devil."

At this moment the dark crowd in the doorway parted, and Jake entered, his arm bound up and in a sling.

"Jake, come here," said the Colonel; "this man would have killed you. What shall we do with him?"

"'Taint for a darky to say dat, massa," said the negro, evidently unaccustomed to the rude administration of justice which the Colonel was about to inaugurate; "he did wuss dan dat to Sam, massa—he orter swing for shootin' him."

"That's *my* affair; we'll settle your account first," replied the Colonel.

The darky looked undecidedly at his master, and then at the overseer, who, overcome by weakness, had sunk again to the floor. The little humanity in him was evidently struggling with his hatred of Moye and his desire for revenge, when the old nurse yelled out from among the crowd, "Gib him fifty lashes, Massa Davy, and den you wash him down.* Be a man, Jake, and say dat."

Jake still hesitated, and when at last he was about to speak, the eye of the octoroon caught his, and chained the words to his tongue, as if by magnetic power.

"Do you say that, boys;" said the Colonel, turning to the other negroes; "shall he have fifty lashes?"

"Yas, massa, fifty lashes—gib de ole debble fifty lashes," shouted about fifty voices.

"He shall have them," quietly said the master.

The mad shout that followed, which was more like the yell of demons than the cry of men, seemed to arouse Moye to a sense of his real position. Springing to his feet, he gazed wildly around; then, sinking on his knees before the octoroon, and clutching the folds of her dress, he shrieked, "Save me, good lady, save me! as you hope for mercy, save me!"

---

* Referring to the common practice of bathing the raw and bleeding backs of the punished slaves with a strong solution of salt and water.

Not a muscle of her face moved, but, turning to the excited crowd, she mildly said, "Fifty lashes would kill him. *Jake* does not say that—your master leaves it to him, and *he* will not whip a dying man—will you, Jake?"

"No, ma'am—not—not ef you gwo agin it," replied the negro, with very evident reluctance.

"But he whipped Sam, ma'am, when Sam war nearer dead than *he* am," said Jim, whose station as house-servant allowed him a certain freedom of speech.

"Because he was brutal to Sam, should you be brutal to him? Can you expect me to tend you when you are sick, if you beat a dying man? Does Pompey say you should do such things?"

"No, good ma'am," said the old preacher, stepping out, with the freedom of an old servant, from the black mass, and taking his stand beside me in the open space left for the "w'ite folks;" "de ole man dusn't say dat, ma'am; he tell 'em dat de Lord want 'em to forgib dar en'mies—to lub dem dat pursyskute 'em;" and, turning to the Colonel, he added, as he passed his hand meekly over his thin crop of white wool and threw his long heel back, "ef massa'll 'low me I'll talk to 'em."

"Fire away," said the Colonel, with evident chagrin. "This is a nigger trial; if you want to screen the d—— hound you can do it."

"I dusn't want to screed him, massa, but I'se bery ole and got soon to gwo, and I dusn't want de blessed Lord to ax me wen I gets dar why I 'lowed dese pore ig'nant brack folks to mudder a man 'fore my bery face. I toted you, massa, 'fore you cud gwo, I'se worked for you till I can't work no more; and I dusn't want to tell de Lord dat *my* massa let a brudder man be killed in cole blood."

"He is no brother of mine, you old fool; preach to the nigs, don't preach to me," said the Colonel, stifling his displeasure, and striding off through the black crowd, without saying another word.

Here and there in the dark mass a face showed signs of relenting; but much the larger number of that strange jury, had the question been put, would have voted— DEATH.

The old preacher turned to them as the Colonel passed out, and said, "My chil'ren, would you hab dis man whipped, so weak, so dyin' as he am, ef he war brack?"

"No, not ef he war a darky—fer den he wouldn't be such an ole debble," replied Jim, and about a dozen of the other negroes.

"De w'ite aint no wuss dan de brack—we'm all 'like—pore sinners all on us. De Lord wudn't whip a w'ite man no sooner dan a brack one—He tinks de w'ite juss so good as de brack (good Southern doctrine, I thought). De porest w'ite trash wudn't strike a man wen he war down."

"We'se had 'nough of dis, ole man," said a large, powerful negro (one of the drivers), stepping forward, and, regardless of the presence of Madam P—— and myself, pressing close to where the overseer lay, now totally unconscious of what was passing around him. "You needn't preach no more; de Cunnel hab say we'm to whip ole Moye, and we'se gwine to do it, by ——."

I felt my fingers closing on the palm of my hand, and in a second more they might have cut the darky's profile, had not Madam P—— cried out, "Stand back, you impudent fellow: say another word, and I'll have you whipped on the spot."

"De Cunnel am my massa, ma'am—*he* say ole Moye am to be whipped, and I'se gwine to do it—shore."

I have seen a storm at sea—I have seen the tempest tear up great trees—I have seen the lightning strike in a dark night—but I never saw any thing half so grand, half so terrible, as the glance and tone of that woman as she cried out, "Jim, take this man—give him fifty lashes this instant."

Quicker than thought, a dozen darkies were on him. His hands and feet were tied and he was under the whipping-rack in a second. Turning then to the other negroes, the brave woman said, "Some of you carry Moye to the house, and you, Jim, see to this man—if fifty lashes don't make him sorry, give him fifty more."

This summary change of programme was silently acquiesced in by the assembled negroes, but many a cloudy face scowled sulkily on the octoroon, as, leaning on my arm, she followed Junius and the other negroes, who bore Moye to the mansion. It was plain that under those dark faces a fire was burning that a breath would have fanned into a flame.

We entered the house by its rear door, and placed Moye in a small room on the ground floor. He was laid on a bed, and stimulants being given him, his senses and reason shortly returned. His eyes opened, and his real position seemed suddenly to flash upon him, for he turned to Madam P——, and in a weak voice, half choked with emotion, faltered out: "May God in heaven bless ye, ma'am; God *will* bless ye for bein' so good to a wicked man like me. I doesn't desarve it, but ye woant leave me—ye woant leave me—they'll kill me ef ye do!"

"Don't fear," said the Madam; "you shall have a fair trial. No harm shall come to you here."

"Thank ye, thank ye," gasped the overseer, raising himself on one arm, and clutching at the lady's hand, which he tried to lift to his lips.

"Don't say any more now," said Madam P——, quietly; "you must rest and be quiet, or you wont get well."

"Shan't I get well? Oh, I can't die—I can't die *now!*"

The lady made a soothing reply, and giving him an opiate, and arranging the bedding so that he might rest more easily, she left the room with me.

As we stepped into the hall, I saw through the front door, which was open, the horses harnessed in readiness for "meeting," and the Colonel pacing to and to on the piazza, smoking a cigar. He perceived us, and halted in the doorway.

"So you've brought that d—— bloodthirsty villain into my house!" he said to Madam P—— in a tone of strong displeasure.

"How could I help it? The negroes are mad, and would kill him anywhere else," replied the lady, with a certain self-confidence that showed she knew her power over the Colonel.

"Why should *you* interfere between them and him? Has he not insulted you enough to make you let him alone? Can you so easily forgive his taunting you with"— He did not finish the sentence, but what I had learned on the previous evening from the old nurse gave me a clue to its meaning. A red flame flushed the face and neck of the octoroon woman—her eyes literally flashed fire, and her very breath seemed to come with pain; in a moment, however, this emotion passed away, and she quietly said, "Let me settle that in my own way. He has served *you* well—*you* have nothing against him that the law will not punish."

"By ——, you are the most unaccountable woman I ever knew," exclaimed the Colonel, striding up and down the piazza, the angry feeling passing from his face, and giving way to a mingled expression of wonder and admiration. The conversation was here interrupted by Jim, who just then made his appearance, hat in hand.

"Well, Jim, what is it?" asked his master.

"We'se gib'n Sam twenty lashes, ma'am, but he beg so hard, and say he so sorry, dat I tole him I'd ax you 'fore we gabe him any more."

"Well, if he's sorry, that's enough; but tell him he'll get fifty another time," said the lady.

"What Sam is it?" asked the Colonel.

"Big Sam, the driver," said Jim.

"Why was he whipped?"

"He told me *you* were his master, and insisted on whipping Moye," replied the lady.

"Did he dare to do that? Give him a hundred, Jim, not one less," roared the Colonel.

"Yas, massa," said Jim, turning to go.

The lady looked significantly at the negro and shook her head, but said nothing, and he left.

"Come, Alice, it is nearly time for meeting, and I want to stop and see Sandy on the way."

"I reckon I wont go," said Madam P——.

"You stay to take care of Moye, I suppose," said the Colonel, with a slight sneer.

"Yes," replied the lady, "he is badly hurt, and in danger of inflammation."

"Well, suit yourself. Mr. K——, come, *we'll* go—you'll meet some of the *natives*."

The lady retired to the house, and the Colonel and I were soon ready. The driver brought the horses to the door, and as we were about to enter the carriage, I noticed Jim taking his accustomed seat on the box.

"Who's looking after Sam?" asked the Colonel.

"Nobody, Cunnel; de ma'am leff him gwo."

"How dare you disobey me? Didn't I tell you to give him a hundred?"

"Yas, massa, but de ma'am tole me notter."

"Well, another time you mind what *I* say—do you hear?" said his master.

"Yas, massa," said the negro, with a broad grin, "I allers do dat."

"You *never* do it, you d—— nigger; I ought to have flogged you long ago."

Jim said nothing, but gave a quiet laugh, showing no sort of fear, and we entered the carriage. I afterward learned from him that he had never been whipped, and that all the negroes on the plantation obeyed the lady when, which was seldom, her orders came in conflict with their master's. They knew if they did not, the Colonel would whip them.

As we rode slowly along the Colonel said to me, "Well, you see that the best people have to flog niggers sometimes."

"Yes, *I* should have given that fellow a hundred lashes, at least. I think the effect on the others would have been bad if Madam P—— had not had him flogged."

"But she generally goes against it. I don't remember of her having it done in ten years before. And yet, though I've the worst gang of niggers in the district, they obey her like so many children."

"Why is that?"

"Well, there's a kind of magnetism about her that makes everybody love her; and then she tends them in sickness, and is constantly doing little things for their comfort; *that* attaches them to her. She is an extraordinary woman."

"Whose negroes are those, Colonel?" I asked, as, after a while, we passed a gang of about a dozen, at work near the roadside. Some were tending a tar-kiln, and some engaged in cutting into fire-wood the pines which a recent tornado had thrown to the ground.

"They are mine, but they are working now for themselves. I let such as will, work on Sunday. I furnish the "raw material," and pay them for what they do, as I would a white man."

"Wouldn't it be better to make them go to hear the old preacher; couldn't they learn something from him?"

"Not much; Old Pomp never read any thing but the Bible, and he doesn't understand that; besides, they can't be taught. You can't make 'a whistle out of a pig's tail;' you can't make a nigger into a white man."

Just here the carriage stopped suddenly, and we looked out to see the cause. The road by which we had come was a mere opening through the pines; no fences separated it from the wooded land, and being seldom travelled, the track was scarcely visible. In many places it widened to a hundred feet, but in others tall trees had grown up on its opposite sides, leaving scarcely width enough for a single carriage to pass along. In one of these narrow passages, just before us, a queer-looking vehicle had upset, and scattered its contents in the road. We had no alternative but to wait till it got out of the way; and we all alighted to reconnoitre.

The vehicle was a little larger than an ordinary hand-cart, and was mounted on wheels that had probably served their time on a Boston dray before commencing their travels in Secessiondom. Its box of pine boarding and its shafts of rough oak poles were evidently of Southern home manufacture. Attached to it by a rope harness, with a primitive bridle of decidedly original construction, was—not a horse, nor a mule, nor even an alligator, but a "three-year-old heifer."

The wooden linch-pin of the cart had given way, and the weight of a half-dozen barrels of turpentine had thrown the box off its balance, and rolled the contents about in all directions.

The appearance of the proprietor of this nondescript vehicle was in keeping with his establishment. His coat, which was much too short in the waist and much too long in the skirts, was of the common reddish gray linsey, and his nether garments, which stopped just below the knees, were of the same material. From there downwards, he wore only the covering that is said to have been the fashion in Paradise before Adam took to fig-leaves. His hat had a rim broader than a political platform, and his skin a color half way between tobacco-juice and a tallow candle.

"Wal, Cunnul, how dy'ge?" said the stranger, as we stepped from the carriage.

"Very well, Ned; how are you?"

"Purty wal, Cunnul; had the nagur lately, right smart, but'm gittin' 'roun'."

"You're in a bad fix here, I see. Can Jim help you?"

"Wal, p'raps he moight. Jim, how dy'ge?"

"Sort o' smart, ole feller. But come, stir yerseff; we want ter gwo 'long," replied Jim, with a lack of courtesy that showed he regarded the white man as altogether too "trashy" to be treated with much ceremony.

With the aid of Jim, a new linch-pin was soon whittled out, the turpentine rolled on to the cart, and the vehicle put in a moving condition.

"Where are you hauling your turpentine?" asked the Colonel.

"To Sam Bell's, at the 'Boro'."

"What will he pay you?"

"Wal, I've four barr'ls of 'dip,' and tu of 'hard.' For the hull, I reckon he'll give three dollar a barr'l."

"By tale?"

"No, for tu hun'red and eighty pound."

"Well, *I'll* give you two dollars and a half, by weight."

"Can't take it, Cunnel; must get three dollar."

"What, will you go sixty miles with this team, and waste five or six days, for fifty cents on six barrels— three dollars!"

"Can't 'ford the time, Cunnel, but must git three dollar a barr'l."

"That fellow is a specimen of our 'natives,'" said the Colonel, as we resumed our seats in the carriage. "You'll see more of them before we get back to the plantation."

"He puts a young cow to a decidedly original use," I remarked.

"Oh no, not original here; the ox and the cow with us are both used for labor."

"You don't mean to say that cows are generally worked here?"

"Of course I do. Our breeds are good for nothing as milkers, and we put them to the next best use. I never have cow's milk on my plantation."

"You don't! I could have sworn it was in my coffee this morning."

"I wouldn't trust you to buy brandy for me, if your organs of taste are not keener than that. It was goat's milk."

"Then how do you get your butter?"

"From the North. I've had mine from my New York factors for over ten years."

We soon arrived at Sandy, the negro-hunter's, and halted to allow the Colonel to inquire as to the health of his family of children and dogs—the latter the less numerous, but, if I might judge by appearances, the more valued of the two.

CHAPTER VIII.

THE NEGRO HUNTER.

ALIGHTING from the carriage, I entered, with my host, the cabin of the negro-hunter. So far as external appearance went, the shanty was a slight improvement on the "Mills House," described in a previous chapter; but internally, it was hard to say whether it resembled more a pig-sty or a dog-kennel. The floor was of the bare earth, covered in patches with loose plank of various descriptions, and littered over with billets of "lightwood," unwashed cooking utensils, two or three cheap stools, a pine settee—made from the rough log and hewn smooth on the upper side—a full-grown bloodhound, two younger canines, and nine half-clad juveniles of the flax-head species. Over against the fire-place three low beds afforded sleeping accommodation to nearly a dozen human beings (of assorted sizes, and dove-tailed together with heads and feet alternating), and in the opposite corner a lower couch, whose finer furnishings told plainly it was the peculiar property of the "wee ones" of the family—a mother's tenderness for her youngest thus cropping out even in the midst of filth and degradation—furnished quarters for an unwashed, uncombed, unclothed, saffron-hued little fellow about fifteen months old, and—the dog "Lady." She was of a dark hazel color—a cross between a pointer and a bloodhound—and one of the most beautiful creatures I ever saw. Her neck and breast were bound about with a coarse cotton cloth, saturated with blood, and emitting a strong odor of bad whiskey; and her whole appearance showed the desperate nature of the encounter with the overseer.

The nine young democrats who were lolling about the room in various attitudes, rose as we entered, and with a familiar but rather deferential "How-dy'ge," to the Colonel, huddled around and stared at me with open mouths and distended eyes, as if I were some strange being, dropped from another sphere. The two eldest were of the male gender, as was shown by their clothes—cast-off suits of the inevitable reddish-gray, much too large, and out at the elbows and the knees—but the sex of the others I was at a loss to determine, for they wore only a single robe, reaching, like their mother's, from the neck to the knees. Not one of the occupants of the cabin boasted a pair of stockings, but the father and mother did enjoy the luxury of shoes—coarse, stout brogans, untanned, and of the color of the legs which they encased.

"Well, Sandy, how is 'Lady?'" asked the Colonel, as he stepped to the bed of the wounded dog.

"Reckon she's a goner, Cunnel; the d—— Yankee orter swing fur it."

This intimation that the overseer was a countryman of mine, took me by surprise, nothing I had observed in his speech or manners having indicated it, but I consoled myself with the reflection that Connecticut had reared him—as she makes wooden hams and nutmegs—expressly for the Southern market.

"He *shall* swing for it, by ——. But are you sure the slut will die?"

"Not shore, Cunnel, but she can't stand, and the blood *will* run. I reckon a hun'red and fifty ar done for thar, sartin."

"D—— the money—I'll make that right. Go to the house and get some ointment from Madam—she can save her—go at once," said my host.

"I will, Cunnel," replied the dirt-eater, taking his broad-brim from a wooden peg, and leisurely leaving the cabin. Making our way then over the piles of rubbish and crowds of children that cumbered the apartment, the Colonel and I returned to the carriage.

"Dogs must be rare in this region," I remarked, as we resumed our seats.

"Yes, well-trained bloodhounds are scarce everywhere. That dog is well worth a hundred and fifty dollars."

"The business of nigger-catching, then, is brisk, just now?"

"No, not more brisk than usual. We always have more or less runaways."

"Do most of them take to the swamps?"

"Yes, nine out of ten do, though now and then one gets off on a trading vessel. It is almost impossible for a strange nigger to make his way by land from here to the free states."

"Then why do you Carolinians make such an outcry about the violation of the Fugitive Slave Law?"

"For the same reason that dogs quarrel over a naked bone. We should be unhappy if we couldn't growl at the Yankees," replied the Colonel, laughing.

"*We*, you say; you mean by that, the hundred and eighty thousand nabobs who own five-sixths of your slaves?"*

"Yes, 1 mean them, and the three millions of poor whites—the ignorant, half-starved, lazy vermin you have just seen. *They* are the real basis of our Southern oli-

---

* The foregoing statistics are correct. That small number of slave-holders sustains the system of slavery, and has caused this terrible rebellion. They are, almost to a man, rebels and secessionists, and we may cover the South with armies, and keep a file of soldiers upon every plantation, and not smother this insurrection, unless we break down the power of that class. Their wealth gives them their power, and their wealth is in their slaves. Free their negroes by an act of emancipation, or confiscation, and the rebellion will crumble to pieces in a day. Omit to do it, and it will last till doomsday.

The power of this dominant class once broken, with landed property at the South more equally divided, a new order of things will arise there. Where now, with their large plantations, not one acre in ten is tilled, a system of small farms will spring into existence, and the whole country be covered with cultivation. The six hundred thousand men who have gone there to fight our battles, will see the amazing fertility of the Southern soil—into which the seed is thrown and springs up without labor into a bountiful harvest—and many of them, if slavery is crushed out, will remain there. Thus a new element will be introduced into the South, an element that will speedily make it a loyal, prosperous, and *intelligent* section of the Union.

I would interfere with no one's rights, but a rebel in arms against his country has no rights; all that he has "is confiscate." Will the loyal people of the North submit to be ground to the earth with taxes to pay the expenditures of a war, brought upon them by these Southern oligarchists, while the traitors are left in undisturbed possession of every thing, and even their slaves are exempted from taxation? It were well that our legislators should ask this question now, and not wait till it is asked of them by THE PEOPLE.

garchy, as you call it," continued my host, still laughing.

"I thought the negroes were the serfs in your feudal system?"

"Both the negroes and the poor whites are the serfs, but the white trash are its real support. Their votes give the small minority of slave-owners all their power. You say we control the Union. We do, and we do it by the votes of these people, who are as far below our niggers as the niggers are below decent white men. Who that reflects that this country has been governed for fifty years by such scum, would give a d—— for republican institutions?"

"It does speak badly for *your* institutions. A system that reduces nearly half of a white population to the level of slaves cannot stand in this country. The late election shows that the power of your 'white trash' is broken."

"Well, it does, that's a fact. If the states should remain together, the West would in future control the Union. We see that, and are therefore determined on dissolution. It is our only way to keep our niggers."

"The West will have to consent to that project. My opinion is, your present policy will, if carried out, free every one of your slaves."

"I dont see how. Even if we are put down—which we cannot be—and are held in the Union against our will, government cannot, by the constitution, interfere with slavery in the states."

"I admit that, but it can confiscate the property of traitors. Every large slave-holder is to-day, at heart, a traitor. If this movement goes on, you will commit overt acts against the government, and in self-defence it will punish treason by taking from you the means of future mischief."

"The Republicans and Abolitionists might do that if they had the power, but nearly one-half of the North is on our side, and will not fight us."

"Perhaps so; but if *I* had this thing to manage, I would put you down without fighting."

"How would you do it—by preaching abolition where even the niggers would mob you? There's not a slave in all South Carolina but would shoot Garrison or Greeley on sight."

"That may be, but if so, it is because you keep them in ignorance. Build a free-school at every cross-road, and teach the poor whites, and what would become of slavery? If these people were on a par with the farmers of New England, would it last for an hour? Would they not see that it stands in the way of their advancement, and vote it out of existence as a nuisance?"

"Yes, perhaps they would; but the school-houses are not at the cross-roads, and, thank God, they will not be there in this generation."

"The greater the pity; but that which will not flourish alongside of a school-house, cannot, in the nature of things, outlast this century. Its time must soon come."

"Enough for the day is the evil thereof. I'll risk the

future of slavery, if the South, in a body, goes out of the Union."

"In other words, you'll shut out schools and knowledge, in order to keep slavery in existence. The Abolitionists claim it to be a relic of barbarism, and you admit it could not exist with general education among the people."

"Of course it could not. If Sandy, for instance, knew he were as good a man as I am—and he would be if he were educated—do you suppose he would vote as I tell him, go and come at my bidding, and live on my charity? No, sir! give a man knowledge, and, however poor he may be, he'll act for himself."

"Then free-schools and general education would destroy slavery?"

"Of course they would. The few cannot rule when the many know their rights. If the poor whites realized that slavery kept them poor, would they not vote it down? But the South and the world are a long way off from general education. When it comes to that, we shall need no laws, and no slavery, for the millennium will have arrived."

"I'm glad you think slavery will not exist during the millennium," I replied, good-humoredly; "but how is it that you insist the negro is naturally inferior to the white, and still admit that the 'white trash,' are far below the black slaves?"

"Education makes the difference. We educate the negro enough to make him useful to us; but the poor white man knows nothing. He can neither read nor write, and not only that, he is not trained to any useful employment. Sandy, here, who is a fair specimen of the tribe, obtains his living just like an Indian, by hunting, fishing, and stealing, interspersed with nigger-catching. His whole wealth consists of two hounds and pups; his house—even the wooden trough his miserable children eat from—belongs to me. If he didn't catch a runaway-nigger once in a while, he wouldn't see a dime from one year to another."

"Then you have to support this man and his family?"

"Yes, what I don't give him he steals. Half a dozen others poach on me in the same way."

"Why don't you set them at work?"

"They can't be made to work. I have hired them time and again, hoping to make something of them, but I never got one to work more than half a day at a time. It's their nature to lounge and to steal."

"Then why do you keep them about you?"

"Well, to be candid, their presence is of use in keeping the blacks in subordination, and they are worth all they cost me, because I control their votes."

"I thought the blacks were said to be entirely contented?"

"No, not contented. I do not claim that. I only say that they are unfit for freedom. I might cite a hundred instances in which it has been their ruin."

"I have not heard of one. It seems strange to me that a man who can support another cannot support himself."

"Oh! no, it's not at all strange. The slave has hands, and when the master gives him brains, he works well enough; but to support himself he needs both hands and brains, and he has only hands. I'll give you a case in point: At Wilmington, N. C., some years ago, there lived a negro by the name of Jack Campbell. He was a slave, and was employed, before the river was deepened so as to admit of the passage of large vessels up to the town, in lightering cargoes to the wharves. He hired his time of his master, and carried on business on his own account. Every one knew him, and his character for honesty, sobriety, and punctuality stood so high that his word was considered among merchants as good as that of the first business-men of the place. Well, Jack's wife and children were free, and he finally took it into his head to be free himself. He arranged with his master to purchase himself within a specified time, at eight hundred dollars, and he was to deposit his earnings in the hands of a certain merchant till they reached the required sum. He went on, and in three years had accumulated nearly seven hundred dollars, when his owner failed in business. As the slave has no right of property, Jack's earnings belonged by law to his master, and they were attached by the Northern creditors (mark that, *by Northern creditors*), and taken to pay the master's debts. Jack, too, was sold. His new owner also consented to his buying himself, at about the price previously agreed on. Nothing discouraged, he went to work again. Night and day he toiled, and it surprised
8*

every one to see so much energy and firmness of purpose in a negro. At last, after four more years of labor, he accomplished his purpose, and received his free-papers. He had worked seven years—as long as Jacob toiled for Rachel—for his freedom, and like the old patriarch he found himself cheated at last. I was present when he received his papers from his owner—a Mr. William H. Lippitt, who still resides at Wilmington—and I shall never forget the ecstasy of joy which he showed on the occasion. He sung and danced, and laughed, and wept, till my conscience smote me for holding my own niggers, when freedom might give them so much happiness. Well, he went off that day and treated some friends, and for three days afterward lay in the gutter, the entreaties of his wife and children having no effect on him. He swore he was free, and would do as he 'd—— pleased.' He had previously been a class-leader in the church, but after getting his freedom he forsook his previous associates, and spent his Sundays and evenings in a bar-room. He neglected his business; people lost confidence in him, and step by step he went down, till in five years he sunk into a wretched grave. That was the effect of freedom on *him*, and it would be the same on all of his race."

"It is clear," I replied, "*he* could not bear freedom, but that does not prove he might not have 'endured' it if he had never been a slave. His overjoy at obtaining liberty, after so long a struggle for it, led to his excesses and his ruin. According to your view, neither the black nor the poor white is competent to take care of himself.

The Almighty, therefore, has laid upon *you* a triple burden; you not only have to provide for yourself and your children, but for two races beneath you, the black and the clay-eater. The poor nigger has a hard time, but it seems to me you have a harder one."

"Well, it's a fact, we do. I often think that if it wasn't for the color and the odor, I'd willingly exchange places with my man Jim."

The Colonel made this last remark in a half-serious, half-comic way, that excited my risibilities, but before I could reply, the carriage stopped, and Jim, opening the door, announced:

"We's har, massa, and de prayin' am gwine on."

CHAPTER IX.

THE COUNTRY CHURCH.

HAD we not been absorbed in conversation, we might have discovered, some time previous to our arrival at the church door, that the services had commenced, for the preacher was shouting at the top of his lungs. He evidently thought the Lord either a long way off, or very hard of hearing. Not wishing to disturb the congregation while at their devotions, we loitered near the doorway until the prayer was over, and in the mean time I glanced around the vicinity.

The "meeting-house," of large unhewn logs, was a story and a half in height, and about large enough to seat comfortably a congregation of two hundred persons. It was covered with shingles, with a roof projecting some four feet over the walls, and was surmounted at the front gable by a tower, about twelve feet square. This also was built of logs, and contained a bell "to call the erring to the house of prayer," though, unfortunately, all of that character thereabouts dwelt beyond the sound of its voice. The building was located at a cross-roads, about equally distant from two little hamlets (the nearer nine miles off), neither of which was populous enough to singly support a church and a preacher. The trees in the vicinity had been thinned out, so that carriages could drive into the woods, and find under the branches shelter from the rain and the sun; and at the time of my visit, about twenty vehicles of all sorts and descriptions, from the Colonel's magnificent barouche to the rude cart drawn by a single two-horned quadruped, filled the openings. There was a rustic simplicity about the whole scene that charmed me. The low, rude church, the grand old pines that towered in leafy magnificence around it, and the soft, low wind, that sung a morning hymn in the green, wavy woods, seemed to lift the soul up to Him who inhabiteth eternity, but who deigns to visit the erring children of men.

The preacher was about to "line out" one of Watts' psalms when we entered the church, but he stopped short on perceiving us, and, bowing low, waited till we had taken our seats. This action, and the sycophantic air which accompanied it, disgusted me, and turning to the Colonel, I asked, jocosely:

"Do the chivalry exact so much obsequiousness from the country clergy? Do you require to be bowed up to heaven?"

In a low voice, but high enough, I thought, for the preacher to hear, for we sat very near, the Colonel replied:

"He's a renegade Yankee—the meanest thing on earth."

I said no more, but entered into the services as seriously as the strange gymnastic performances of the preacher would allow of my doing; for he was quite as amusing as a circus clown.

With the exception of the Colonel's, and a few other pews in the vicinity of the pulpit, all of the seats were mere rough benches, without backs, and placed so closely together as to interfere uncomfortably with the knees of the sitters. The house was full, and the congregation as attentive as any I ever saw. All classes were there; the black serving-man away off by the door way, the poor white a little higher up, the small turpentine-farmer a little higher still, and the wealthy planter, of the class to which the Colonel belonged, on "the highest seats of the synagogue," and in close proximity to the preacher.

The "man of prayer" was a tall, lean, raw-boned, angular-built individual, with a thin, sharp, hatchet-face, a small sunken eye, and long, loose hair, brushed back and falling over the collar of a seedy black coat. He looked like a dilapidated scare-crow, and his pale, sallow face, and cracked, wheezy voice, were in odd and comic keeping with his discourse. His text was: "Speak unto the children of Israel, that they go forward." And addressing the motley gathering of poor whites and small planters before him as the "chosen people of God," he urged them to press on in the mad course their state had taken. It was a political harangue, a genuine stump-speech, but its frequent allusions to the auditory as the legitimate children of the old patriarch, and the rightful heirs of all the promises, struck me as out of place in a rural district of South Carolina, however appropriate it might have been in one of the large towns, before an audience of merchants and traders, who are, almost to a man, Jews.

The services over, the congregation slowly left the church. Gathered in groups in front of the "meeting-house," they were engaged in a general discussion of the affairs of the day, when the Colonel and I emerged from the doorway. The better class greeted my host with considerable cordiality, but I noticed that the well-to-do small planters, who composed the greater part of the assemblage, received him with decided coolness. These people were the "North County folks," on whom the overseer had invoked a hanging. Except that their clothing was more uncouth and ill-fashioned, and their faces generally less "cute" of expression, they did not materially differ in appearance from the rustic citizens who may be seen on any pleasant Sunday gathered around the doorways of the rural meeting-houses of New England.

One of them, who was leaning against a tree, quietly lighting a pipe, was a fair type of the whole, and as he took a part in the scene which followed, I will describe him. He was tall and spare, with a swinging, awkward gait, and a wiry, athletic frame. His hair, which he wore almost as long as a woman's, was coarse and black, and his face strongly marked, and of the precise color of two small rivulets of tobacco-juice that escaped from the corners of his mouth. He had an easy, self-possessed manner, and a careless, devil-may-care way about him, that showed he had measured his powers, and was accustomed to "rough it" with the world. He wore a broadcloth coat of the fashion of some years ago, but his waistcoat and nether garments of the common, reddish homespun, were loose and ill-shaped, as if their owner did not waste thought on such trifles. His hat, as shockingly bad as Horace Greeley's, had the inevitable broad brim, and fell over his face like a calash-awning over a shop-window. As I approached him he extended his hand with a pleasant "How are ye, stranger?"

"Very well," I replied, returning his grasp with equal warmth, "how are you?"

"Right smart, right smart, thank ye. You're ——" the rest of the sentence was cut short by a gleeful exclamation from Jim, who, mounted on the box of the carriage, which was drawn up on the cleared plot in front of the meeting-house, waved an open newspaper over his head, and called out, as he caught sight of the Colonel:

"Great news, massa—great news from Charls'on!"

(The darky, while we were in church, had gone to the post-office, some four miles away, and got the Colonel's mail, which consisted of letters from his New York and Charleston factors, the Charleston *Courier* and *Mercury* and the New York *Journal of Commerce*. The latter sheet, at the date of which I am writing, was in wide circulation at the South, its piety (!) and its politics being then calculated with mathematical precision for secession latitudes.)

"What is it, Jim?" shouted his master. "Give it to us."

The darky had somehow learned to read, but holding the paper at arm's length, and throwing himself into a theatrical attitude, he cried out, with any amount of gesticulation:

"De news am, massa, and gemmen and ladies, dat de ole fort fore Charls'on hab ben devacuated by Major Andersin and de sogers, and dey hab stole 'way in de dark night and gone to Sumter, whar dey can't be took; and dat de ole Gubner hab got out a procdemation dat all dat don't lub de Aberlishen Yankees shill cum up dar and clar 'em out; and de paper say dat lots ob sogers hab cum from Georgi and Al'bama, and 'way down Souf, to help 'em. Dis am w'at de *Currer* say," he continued, holding the paper up to his eyes and reading: 'Major Andersin, ob de United States army hab 'chieved de 'stinction ob op'ning cibil war 'tween American citizens; he hab desarted Moulfrie, and by false fretexts hab took dat ole Garrison and all his millinery stores to Fort Sumter."

"Get down, you d——d nigger," said the Colonel, laughing, and mounting the carriage-box beside him. "You can't read. Old Garrison isn't there—he's the d——d Northern Abolitionist."

"I knows dat, Cunnel, but see dar," replied Jim, holding the paper out to his master, "don't dat say he'm dar? It'm him dat make all de trubble. P'raps dis nig can't read, but ef dat aint readin' I'd like to know it!"

"Clear out," said the Colonel, now actually roaring with laughter; "it's the garrison of soldiers that the *Courier* speaks of, not the Abolitionist."

"Read it yoursef, den, massa, I don't seed it dat way."

Jim was altogether wiser than he appeared, but while equally as well pleased with the news as his master, he was so for an entirely different reason. In the crisis which these tidings announced, he saw hope for his race.

The Colonel then read the paper to the assemblage. The news was received with a variety of manifestations by the auditory, the larger portion, I thought, hearing it, as I did, with sincere regret.

"Now is the time to stand by the state, my friends," said my host, as he finished the reading. "I hope every man here is ready to do his duty by old South Carolina."

"Yes, *sar!* if she does *har* duty by the Union. We'll go to the death for har just so long as she's in the right, but not a d——d step if she arn't," said the long-legged native I have introduced to the reader.

"And what have *you* to say about South Carolina? What does she owe to *you?*" asked the Colonel, turning on the speaker with a proud and angry look.

"More, a darned sight, than she'll pay, if ye cursed 'ristocrats run her to h— as ye'r doin'. She owes me, and 'bout ten as likely niggers as ye ever seed, a living, and we've d——d hard work to get it out on her *now*, let alone what's comin'."

"Don't talk to me, you ill-mannered cur," said my host, turning his back on his neighbor, and directing his attention to the remainder of the assemblage.

"Look har, Cunnel," replied the native, "if ye'll jest come down from thar, and throw 'way yer shootin'-irons, I'll give ye the all-firedest thrashing ye ever did get."

The Colonel gave no further heed to him, but the speaker mounted the steps of the meeting-house and harangued the natives in a strain of rude and passionate declamation, in which my host, the aristocrats, and the secessionists came in for about equal shares of abuse. Seeing that the native (who, it appeared, was quite popular as a stump-speaker) was drawing away his audience, the Colonel descended from the driver's seat, and motioning for me to follow, entered the carriage. Turning the horses homeward, we rode off at a brisk pace.

"Not much secession about that fellow, Colonel," I remarked, after a while.

"No," he replied, "he's a North Carolina 'corn-cracker,' one of the ugliest specimens of humanity extant. They're as thick as fleas in this part of the state, and about all of them are traitors."

"Traitors to the state, but true to the Union. As far as I've seen, that is the case with the middling class throughout the South."

"Well, it may be, but they generally go with us, and I reckon they will now, when it comes to the rub. Those in the towns—the traders and mechanics—will, certain; its only these half-way independent planters that ever kick the traces. By the way," continued my host, in a jocose way, "what did you think of the preaching?"

"I thought it very poor. I'd rather have heard the stump-speech, had it not been a little too personal on you."

"Well, it was the better of the two," he replied, laughing, "but the old devil can't afford any thing good, he don't get enough pay."

"Why, how much does he get?"

"Only a hundred dollars."

"That *is* small. How does the man live?"

"Well, he teaches the daughter of my neighbor, Captain Randall, who believes in praying, and gives him his board. Randall thinks that enough. The rest of the parish can't afford to pay him, and I *wont*."

"Why wont you?"

"Because he's a d——d old hypocrite. He believes in the Union with all his heart—at least so Randall, who's a sincere Union man, says—and yet, he never sees me at meeting but he preaches a red-hot secession sermon."

"He wants to keep you in the faith," I replied.

A few more miles of sandy road took us to the mansion, where we found dinner in waiting. Meeting

"Massa Tommy"—who had staid at home with his mother—as we entered the doorway, the Colonel asked after the overseer.

"He seems well enough, sir; I believe he's coming the possum over mother."

"I'll bet on it, Tommy; but he wont fool you and me, will he, my boy?" said his father, slapping him affectionately on the back.

After dinner I went, with my host to the room of the wounded man. His head was still bound up, and he was groaning piteously, as if in great pain; but I thought there was too fresh a color in his face to be entirely natural in one who had lost so much blood, and been so severely wounded as he affected to have been.

The Colonel mentioned our suspicions to Madam P——, and suggested that the shackles should be put on him.

"Oh! no, don't do that; it would be inhuman," said the lady; "the color is the effect of fever. If you fear he is plotting to get away, let him be watched."

The Colonel consented, but with evident reluctance, to the arrangement, and retired to his room to take a *siesta*, while I lit a segar, and strolled out to the negro quarters.

Making my way through the woods to the scene of the morning's jollification, I found about a hundred darkies gathered around Jim, on the little plot in front of old Lucy's cabin. He had evidently been giving them the news. Pausing when I came near, he exclaimed:

"Har's Massa K——, he'll say dat I tells you de trufh;" and turning to me, he said: "Massa K——, dese darkies say dat Massa Andersin am an ab'lisherner, and dat none but de ab'lisherners will fight for de Union; am dat so, sar?"

"No, I reckon not, Jim; I think the whole North would fight for it if it were necessary."

"Am dat so, massa? am dat so?" eagerly inquired a dozen of the darkies; "and am dar great many folks at de Norf—more dan dar am down har?"

"Yas, you fools, didn't I tell you dat?" said Jim, as I, not exactly relishing the idea of preaching treason, in the Colonel's absence, to his slaves, hesitated to reply. "Haint I tole you," he continued, "dat in de big city ob New York dar'm more folks dan in all Car'lina? I'se been dar, and I knows; and Massa K——'ll tell you dat dey—most on 'em—feel mighty sorry for de brack man."

"No he wont," I replied, "and besides, Jim, you should not talk in this way before me; I might tell your master."

"No! you wont do dat; I knows you wont, massa. Scipio tole us he'd trust his bery life wid *you*."

"Well, perhaps he might; it's true I would not injure you;" saying that, I turned away, though my curiosity was greatly excited to hear more.

I wandered farther into the woods, and a half-hour found me near one of the turpentine distilleries. Seating myself on a rosin barrel, I quietly finished my segar, and was about lighting another, when Jim made his appearance.

"Beg pardon, Massa K——," said the negro, bowing very low, "but I wants to ax you one or two tings, ef you please, sar."

"Well," I replied, "I'll tell you any thing that I ought to."

"Der yer tink, den, massa, dat dey'll git to fightin' at Charl'son?"

"Yes, judging by the tone of the Charleston papers you've read to-day, I think they will."

"And der yer tink dat de rest ob de Souf will jine wid Souf Car'lina, if she go at it fust?"

"Yes, Jim, I'm inclined to think so."

"I hard you say to massa, dat ef dey goes to war, 'twill free all de niggers—der you raily b'lieve dat, sar?"

"*You* heard me say that; how did you hear it?" I exclaimed, in surprise.

"Why, sar, de front winder ob de carriage war down jess a crack, so I hard all you said."

"Did you let it down on purpose?"

"P'r'aps so, massa. Whot's de use ob habin' ears, ef you don't har?"

"Well, I suppose not much; and you tell all you hear to the other negroes?"

"I reckon so, massa," said the darky, looking very demure.

"That's the use of having a tongue, eh?" I replied, laughing.

"Dat's it 'zactly, massa."

"Well, Jim, I do think the slaves will be finally freed; but it will cost more white blood to do it than all the niggers in creation are worth. Do you think the darkies would fight for their freedom?"

"Fight, sar!" exclaimed the negro, straightening up his fine form, while his usual good-natured look passed from his face, and gave way to an expression that made him seem more like an incarnate devil than a human being; "FIGHT, sar; gib dem de chance, and den see."

"Why are you discontented? You have been at the North, and you know the blacks are as well off as the majority of the poor laboring men there."

"You says dat to *me*, Massa K——; you don't say it to de *Cunnel*. We am *not* so well off as de pore man at de Norf! You knows dat, sar. He hab his wife and chil'ren, and his own home. What hab we, sar? No wife, no chil'ren, no home; all am de white man's. Der yer tink we wouldn't fight to be free?" and he pressed his teeth together, and there passed again over his face the same look it wore the moment before.

"Come, come, Jim, this may be true of your race; but it don't apply to yourself. Your master is kind and indulgent to *you*."

"He am kine to me, sar; he orter be," said the negro, the savage expression coming again into his eyes. For a moment he hesitated; then, taking a step toward me, he placed his face down to mine, and hissed out these words, every syllable seeming to come from the very bottom of his being. "I tell you he orter be, sar, FUR I AM HIS OWN FATHER'S SON!"

"His brother!" I exclaimed, springing to my feet, and looking at him in blank amazement. "It can't be true!"

"It am true, sar—as true as there's a hell! His father had my mother—when he got tired of her, he sold her Souf. *I war too young den eben to know her!*"

"This is horrible—too horrible!" I said.

"It am slavery, sar! Shouldn't we be contented?" replied the negro with a grim smile. Drawing, then, a large spring-knife from his pocket, he waved it above his head, and added: "Ef I had de hull white race dar—right dar under dat knife, don't yer tink I'd take all dar lives—all at one blow—to be FREE!"

"And yet you refused to run away when the Abolitionists tempted you, at the North. Why didn't you go then?"

"'Cause I had promised, massa."

"Promised the Colonel before you went?"

"No, sar; he neber axed me; but *I* can't tell you no more. P'raps Scipio will, ef you ax him."

"Oh! I see; you're in that league of which Scip is a leader. You'll get into trouble, *sure*," I replied, in a quick, decided tone, which startled him.

"You tole Scipio dat, sar, and what did *he* tell you?"

"That he didn't care for his life."

"No more do I, sar," said the negro, turning on his heel with a proud, almost defiant gesture, and starting to go

9

"A moment, Jim. You are very imprudent; never say these things to any other mortal; promise me that."

"You'se bery good, massa, bery good. Scipio say you's true, and he'm allers right. I ortent to hab said what I hab; but sumhow, sar, dat news brought it all up *har*" (laying his hand on his breast), "and it wud come out."

The tears filled his eyes as he said this, and turning away without another word, he disappeared among the trees.

I was almost stunned by this strange revelation, but the more I reflected on it, the more probable it appeared. Now, too, that my thoughts were turned in that direction, I called to mind a certain resemblance between the colonel and the negro that I had not heeded before. Though one was a high-bred Southern gentleman, claiming an old and proud descent, and the other a poor African slave, they had some striking peculiarities which might indicate a common origin. The likeness was not in their features, for Jim's face was of the unmistakable negro type, and his skin of a hue so dark that it seemed impossible he could be the son of a white man (I afterward learned that his mother was a black of the deepest dye), but it was in their form and general bearing. They had the same closely-knit and sinewy frame, the same erect, elastic step, the same rare blending of good-natured ease and dignity—to which I have already alluded as characteristic of the Colonel—and in the wild burst of passion that accompanied the negro's disclosure of their relationship, I saw the same fierce, unbridled temper, whose outbreaks I had witnessed in my host.

What a strange fate was theirs! Two brothers—the one the owner of three hundred slaves, and the first man of his district—the other, a bonded menial, and so poor that the very bread he ate, and the clothes he wore, were another's!

I passed the remainder of the afternoon in my room, and did not again meet my host until the family assembled at the tea-table. Jim then occupied his accustomed seat behind the Colonel's chair, and that gentleman was in more than his usual spirits, though Madam P——, I thought, wore a sad and absent look.

The conversation rambled over a wide range of subjects, and was carried on mainly by the Colonel and myself; but toward the close of the meal the lady said to me:

"Mr. K——, Sam and young Junius are to be buried this evening; if you have never seen a negro funeral, perhaps you'd like to attend."

"I will be happy to accompany you, Madam, if you go," I replied.

"Thank you," said the lady.

"Pshaw! Alice, you'll not go into the woods on so cold a night as this!" said the Colonel.

"Yes, I think I ought to. Our people will expect me."

CHAPTER X.

THE NEGRO FUNERAL.

IT was about an hour after nightfall when we took our way to the burial-ground. The moon had risen, but the clouds which gathered when the sun went down, covered its face, and were fast spreading their thick, black shadows over the little collection of negro-houses. Near two new-made graves were gathered some two hundred men and women, as dark as the night that was setting around them. As we entered the circle the old preacher pointed to seats reserved for us, and the sable crowd fell back a few paces, as if, even in the presence of death, they did not forget the difference between their race and ours.

Scattered here and there among the trees, torches of lightwood threw a wild and fitful light over the little cluster of graves, revealing the long, straight boxes of rough pine that held the remains of the two negroes, and lighting up the score or two of russet mounds where slept the dusky kinsmen who had gone before them.

The simple head-boards that marked these humble graves chronicled no bad biography or senseless rhyme, and told no false tales of lives that might better not have been, but "SAM, AGE 22;" "POMPEY;" "JAKE'S ELIZA;"

"Aunt Sue;" "Aunt Lucy's Tom;" "Joe;" and other like inscriptions, scratched in rough characters on the unplaned boards, were all the records there. The rude tenants had passed away and "left no sign;" their birth, their age, their deeds, were alike unknown—unknown, but not forgotten! for are they not written in the book of His remembrance—and when he counteth up his jewels, may not some of them be there?

The queer, grotesque dress, and sad, earnest looks of the black group; the red, fitful glare of the blazing pine, and the white faces of the tapped trees, gleaming through the gloom like so many sheeted ghosts gathered to some death-carnival, made up a strange, wild scene —the strangest and the wildest I had ever witnessed.

The covers of the rude coffins were not yet nailed down, and when we arrived, the blacks were, one by one, taking a last look at the faces of the dead. Soon, Junius, holding his weeping wife by the hand, approached the smaller of the two boxes, which held all that was left of their first-born. The mother, kneeling by its side, kissed again and again the cold, shrunken lips, and sobbed as if her heart would break; and the strong frame of the father shook convulsively, as he choked down the great sorrow which welled up in his throat, and turned away from his boy forever. As he did so, old Pompey said:

"Don't grebe, June, he'm whar de wicked cease from trubling, whar de weary am at rest."

"I knows it; I knows it, Uncle. I knows de Lord

am bery good to take 'im 'way; but why did he take de young chile, and leab de ole man har?"

"De little sapling dat grow in de shade may die while it'm young; de great tree dat grow in de sun must lib till he'm rotted down."

These words were the one drop wanting to make the great grief which was swelling in the negro's heart overflow. Giving one low, wild cry, he folded his wife in his arms, and burst into a paroxysm of tears.

"Come now, my chil'ren," said the old preacher, kneeling down, "let us pray."

The whole assemblage then knelt on the cold ground, while the old man prayed, and a more sincere, heart-touching prayer never went up from human lips to that God "who hath made of one blood all nations that dwell on the face of the earth." Though clothed in rags, and in feeble age at the mercy of a cruel task-master, that old slave was richer far than his master. His simple faith, which saw through the darkness around him into the clear and radiant light of the unseen day, was of far more worth than all the wealth and glory of this world. I know not why it was, but as I looked at him in the dim red light, which fell on his bent form and cast a strange halo around his upturned face, I thought of Stephen, as he gazed upward and behold heaven open, and "the Son of Man seated at the right hand of the throne of God."

Rising from his knees, the old preacher turned slowly to the black mass that encircled him, and said:

"My dear brederin and sisters, de Lord say dat 'de dust shill return to de earth as it war, and de spirit to Him who gabe it,' and now, 'cordin' to dat text, my friends, we'm gwine to put dis dust (pointing to the two coffins) in de groun' whar it cum from, and whar it shill lay till de bressed Lord blow de great trumpet on de resumrection mornin'. De spirits of our brudders har de Lord hab already took to hisseff. 'Our brudders,' I say, my chil'ren, 'case ebery one dat de Lord hab made am brudders to you and to me, whedder dey'm bad or good, white or brack.

"Dis young chile, who hab gone 'way and leff his pore fader and mudder suffrin' all ober wid grief, *he* hab gone to de Lord, *shore*. *He* neber done no wrong he allers 'bey'd his massa, and neber said no hard word, nor found no fault, not eben w'en de cruel, bad oberseer put de load so heaby on him dat it kill him. Yes, my brederin and sisters, *he* hab gone to de Lord; gone whar dey don't work in de swamps; whar de little chil'ren don't tote de big shingles fru de water up to dar knees. No swamps am dar; no shingles am dar; dey doan't need 'em, 'case dar de hous'n haint builded wid hands, for dey'm all builded by de Lord, and gib'n to de good niggers, ready-made, and for nuffin'. De Lord don't say, like as ded massa say, 'Pomp, dar's de logs and de shingles' (dey'm allers pore shingles, de kine dat woant sell; but massa say, 'dey'm good 'nuff for niggers,' ef de roof do leak). De Lord doan't say: 'Now, Pomp, you go to work and build you' own house; but

mine dat you does you, task all de time, jess de same!'
But de Lord—de bressed Lord—He say, w'en we goes
up dar, 'Dar, Pomp, dar's de house dat I'se been a
buildin' for you eber sence ' de foundation ob de worle.'
It'm done now, and you kin cum in; your room am
jess ready, and ole Sal and de chil'ren dat I tuk 'way
from you eber so long ago, and dat you mourned ober
and cried ober as ef you'd neber see dem agin, dey'm dar
too, all on 'em, a waitin, for you. Dey'm been fixin' up
de house 'spressly for you all dese long years, and dey'b
got it all nice and comfible now.' Yas, my friends,
glory be to Him, dat's what our Heabenly massa say,
and who ob you wouldn't hab sich a massa as dat? A
massa dat doant set you no hard tasks, and dat gibs you
'nuff to eat, and time to rest and to sing and to play! A
massa dat doan't keep no Yankee oberseer to foller you
'bout wid de big free-lashed whip; but dat leads you
hisseff to de green pastures and de still waters; and
w'en you'm a-faint and a-tired, and can't go no furder,
dat takes you up in his arms, and carries you in his
bosom! What pore darky am dar dat wudn't hab sich
a massa? What one ob us, eben ef he had to work
jess so hard as we works now, wudn't tink heseff de
happiest nigger in de hull worle, ef he could hab sich
hous'n to lib in as dem? dem hous'n ' not made wid
hands, eternal in de heabens!'

"But glory, glory to de Lord! my chil'ren, wese all
got dat massa, ef we only knowd it, and He'm buildin'
dem hous'n up dar, now, for ebery one ob us dat am try-

in' to be good and to lub one anoder. *For ebery one ob us*, I say, and we kin all git de fine hous'n ef we try.

"Recolember, too, my brudders, dat our great Massa am rich, bery rich, and he kin do all he promise. He doant say, w'en wese worked ober time to git some little ting to comfort de sick chile, 'I knows, Pomp, you'se done de work, an' I did 'gree to gib you de pay; but de fact am, Pomp, de frost hab come so sudden dis yar, dat I'se loss de hull ob de sebenfh dippin', and I'se pore, so pore, de chile muss go widout dis time.' No, no, brudders, de bressed Lord He neber talk so. He neber break, 'case de sebenfh dip am shet off, or 'case de price of turpentime gwo down at de Norf. He neber sell his niggers down Souf, 'case he lose his money on he hoss-race. No, my chil'ren, our HEABENLY Massa am rich, RICH, I say. He own all dis worle, and all de oder worles dat am shinin' up dar in de sky. He own dem all; but he tink more ob one ob you, more ob one ob you—pore, ign'rant brack folks dat you am—dan ob all dem great worles! Who wouldn't belong to sich a Massa as dat? Who wouldn't be his nigger—not his slave—He doant hab no slaves—but his chile; and 'ef his chile, den his heir, de heir ob God, and de jined heir wid de bressed Jesus.' O my chil'ren! tink of dat! de heir ob de Lord ob all de 'arth and all de sky! What white man kin be more'n dat?

"Don't none ob you say you'm too wicked to be His chile; 'ca'se you haint. He lubs de wicked ones de best, 'ca'se dey need his lub de most. Yas, my brudders, eben de wickedest, ef dey's only sorry, and turn roun' and leab off dar bad ways, he lub de bery best ob all, 'ca'se he'm all lub and pity.

"Sam, har, my chil'ren, war wicked, but don't *we* pity him; don't *we* tink he hab a hard time, and don't we tink de bad oberseer, who'm layin' dar in de house jess ready to gwo and answer for it—don't we tink he gabe Sam bery great probincation?

"Dat's so," said a dozen of the auditors.

"Den don't you 'spose dat de bressed Lord know all dat, and dat He pity Sam too. If we pore sinners feel sorrer for him, haint de Lord's heart bigger'n our'n, and haint he more sorrer for him? Don't you tink dat ef He lub and pity de bery worse whites, dat He lub and pity pore Sam, who warn't so bery bad, arter all? Don't you tink He'll gib Sam a house? P'r'aps' 'twont be one ob de fine hous'n, but wont it be a comfible house, dat hain't no cracks, and one dat'll keep out de wind and de rain? And don't you s'pose, my chil'ren, dat it'll be big 'nuff for Jule, too—dat pore, repentin' chile, whose heart am clean broke, 'ca'se she hab broughten dis on Sam—and won't de Lord—de good Lord—de tender-hearted Lord—won't He touch Sam's heart, and coax him to forgib Jule, and to take her inter his house up dar? I knows he will, my chil'ren. I knows——"

The old negro paused abruptly; there was a quick swaying in the black crowd—a hasty rush—a wild cry—and Sam's wife burst into the open space around the preacher, and fell at his feet. Throwing her arms wildly about him, she shrieked out:

"Say dat agin, Uncle Pomp! for de lub ob de good Lord, oh! say dat agin!"

Bending down, the old man raised her gently in his arms, and folding her there, as he would have folded a child, he said, in a voice thick with emotion:

"It am so, Juley. I knows dat Sam will forgib you, and take you wid him up dar."

Fastening her arms frantically around Pompey's neck, the poor woman burst into a paroxysm of grief, while the old man's tears fell in great drops on her upturned face, and many a dark cheek was wet, as with rain.

The scene had lasted a few minutes, and I was turning away to hide the emotion that fast filled my eyes, and was creeping up, with a choking feeling, to my throat, when the Colonel, from the farther edge of the group, called out:

"Take that d—d —— away—take her away, Pomp!"

The old negro turned toward his master with a sad, grieved look, but gave no heed to the words.

"Take her away, some of you, I say," again cried the Colonel. "Pomp, you mustn't keep these niggers all night in the cold."

At the sound of her master's voice the metif woman fell to the ground as if struck by a Minie-ball. Soon several negroes lifted her up to bear her off; but she struggled violently, and rent the woods with her wild cries for "one more look at Sam."

"Look at him, you d—d ——; then go, and don't let me see you again."

She threw herself on the face of the dead, and covered the cold lips with her kisses; then she rose, and with a weak, uncertain step, staggered out into the darkness.

Was not the system which had so seared and hardened that man's heart, begotten in the lowest hell?

The old preacher said no more, but four stout negro men stepped forward, nailed down the lids, and lowered the rough boxes into the ground. Turning to Madam P——, I saw her face was red with weeping. She turned to go as the first earth fell, with a dull, heavy sound, on the rude coffins; and giving her my arm, I led her from the scene.

As we walked slowly back to the house, a low wail—half a chant, half a dirge—rose from the black crowd, and floated off on the still night air, till it died away amid the far woods, in a strange, unearthly moan. With that sad, wild music in our ears, we entered the mansion.

As we seated ourselves by the bright wood-fire on the library hearth, obeying a sudden impulse which I could not restrain, I said to Madam P——:

"The Colonel's treatment of that poor woman is inexplicable to me. Why is he so hard with her? It is not in keeping with what I have seen of his character."

"The Colonel is a peculiar man," replied the lady. "Noble, generous, and a true friend, he is also a bitter, implacable enemy. When he once conceives a dislike, his feelings become even vindictive. Never having had an ungratified wish, he does not know how to feel for the sorrows of those beneath him. Sam, though a proud, headstrong, unruly character, was a great favorite with him; he felt his death much; and as he attributes it to Jule, he feels terribly bitter toward her. She will have to be sold to get her out of his way, for he will *never* forgive her."

It was some time before the Colonel joined us, and when at last he made his appearance, he seemed in no mood for conversation. The lady soon retired; but feeling unlike sleep, I took down a book from the shelves, drew my chair near the fire, and fell to reading. The Colonel, too, was deep in the newspapers, till, after a while, Jim entered the room:

"I'se cum to ax ef you've nuffin more to-night, Cunnel?" said the negro.

"No, nothing, Jim," replied his master; "but, stay—hadn't you better sleep in front of Moye's door?"

"Dunno, sar; jess as you say."

"I think you'd better," returned the Colonel.

"Yas, massa," and the darky left the apartment.

The Colonel shortly rose, and bade me "good-night." I continued reading till the clock struck eleven, when I laid the book aside and went to my room.

I lodged, as I have said before, on the first floor, and was obliged to pass by the overseer's apartment in going to mine. Wrapped in his blanket, and stretched at full length on the ground, Jim lay there, fast asleep.

I passed on, thinking of the wisdom of placing a tired negro on guard over an acute and desperate Yankee.

I rose in the morning with the sun, and had partly donned my clothing, when I heard a loud uproar in the hall. Opening my door, I saw Jim pounding vehemently at the Colonel's room, and looking as pale as is possible with a person of his complexion.

"What the d—l is the matter?" asked his master, who now, partly dressed, stepped into the hall.

"Moye hab gone, sar—he'm gone and took Firefly (my host's five-thousand-dollar thorough-bred) wid him."

For a moment the Colonel stood stupified; then, his face turning to a cold, clayey white, he seized the black by the throat, and hurled him to the floor. With his thick boot raised, he seemed about to dash out the man's brains with its ironed heel, when, on the instant, the octoroon woman rushed, in her night-clothes, from his room, and, with desperate energy, pushed him aside, exclaiming: "What would you do? Remember WHO HE IS!"

The negro rose, and the Colonel, without a word, passed into his own apartment.

CHAPTER XI.

THE PURSUIT.

I SAUNTERED out, after the events recorded in the last chapter, to inhale the fresh air of the morning. A slight rain had fallen during the night, and it still moistened the dead leaves which carpeted the woods, making an extended walk out of the question; so, seating myself on the trunk of a fallen tree, in the vicinity of the house, I awaited the hour for breakfast. I had not remained there long before I heard the voices of my host and Madam P—— on the front piazza:

"I tell you, Alice, I cannot—must not do it. If I overlook this, the discipline of the plantation is at an end."

"Do what you please with him when you return," replied the lady, "but do not chain him up, and leave me, at such a time, alone. You know Jim is the only one I can depend on."

"Well, have your own way. You know, my darling, I would not cause you a moment's uneasiness, but I must follow up this d——d Moye."

I was seated where I could hear, though I could not see the speakers, but it was evident from the tone of the last remark, that an action accompanied it quite as tender as the words. Being unwilling to overhear more of a private conversation, I rose and approached them.

"Ah! my dear fellow," said the Colonel, on perceiving me, "are you stirring so early? I was about to send to your room to ask if you'll go with me up the country. My d——d overseer has got away, and I must follow him at once."

"I'll go with pleasure," I replied. "Which way do you think Moye has gone?"

"The shortest cut to the railroad, probably; but old Cæsar will track him."

A servant then announced breakfast—an early one having been prepared. We hurried through the meal with all speed, and the other preparations being soon over, were in twenty minutes in our saddles, and ready for the journey. The mulatto coachman, with a third horse, was at the door, ready to accompany us. As we mounted, the Colonel said to him:

"Go and call Sam, the driver."

The darky soon returned with the heavy, ugly-visaged black who had been whipped, by Madam P——'s order, the day before.

"Sam," said his master, "I shall be gone some days, and I leave the field-work in your hands. Let me have a good account of you when I return."

"Yas, massa, you shill dat," replied the negro.

"Put Jule—Sam's Jule—into the woods, and see that she does full tasks," continued the Colonel.

"Haint she wanted 'mong de nusses, massa?"

"Put some one else there—give her field-work; she needs it."

On large plantations the young children of the field-women are left with them only at night, and are herded together during the day, in a separate cabin, in charge of nurses. These nurses are feeble, sickly women, or recent mothers; and the fact of Jule's being employed in that capacity was evidence that she was unfit for outdoor labor.

Madam P——, who was waiting on the piazza to see us off, seemed about to remonstrate against this arrangement, but she hesitated a moment, and in that moment we had bidden her "Good-bye," and galloped away.

We were soon at the cabin of the negro-hunter, and the coachman, dismounting, called him out.

"Hurry up, hurry up," said the Colonel, as Sandy appeared, "we haven't a moment to spare."

"Jest so—jest so, Cunnel; I'll jine ye in a jiffin," replied he of the reddish extremities.

Emerging from the shanty with provoking deliberation—the impatience of my host had infected me—the clay-eater slowly proceeded to mount the horse of the negro, while his dirt-bedraggled wife, and clay-encrusted children, followed close at his heels, the younger ones huddling around for the tokens of paternal affection usual at parting. Whether it was the noise they made, or their frightful aspect, I know not, but the horse, a spirited animal, took fright on their appearance, and nearly broke away from the negro, who was holding him. Seeing this, the Colonel said:

"Clear out, you young scare-crows. Into the house with you."

"They arn't no more scare-crows than yourn, Cunnel J——," said the mother, in a decidedly belligerent tone. "You may 'buse my old man—he kin stand it—but ye shan't blackguard my young 'uns!"

The Colonel laughed, and was about to make a good-natured reply, when Sandy yelled out:

"Gwo enter the house and shet up, ye —— ——."

With this affectionate farewell, he turned his horse and led the way up the road.

The dog, who was a short distance in advance, soon gave a piercing howl, and started off at the speed of a reindeer. He had struck the trail, and urging our horses to their fastest speed, we followed.

We were all well mounted, but the mare the Colonel had given me was a magnificent animal, as fleet as the wind, and with a gait so easy that her back seemed a rocking-chair. Saddle-horses at the South are trained to the gallop—Southern riders not deeming it necessary that one's breakfast should be churned into a Dutch cheese by a trotting nag, in order that he may pass for a horseman.

We had ridden on at a perfect break-neck pace for half an hour, when the Colonel shouted to our companion:

"Sandy, call the dog in; the horses wont last ten miles at this gait—we've a long ride before us."

The dirt-eater did as he was bidden, and we soon settled into a gentle gallop.

We had passed through a dense forest of pines, but were emerging into a "bottom country," where some of the finest deciduous trees—then brown and leafless, but bearing promise of the opening beauty of spring—reared, along with the unfading evergreen, their tall stems in the air. The live-oak, the sycamore, the Spanish mulberry, the holly, and the persimmon—gaily festooned with wreaths of the white and yellow jessamine, the woodbine and the cypress-moss, and bearing here and there a bouquet of the mistletoe, with its deep green and glossy leaves upturned to the sun—flung their broad arms over the road, forming an archway grander and more beautiful than any the hand of man ever wove for the greatest hero the world has worshipped.

The woods were free from underbrush, and a coarse, wiry grass, unfit for fodder, and scattered through them in detatched patches, was the only vegetation visible. The ground was mainly covered with the leaves and burrs of the pine.

We passed great numbers of swine, feeding on these burrs, and now and then a horned animal browsing on the cypress-moss where it hung low on the trees. I observed that nearly all the swine were marked, though they seemed too wild to have ever seen an owner, or a human habitation. They were a long, lean, slab-sided race, with legs and shoulders like deer, and bearing no sort of resemblance to the ordinary hog, except in the snout, and that feature was so much longer and sharper than the nose of the Northern swine, that I doubt if Agassiz would class the two as one species. However, they have their uses—they make excellent bacon, and are " death on snakes." Ireland itself is not more free from the serpentine race than are the districts frequented by these long-nosed quadrupeds.

"We call them Carolina race-horses," said the Colonel, as he finished an account of their peculiarities.

"Race-horses! Why, are they fleet of foot?"

"Fleet as deer. I'd match one against an ordinary horse at any time."

"Come, my friend, you're practising on my ignorance of natural history."

"Not a bit of it. See! there's a good specimen yonder. If we can get him into the road, and fairly started, I'll bet you a dollar he'll beat Sandy's mare on a half-mile stretch—Sandy to hold the stakes and have the winnings."

"Well, agreed," I said, laughing, " and I'll give the pig ten rods the start."

"No," replied the Colonel, "you can't afford it. He'll *have* to start ahead, but you'll need that in the count. Come, Sandy, will you go in for the pile?"

I'm not sure that the native would not have run a race with Old Nicholas himself, for the sake of so much money. To him it was a vast sum; and as he thought of it, his eyes struck small sparks, and his enormous beard and mustachio vibrated with something that faintly resembled a laugh. Replying to the question, he said:

"Kinder reckon I wull, Cunnel; howsomdever, I keeps the stakes, ony how?"

"Of course," said the planter, "but be honest—win if you can."

Sandy halted his horse in the road, while the planter and I took to the woods on either side of the way. The Colonel soon manœuvred to separate the selected animal from the rest of the herd, and, without much difficulty, got him into the road, where, by closing down on each flank, we kept him till he and Sandy were fairly under way.

"He'll keep to the road when once started," said the Colonel, laughing: "and he'll show you some of the tallest running you ever saw in your life."

Away they went. At first the pig, seeming not exactly to comprehend the programme, cantered off at a leisurely pace, though he held his own. Soon, however, he cast an eye behind him—halted a moment to collect his thoughts and reconnoitre—and then, lowering his head and elevating his tail, put forth all his speed. And such speed! Talk of a deer, the wind, or a steam-engine—they are not to be compared with it. Nothing in nature I ever saw run—except, it may be, a Southern tornado, or a Sixth Ward politician—could hope to distance that pig. He gained on the horse at every step, and it was soon evident that my dollar was gone!

"'In for a shilling, in for a pound,' is the adage, so, turning to the Colonel, I said, as intelligibly as my horse's rapid pace and my excited risibilities would allow:

"I see I've lost, but I'll go you another dollar that *you* can't beat the pig!"

"No—sir!" the Colonel got out in the breaks of his laughing explosions; "you can't hedge on me in that manner. I'll go a dollar that *you* can't do it, and your mare is the fastest on the road. She won me a thousand not a month ago."

"Well, I'll do it—Sandy to have the stakes."

"Agreed," said the Colonel, and away *we* went.

The swinish racer was about a hundred yards ahead when I gave the mare the reins, and told her to go. And she *did* go. She flew against the wind with a motion so rapid that my face, as it clove the air, felt as if cutting its way through a solid body, and the trees, as we passed, seemed struck with panic, and running for dear life in the opposite direction.

For a few moments I thought the mare was gaining, and I turned to the Colonel with an exultant look.

"Don't shout till you win, my boy," he called out from the distance where I was fast leaving him and Sandy.

I *did not shout*, for spite of all my efforts the space between me and the pig seemed to widen. Yet I kept on, determined to win, till, at the end of a short half-mile, we reached the Waccamaw—the swine still a hundred yards ahead! There his pigship halted, turned coolly around, eyed me for a moment, then with a quiet, deliberate trot, turned off into the woods.

A bend in the road kept my companions out of sight for a few moments, and when they came up I had somewhat recovered my breath, though the mare was blowing hard, and reeking with foam.

"Well," said the Colonel, "what do you think of our bacon 'as it runs?'"

"I think the Southern article can't be beat, whether raw or cooked, standing or running."

At this moment the hound, who had been leisurely jogging along in the rear, disdaining to join in the race in which his dog of a master and I had engaged, came up, and dashing quickly on to the river's edge, set up a most dismal howling. The Colonel dismounted, and clambering down the bank, which was there twenty feet high, and very steep, shouted:

"The d—d Yankee has swum the stream!"

"Why so?" I asked.

"To cover his tracks and delay pursuit; but he has overshot the mark. There is no other road within ten miles, and he must have taken to this one again beyond here. He's lost twenty minutes by this manœuvre. Come, Sandy, call in the dog, we'll push on a little faster."

"But he tuk to t'other bank, Cunnel. Shan't we trail him thar?" asked Sandy.

"And suppose he found a boat here," I suggested, "and made the shore some ways down?"

"He couldn't get Firefly into a flat—we should only waste time in scouring the other bank. The swamp this side the next run has forced him into the road within five miles. The trick is transparent. He took me for a fool," replied the Colonel, answering both questions at once.

I had reined my horse out of the road, and when my companions turned to go, was standing at the edge of the bank, overlooking the river. Suddenly I saw, on one of the abutments of the bridge, what seemed a long, black log—strange to say, *in motion!*

"Colonel," I shouted, "see there! a live log as I'm a white man!"

"Lord bless you," cried the planter, taking an observation, "it's an alligator!"

I said no more, but pressing on after the hound, soon left my companions out of sight. For long afterward, the Colonel, in a doleful way, would allude to my lamentable deficiency in natural history—particularly in such branches as bacon and "live logs."

I had ridden about five miles, keeping well up with the hound, and had reached the edge of the swamp, when suddenly the dog darted to the side of the road, and began to yelp in the most frantic manner. Dismounting, and leading my horse to the spot, I made out plainly the print of Firefly's feet in the sand. There was no mistaking it—that round shoe on the off forefoot. (The horse had, when a colt, a cracked hoof, and though the wound was outgrown, the foot was still tender.) These prints were dry, while the tracks we had seen at the river were filled with water, thus proving that the rain had ceased while the overseer was passing between the two places. He was therefore not far off.

The Colonel and Sandy soon rode up.

"Caught a live log! eh, my good fellow?" asked my host, with a laugh.

"No; but here's the overseer as plain as daylight; and his tracks not wet!"

Quickly dismounting, he examined the ground, and then exclaimed:

"The d—l——it's a fact—here not four hours ago! He has doubled on his tracks since, I'll wager, and not made twenty miles—we'll have him before night, sure! Come, mount—quick."

We sprang into our saddles, and again pressed rapidly on after the dog, who followed the scent at the top of his speed.

Some three miles more of wet, miry road took us to the run of which the Colonel had spoken. Arrived there, we found the hound standing on the bank, wet to the skin, and looking decidely chop-fallen.

"Death and d——n!" shouted the Colonel; "the dog has swum the run, and lost the trail on the other side! The d—d scoundrel has taken to the water, and balked us after all! Take up the dog, Sandy, and try him again over there."

The native spoke to Cæsar, who bounded on to the horse's back in front of his master. They then crossed the stream, which there was about fifty yards wide, and so shallow that in the deepest part the water merely touched the horse's breast; but it was so roiled by the recent rain that we could not distinguish the foot-prints of the horse beneath the surface.

The dog ranged up and down the opposite bank, but all to no purpose: the overseer had not been there. He had gone either up or down the stream—in which direction, was now the question. Calling Sandy back to our side of the run, the Colonel proceeded to hold a 'council of war.' Each one gave his opinion, which was canvassed by the others, with as much solemnity as if the fate of the Union hung on the decision.

The native proposed we should separate—one go up, another down the stream, and the third, with the dog, follow the road; to which he thought Moye had finally returned. Those who should explore the run would easily detect the horse's tracks where he had left it, and then taking a straight course to the road, all might meet some five miles further on, at a place indicated.

I gave my adhesion to Sandy's plan, but the Colonel overruled it on the ground of the waste of time that would be incurred in thus recovering the overseer's trail.

"Why not," he said, "strike at once for the end of his route? Why follow the slow steps he took in order to throw us off the track? He has not come back to this road. Ten miles below there is another one leading also to the railway. He has taken that. We might as well send Sandy and the dog back and go on by ourselves."

"But if bound for the Station, why should he wade through the creek here, ten miles out of his way? Why not go straight on by the road?" I asked.

"Because he knew the dog would track him, and he hoped by taking to the run to make me think he had crossed the country instead of striking for the railroad."

I felt sure the Colonel was wrong, but knowing him to be tenacious of his own opinions, I made no further objection.

Directing Sandy to call on Madam P——and acquaint her with our progress, he then dismissed the negro-hunter, and once more led the way up the road.

The next twenty miles, like our previous route, lay through an unbroken forest. As we left the watercourses, we saw only the gloomy pines, which there—the region being remote from the means of transportation—were seldom tapped, and presented few of the openings that invite the weary traveller to the dwelling of the hospitable planter.

After a time the sky, which had been bright and cloudless all the morning, grew overcast, and gave out tokens of a coming storm. A black cloud gathered in the west, and random flashes darted from it far off in the distance; then gradually it neared us; low mutterings sounded in the air, and the tops of the tall pines a few miles away, were lit up now and then with a fitful blaze, all the brighter for the deeper gloom that succeeded. Then a terrific flash and peal broke directly over us, and a great tree, struck by a red-hot bolt, fell with a deafening crash, half way across our path. Peal after peal followed, and then the rain—not filtered into drops as it falls from our colder sky, but in broad, blinding sheets—poured full and heavy on our shelterless heads.

"Ah! there it comes!" shouted the Colonel. "God have mercy upon us!"

As he spoke, a crashing, crackling, thundering roar rose above the storm, filling the air, and shaking the solid earth till it trembled beneath our horses' feet, as if upheaved by a volcano. Nearer and nearer the sound came, till it seemed that all the legions of darkness were unloosed in the forest, and were mowing down the great pines as the mower mows the grass with his scythe. Then an awful, sweeping crash thundered directly at our backs, and turning round, as if to face a foe, my horse, who had borne the roar and the blinding flash till then unmoved, paralyzed with dread, and panting for breath, sunk to the ground; while close at my side the Colonel, standing erect in his stirrups, his head uncovered to the pouring sky, cried out:

"THANK GOD, WE ARE SAVED!"

There—not three hundred yards in our rear, had passed the TORNADO—uprooting trees, prostrating dwellings, and sending many a soul to its last account, but sparing *us* for another day! For thirty miles through the forest it had mowed a swath of two hundred feet, and then moved on to stir the ocean to its briny depths.

With a full heart, I remounted, and turning my horse, pressed on in the rain. We said not a word till a friendly opening pointed the way to a planter's dwelling. Then calling to me to follow, the Colonel dashed up the by-path which led to the mansion, and in five minutes we were warming our chilled limbs before the cheerful fire that roared and crackled on its broad hearth-stone.

CHAPTER XII.

THE YANKEE-SCHOOL-MISTRESS.

The house was a large, old-fashioned frame building, square as a packing-box, and surrounded, as all country dwellings at the South are, by a broad, open piazza. Our summons was answered by its owner, a well-to-do, substantial, middle-aged planter, wearing the ordinary homespun of the district, but evidently of a station in life much above the common "corn-crackers" I had seen at the country meeting-house. The Colonel was an acquaintance, and greeting us with great cordiality, our host led the way directly to the sitting-room. There we found a bright, blazing fire, and a pair of bright sparkling eyes, the latter belonging to a blithesome young woman of about twenty, with a cheery face, and a half-rustic, half-cultivated air, whom our new friend introduced to us as his wife.

"I regret not having had the pleasure of meeting Mrs. S—— before, but am very happy to meet her now," said the Colonel, with all the well-bred, gentlemanly ease that distinguished him.

"The pleasure is mutual, Colonel J——," replied the lady, "but thirty miles in this wild country, should not have made a neighbor so distant as you have been."

"Business, madam, is at fault, as your husband knows. I have much to do; and besides, all my connections are in the other direction—with Charleston."

"It's a fact, Sally, the Colonel is the d—— busy man in these parts. Not content with a big plantation and three hundred niggers, he looks after all South Carolina, and the rest of creation to boot," said our host.

"Tom will have his joke, Madam, but he's not far from the truth."

Seeing we were dripping wet, the lady offered us a change of clothing, and retiring to a chamber, we each appropriated a suit belonging to our host, giving our own to a servant, to be dried.

Arrayed in our fresh apparel, we soon rejoined our friends in the sitting-room. The new garments fitted the Colonel tolerably well, but, though none too long, they were a world too wide for me, and as my wet hair hung in smooth flat folds down my cheeks, and my limp shirt-collar fell over my linsey coat, I looked for all the world like a cross between a theatrical Aminodab Sleek and Sir John Falstaff, with the stuffing omitted. When our hostess caught sight of me in this new garb, she rubbed her hands together in great glee, and, springing to her feet, gave vent to a perfect storm of laughter—jerking out between the explosions:

"Why—you—you—look jest like—a scare-crow."

There was no mistaking that hearty, hoydenish manner; and seizing both of her hands in mine, I shouted:

"I've found you out—you're a "country-woman" of mine—a clear-blooded Yankee!"

"What! *you* a Yankee!" she exclaimed, still laughing, "and here with this horrid 'secesherner,' as they call him."

"True as preachin', Ma'am," I replied, adopting the drawl—"all the way from Down East, and Union, tu, stiff as buckram."

"Du tell!" she exclaimed, swinging my hands together as she held them in hers. "If I warn't hitched to this 'ere feller, I'd give ye a smack right on the spot. I'm *so* glad to see ye."

"Do it, Sally—never mind *me*," cried her husband, joining heartily in the merriment.

Seizing the collar of my coat with both hands, she drew my face down till my lips almost touched hers (I was preparing to blush, and the Colonel shouted, "Come, come, I shall tell his wife"): but then turning quickly on her heel, she threw herself into a chair, exclaiming, "*I* wouldn't mind, but the *old man would be jealous*." Addressing the Colonel, she added, "*You* needn't be troubled, sir, no Yankee girl will kiss *you* till you change your politics."

"Give me that inducement, and I'll change them on the spot," said the Colonel.

"No, no, Dave, 'twouldn't do," replied the planter; "the conversion wouldn't be genuwine—besides such things arn't proper, except 'mong blood-relations—and all the Yankees, you know are first-cousins."

The conversation then subsided into a more placid mood, but lost none of its 'genial, good humor. Refreshments were soon set before us, and while partaking of them I gathered from our hostess that she was a Vermont country-girl, who, some three years before, had been induced by liberal pay to come South as a teacher. A sister accompanied her, and about a year after their arrival, she married a neighboring planter. Wishing to be near her sister, our hostess had also married and settled down for life in that wild region. "I like the country very well," she added; "it's a great sight easier living here than in Vermont; but I do hate these lazy, shiftless, good-for-nothing niggers; they are *so* slow, and *so* careless, and *so* dirty, that I sometimes think they will worry the very life out of me. I do believe I'm the hardest mistress in all the district."

I learned from her that a majority of the teachers at the South are from the North, and principally, too, from New England. Teaching is a very laborious employment there, far more so than with us, for the Southerners have no methods like ours, and the same teacher usually has to hear lessons in branches all the way from Greek and Latin to the simple A B C. The South has no system of public instruction; no common schools; no means of placing within the reach of the sons and daughters of the poor even the elements of knowledge. While the children of the wealthy are most carefully educated, it is the policy of the ruling class to keep the great mass of the people in ignorance; and so long

10*

as this policy continues, so long will that section be as far behind the North as it now is, in all that constitutes true prosperity and greatness.

The afternoon wore rapidly and pleasantly away in the genial society of our wayside-friends. Politics were discussed (our host was a Union man), the prospects of the turpentine crop talked over, the recent news canvassed, the usual neighborly topics touched upon, and—I hesitate to confess it—a considerable quantity of corn whiskey disposed of, before the Colonel discovered, all at once, that it was six o'clock, and we were still seventeen miles from the railway station. Arraying ourselves again in our dried garments, we bade a hasty but regretful "good-bye" to our hospitable entertainers, and once more took to the road.

The storm had cleared away, but the ground was heavy with the recent rain, and our horses were sadly jaded with the ride of the morning. We gave them the reins, and, jogging on at their leisure, it was ten o'clock at night before they landed us at the little hamlet of W—— Station, in the state of North Carolina.

CHAPTER XIII.

THE RAILWAY STATION.

A LARGE hotel, or station-house, and about a dozen log shanties made up the village. Two of these structures were negro-cabins; two were small groceries, in which the vilest alcoholic compounds were sold at a bit (ten cents) a glass; one was a lawyer's office, in which was the post-office, and a justice's court, where, once a month, the small offenders of the vicinity "settled up their accounts;" one was a tailoring and clothing establishment, where breeches were patched at a dime a stitch, and payment taken in tar and turpentine; and the rest were private dwellings of one apartment, occupied by the grocers, the tailor, the switch-tenders, the postmaster, and the negro *attachés* of the railroad. The church and the school-house—the first buildings to go up in a Northern village—I have omitted to enumerate, because—they were not there.

One of the natives told me that the lawyer was a "stuck-up critter;" "he don't live; he don't—he puts-up at th' hotel." And the hotel! Would Shakspeare, had he have known it, have written of taking one's *ease* at his inn? It was a long, framed building, two stories high, with a piazza extending across the side and a front door crowded as closely into one corner as the width of the joist would permit. Under the piazza, ranged along the wall, was a low bench, occupied by about forty tin wash-basins and water-pails, and with coarse, dirty crash towels suspended on rollers above it. By the side of each of these towels hung a comb and a brush, to which a lock of everybody's hair was clinging, forming in the total a stock sufficient to establish any barber in the wig business.

It was, as I have said, ten o'clock when we reached the Station. Throwing the bridles of our horses over the hitching-posts at the door, we at once made our way to the bar-room. That apartment, which was in the rear of the building, and communicated with by a long, narrow passage, was filled almost to suffocation, when we entered, by a cloud of tobacco smoke, the fumes of bad whiskey, and a crowd of drunken chivalry, through whom the Colonel with great difficulty elbowed his way to the counter, where "mine host" and two assistants were dispensing "liquid death," at the rate of ten cents a glass, and of ten glasses a minute.

"Hello, Cunnel, how ar' ye," cried the red-faced liquor-vender, as he caught sight of my companion, and, relinquishing his lucrative employment for a moment, took the Colonel's hand, "how ar' ye?"

"Quite well, thank you, Miles," said the Colonel, with a certain patronizing air, "have you seen my man, Moye?"

"Moye, no! What's up with him?"

"He's run away with my horse, Firefly—I thought he would have made for this station. At what time does the next train go up?"

"Wal, it's due half arter 'leven, but 'taint gin'rally 'long till nigh one."

The Colonel was turning to join me at the door, when a well-dressed young man of very unsteady movements, who was filling a glass at the counter, and staring at him with a sort of dreamy amazement, stammered out, "Moye—run—run a—way, zir! that—k—kant be —by G——. I know—him, zir—he's a—a friend of mine, and—I'm—I'm d——d if he ain't hon—honest."

"About as honest as the Yankees run," replied the Colonel, "he's a d——d thief, sir!"

"Look here—here, zir—don't—don't you—you zay any—thing 'gainst—the Yankees. D——d if—if I aint—one of 'em mezelf—zir," said the fellow staggering toward the Colonel.

"*I* don't care *what* you are; you're drunk."

"You lie—you—you d——d 'ris—'ristocrat," was the reply, as the inebriated gentleman aimed a blow, with all his unsteady might, at the Colonel's face.

The South Carolinian stepped quickly aside, and dexterously threw his foot before the other, who—his blow not meeting the expected resistance—was unable to recover himself, and fell headlong to the floor. The planter turned on his heel, and was walking quietly away, when the sharp report of a pistol sounded through the apartment, and a ball tore through the top of his boot, and lodged in the wall within two feet of where I was standing. With a spring, quick and sure as the tiger's, the Colonel was on the drunken man. Wrenching away the weapon, he seized the fellow by the neck-tie, and drawing him up to nearly his full height, dashed him at one throw to the other end of the room. Then raising the revolver he coolly levelled it to fire!

But a dozen strong men were on him. The pistol was out of his hand, and his arms were pinioned in an instant; while cries of "Fair play, sir!" "He's drunk!" "Don't hit a man when he's down," and other like exclamations, came from all sides.

"Give *me* fair play, you d——d North Carolina hounds," cried the Colonel, struggling violently to get away, "and I'll fight the whole posse of you."

"One's 'nuff for *you*, ye d——d fire-eatin' 'ristocrat;" said a long, lean, bushy-haired, be-whiskered individual, who was standing near the counter: "ef ye want to fight, *I'll* 'tend to yer case to onst. Let him go, boys," he continued as he stepped toward the Colonel, and parted the crowd that had gathered around him: "give him the shootin'-iron, and let's see ef he'll take a man thet's sober."

I saw serious trouble was impending, and stepping forward, I said to the last speaker, "My friend, you have no quarrel with this gentleman. He has treated that man only as you would have done."

"P'raps thet's so; but he's a d——d hound of a

Secesherner thet's draggin' us all to h—ll; it'll du the country good to git quit of one on 'em."

"Whatever his politics are, he's a gentleman, sir, and has done you no harm—let me beg of you to let him alone."

"Don't beg any thing for me, Mr. K——," growled the Colonel through his barred teeth, "I'll fight the d——d corn-cracker, and his whole race, at once."

"No you won't, my friend. For the sake of those at home you won't;" I said, taking him by the arm, and partly leading, partly forcing him, toward the door.

"And who in h—ll ar you?" asked the corn-cracker, planting himself squarely in my way.

"I'm on the same side of politics with you, Union to the core!" I replied.

"Ye ar! Union! Then give us yer fist," said he, grasping me by the hand; "by —— it does a feller good to see a man dressed in yer cloes thet haint 'fraid to say he's Union, so close to South Car'lina, tu, as this ar! Come, hev a drink: come boys—all round—let's liquor!"

"Excuse me now, my dear fellow—some other time I'll be glad to join you."

"Jest as ye say, but thar's my fist, enyhow."

He gave me another hearty shake of the hand, and the crowd parting, I made my way with the Colonel out of the room. We were followed by Miles, the landlord, who, when we had reached the front of the entrance-way, said, "I'm right sorry for this row, gentlemen; the boys will hev a time when they gets together."

"Oh, never mind:" said the Colonel, who had recov-covered his coolness; "but why are all these people here?"

"Thar's a barbacue cumin' off to-morrer on the camp-ground, and the house is cram full."

"Is that so?" said the Colonel, then turning to me he added, "Moye has taken the railroad somewhere else; I must get to a telegraph office at once, to head him off. The nearest one is Wilmington. With all these rowdies here, it will not do to leave the horses alone—will you stay and keep an eye on them over to-morrow?"

"Yes, I will, cheerfully."

"Thar's a mighty hard set, round har now, Cunnel," said the landlord; "and the most peaceable get enter scrapes ef they hain't no friends. Hadn't ye better show the gentleman some of your'n, 'fore you go?"

"Yes, yes, I didn't think of that. Who is here?"

"Wal, thar's Cunnel Taylor, Bill Barnes, Sam Heddleson, Jo Shackelford, Andy Jones, Rob Brown, and lots of others."

"Where's Andy Jones?"

"Reckon he's turned in; I'll see."

As the landlord opened a door which led from the hall, the Colonel said to me, "Andy is a Union man; but he'd fight to the death for me."

"Sal!" called out the hotel keeper.

"Yas, massa, I'se har," was the answer from a slatternly woman, awfully black in the face, who soon thrust her head from the door-way.

"Is Andy Jones har?" asked Miles.

"Yas, massa, he'm turned in up thar on de table."

We followed the landlord into the apartment. It was the dining-room of the hotel, and by the dim light which came from a smoky fire on the hearth, I saw it contained about a hundred people, who, wrapped in blankets, bed-quilts and travelling-shawls, were disposed in all conceivable attitudes, and scattered about on the hard floor and tables, sleeping soundly. The room was a long, low apartment—extending across the entire front of the house—and had a wretched, squalid look. The fire, which was tended by the negro-woman—(she had spread a blanket on the floor, and was keeping a drowsy watch over it for the night)—had been recently replenished with green wood, and was throwing out thick volumes of black smoke, which, mixing with the effluvia from the lungs of a hundred sleepers, made up an atmosphere next to impossible to breathe. Not a window was open, and not an aperture for ventilation could be seen!

Carefully avoiding the arms and legs of the recumbent chivalry, we picked our way, guided by the negro-girl, to the corner of the room where the Unionist was sleeping. Shaking him briskly by the shoulder, the Colonel called out: "Andy! Andy! wake up!"

"What—what the d——l is the matter?" stammered the sleeper, gradually opening his eyes, and raising himself on one elbow, "Lord bless you, Cunnel, is that you? what in —— brought *you* har?"

"Business, Andy. Come, get up, I want to see you, and I can't talk here."

The North Carolinian slowly rose, and throwing his blanket over his shoulders, followed us from the room. When we had reached the open air the Colonel introduced me to his friend, who expressed surprise, and a great deal of pleasure, at meeting a Northern Union man in the Colonel's company.

"Look after our horses, now, Miles; Andy and I want to talk," said the planter to the landlord, with about as little ceremony as he would have shown to a negro.

I thought the white man did not exactly relish the Colonel's manner, but saying, "All right, all right, sir," he took himself away.

The night was raw and cold, but as all the rooms of the hotel were occupied, either by sleepers or carousers, we had no other alternative than to hold our conference in the open air. Near the railway-track a light-wood fire was blazing, and, obeying the promptings of the frosty atmosphere, we made our way to it. Lying on the ground around it, divested of all clothing except a pair of linsey trousers and a flannel shirt, and with their naked feet close to its blaze—roasting at one extremity, and freezing at the other—were several blacks, the switch-tenders and woodmen of the Station—fast asleep. How human beings could sleep in such circumstances seemed a marvel, but further observation convinced me that the Southern negro has a natural aptitude for that exercise, and will, indeed, bear more exposure than any other living thing. Nature in giving him such powers of endurance, appears to have specially fitted him for the life of hardship and privation to which he is born.

The fire-light enabled me to scan the appearance of my new acquaintance. He was rather above the medium height, squarely and somewhat stoutly built, and had an easy and self-possessed, though rough and unpolished manner. His face, or so much of it as was visible from underneath a thick mass of reddish gray hair, denoted a firm, decided character; but there was a manly, open, honest expression about it that gained one's confidence in a moment. He wore a slouched hat and a suit of the ordinary "sheep's-grey," cut in the "sack" fashion, and hanging loosely about him. He seemed a man who had made his own way in the world, and I subsequently learned that appearances did not belie him. The son of a "poor white" man, with scarcely the first rudiments of book-education, he had, by sterling worth, natural ability, and great force of character, accumulated a handsome property, and acquired a leading position in his district. Though on "the wrong side of politics," his personal popularity was so great that for several successive years he had been elected to represent the county in the state legislature. The Colonel, though opposed to him in politics—and party feeling at the South runs so high that political opponents are seldom personal friends—had, in the early part of his career, aided him by his endorsements; and Andy had not forgotten the service. It was easy to see that while two men could not be more unlike in character and appearance than my host and the North Carolinian, they were warm and intimate friends.

"So, Moye has been raising h—ll gin'rally, Colonel," said my new acquaintance after a time. "I'm not surprised. I never did b'lieve in Yankee nigger-drivers—sumhow it's agin natur' for a Northern man to go Southern principles quite so strong as Moye did."

"Which route do you think he has taken?" asked the Colonel.

"Wal, I reckon arter he tuk to the run, he made fur the mountings. He know'd you'd head him on the travelled routes; so he's put, I think, fur the Mississippe, where he'll sell the horse and make North."

"I'll follow him," said the Colonel, "to the ends of the earth. If it costs me five thousand dollars, I'll see him hung."

"Wal," replied Andy, laughing, "if he's gone North you'll need a extradition treaty to kotch him. South Car'lina, I b'lieve, has set up fur a furrin country."

"That's true," said the Colonel, also laughing, "she's "furrin" to the Yankees, but not to the old North State."

"D——d if she haint," replied the North Carolinian, "and now she's got out on our company, I swear she must keep out. We'd as soon think of goin' to h—ll in summer time, as of jining partnership with her. Cunnel, you'r the only decent man in the State—d——d if you haint—and *your* politics are a'most bad 'nuff to spile a township. It allers seemed sort o'queer to me, that a man with such a mighty good heart as your'n, could be so short in the way of brains."

"Well, you're complimentary," replied the Colonel. with the utmost good-nature, "but let's drop politics we never could agree, you know. What shall I dc about Moye?"

"Go to Wilmington and telegraph all creation: wait a day to har, then if you don't har, go home, hire a native overseer, and let Moye go to the d——l. Ef it'l do you any good I'll go to Wilmington with you, though I did mean to give you Secesherners a little h—har to-morrer."

"No, Andy, I'll go alone. 'Twouldn't be patriotic to take you away from the barbacue. You'd 'spile if you couldn't let off some gas soon."

"I do b'lieve I shud. Howsumdever, thar's nary a thing I wouldn't do for you—you knows that."

"Yes, I do, and I wish you'd keep an eye on my Yankee friend here, and see he don't get into trouble with any of the boys—there'll be a hard set 'round, I reckon."

"Wal, I will," said Andy, "but all he's to do is to keep his mouth shet."

"That seems easy enough," I replied, laughing.

A desultory conversation followed for about an hour when the steam-whistle sounded, and the up-train arrived. The Colonel got on board and bidding us "good-night," went on to Wilmington. Andy then proposed we should look up sleeping accommodations. It was useless to seek quarters at the hotel, but an empty car was on the turn-out, and bribing one of the negroes we got access to it, and were soon stretched at full length on two of its hard-bottomed seats.

CHAPTER XIV.

THE BARBACUE.

THE camp-ground was about a mile from the station, and pleasantly situated in a grove, near a stream of water. It was in frequent use by the camp-meetings of the Methodist denomination—which sect at the South is partial to these rural religious gatherings. Scattered over it, with an effort at regularity, were about forty small but neat log cottages, thatched with the long leaves of the turpentine pine, and chinked with branches of the same tree. Each of these houses was floored with leaves or straw, and large enough to afford sleeping accommodations for about ten persons, provided they spread their bedding on the ground, and lay tolerably close together. Interspersed among the cabins were about a dozen canvas tents which had been erected for this especial occasion.

Nearly in the centre of the group of huts a rude sort of scaffold, four or five feet high, and surrounded by a rustic railing, served for the speaker's stand. It would seat about a dozen persons, and was protected by a roof of pine-boughs, interlaced together so as to keep off the sun, without affording protection from the rain. In the rear of this stand were two long tables, made of rough boards, and supported on stout joists, crossed on each other in the form of the letter X. A canopy of green leaves shaded the grounds, and the whole grove, which was perfectly free from underbrush, was carpeted with the soft, brown tassels of the pine.

Being fatigued with the ride of the previous day, I did not awake till the morning was far advanced, and it was nearly ten o'clock when Andy and I took our way to the camp-ground. Avoiding the usual route, we walked on through the forest. It was mid-winter, and vegetation lay dead all around us, awaiting the time when spring should breathe into it the breath of life, and make it a living thing. There was silence and rest in the deep woods. The birds were away on their winter wanderings; the leaves hung motionless on the tall trees, and nature seemed resting from her ceaseless labors, and listening to the soft music of the little stream which sung a cheerful song as it rambled on over the roots and fallen branches that blocked its way. Soon a distant murmur arose, and we had not proceeded far before as many sounds as were heard at Babel made a strange concert about our ears. The lowing of the ox, the neighing of the horse, and the deep braying of another animal, mingled with a thousand human voices, came through the woods. But above and over all rose the stentorian tones of the stump speaker,

"As he trod the shaky platform,
With the sweat upon his brow."

About a thousand persons were already assembled on

the ground, and a more motley gathering I never witnessed. All sorts of costumes and all classes of people were there; but the genuine back-woods corn-crackers composed the majority of the assemblage. As might be expected much the larger portion of the audience were men, still I saw some women and not a few children; many of the country people having taken advantage of the occasion to give their families a holiday. Some occupied benches in front of the stand, though a larger number were seated around in groups, within hearing of the speaker, but paying very little attention to what he was saying. A few were whittling—a few pitching quoits, or playing leap-frog, and quite a number were having a quiet game of whist, euchre or "seven-up."

The speaker was a well-dressed, gentlemanly-looking man and a tolerably good orator. He seemed accustomed to addressing a jury, for he displayed all the adroitness in handling his subject, and in appealing to the prejudices of his hearers, that we see in successful special pleaders. But he overshot his mark. To nine out of ten of his audience, his words and similes, though correct, and sometimes beautiful, were as unintelligible as the dead languages. He advocated immediate, unconditional secession; and I thought from the applause which met his remarks, whenever he seemed to make himself understood, that the large majority of those present were of the same way of thinking.

He was succeeded by a heavy-browed, middle-aged man, slightly bent, and with hair a little turned to gray, but still hale, athletic, and in the prime and vigor of manhood. His pantaloons and waistcoat were of the common homespun, and he used, now and then, a word of the country dialect, but as a stump-speaker he was infinitely superior to the more polished orator who had preceded him.

He, too, advocated secession, as a right and a duty— separation, now and forever, from the dirt-eating, money-loving Yankees, who, he was ashamed to say, had the same ancestry, and worshipped the same God, as himself. He took the bold ground that slavery is a curse to both the black and the white, but that it was forced upon this generation before its birth, by these same greedy, grasping Yankees, who would sell not only the bones and sinews of their fellow men, but—worse than that— their own souls, for gold. It was forced upon them without their consent, and now that it had become interwoven with all their social life, and was a necessity of their very existence, the hypocritical Yankees would take it from them, because, forsooth, it is a sin and a wrong—as if *they* had to bear its responsibility, or the South could not settle its own affairs with its MAKER!

"Slavery is now," he continued, "indispensable to us. Without it, cotton, rice, and sugar will cease to grow, and the South will starve. What if it works abuses? What if the black, at times, is overburdened, and his wife and daughters debauched? Man is not perfect anywhere—there are wrongs in every society. It is for each one to give his account, in such matters, to his God.

But in this are we worse than they? Are there not abuses in society at the North? Are not their laborers overworked? While sin here hides itself under cover of the night, does it not there stalk abroad at noon-day? If the wives and daughters of blacks are debauched here, are not the wives and daughters of whites debauched there? and will not a Yankee barter away the chastity of his own mother for a dirty dollar? Who fill our brothels? Yankee women! Who load our penitentiaries, crowd our whipping-posts, debauch our slaves, and cheat and defraud us all? Yankee men! And I say unto you, fellow-citizens," and here the speaker's form seemed to dilate with the wild enthusiasm which possessed him, 'come out from among them; be ye separate, and touch not the unclean thing,' and thus saith the Lord God of Hosts, who will guide you, and lead you, if need be, to battle and to victory!"

A perfect storm of applause followed. The assemblage rose, and one long, wild shout rent the old woods, and made the tall trees tremble. It was some minutes before the uproar subsided; when it did, a voice near the speaker's stand called out, "Andy Jones!" The call was at once echoed by another voice, and soon a general shout for "Andy!" "Union Andy!" "Bully Andy!" went up from the same crowd which a moment before had so wildly applauded the secession speaker.

Andy rose from where he was seated beside me, and quietly ascended the steps of the platform. Removing his hat, and passing to his mouth a huge quid of tobacco from a tin box in his pantaloons-pocket, he made several rapid strides up and down the speaker's stand, and then turned squarely to the audience.

The reader has noticed a tiger pacing up and down in his cage, with his eyes riveted on the human faces before him. He has observed how he will single out some individual, and finally stopping short in his rounds, turn on him with a look of such intense ferocity as makes a man's blood stand still, and his very breath come thick and hard, as he momentarily expects the beast will tear away the bars of the cage and leap forth on the obnoxious person. Now, Andy's fine, open, manly face had nothing of the tiger in it, but, for a moment, I could not divest myself of the impression, as he halted in his walk up and down the stage, and turned full and square on the previous speaker—who had taken a seat among the audience near me—that he was about to spring upon him. Riveting his eye on the man's face, he at last slowly said:

"A man stands har and quotes Scriptur agin his feller man, and forgets that 'God made of one blood all nations that dwell on the face of the 'arth.' A man stands har and calls his brother a thief, and his mother a harlot, and axes us to go his doctrin's! I don't mean his brother in the Scriptur sense, nor his mother in a fig'rative sense, but I mean the brother of his own blood, and the mother that bore him; for HE, gentlemen (and he pointed his finger directly at the recent speaker, while his words came slow and heavy with intense scorn), HE is a Yankee! And now, I say, gentlemen, d—n sech doctrin's; d——n sech principles, and d——n the man that's got a soul so black as to utter 'em!"

A breathless silence fell on the assemblage, while the person alluded to sprang to his feet, his face on fire, and his voice thick and broken with intense rage, as he yelled out: "Andy Jones, by ——, you shall answer for this!"

"Sartin," said Andy, coolly inserting his thumbs in the armholes of his waistcoat; "enywhar you likes—har—now—ef 'greeable to you."

"I've no weapon here, sir, but I'll give you a chance mighty sudden," was the fierce reply.

"Suit yourself," said Andy, with perfect imperturbability; "but as you haint jest ready, s'pose you set down, and har me tell 'bout your relations: they're a right decent set—them as I knows—and I'll swar they're 'shamed of you."

A buzz went through the crowd, and a dozen voices called out: "Be civil, Andy"—"Let him blow"—"Shut up"—"Go in, Jones"—with other like elegant exclamations.

A few of his friends took the aggrieved gentleman aside, and, soon quieting him, restored order.

"Wal, gentlemen," resumed Andy, "all on you know whar I was raised—over thar in South Car'lina. I'm sorry to say it, but it's true. And you all know my father was a pore man, who couldn't give his boys no chance—and ef he could, thar warn't no schules in the district—so we couldn't hev got no book-larning ef we'd been a minded to. Wal, the next plantation to whar we lived was old Cunnel J——'s, the father of this cunnel. He was a d——d old nullifier, jest like his son— but not half so decent a man. Wal, on his plantation was an old nigger called Uncle Pomp, who'd sumhow larned to read. He was a mighty good nigger, and he'd hev been in heaven long afore now ef the Lord hadn't a had sum good use for him down har—but he'll be thar yet a d——d sight sooner than sum on us white folks— that's sartin. Wal, as I was saying, Pomp could read, and when I was 'bout sixteen, and had never seen the inside of a book, the old darky said to me one day—he was old then, and that was thirty years ago—wal, he said to me, 'Andy, chile, ye orter larn to read, 'twill be ob use to ye when you'se grow'd up, and it moight make you a good and 'spected man—now, come to ole Pomp's cabin, and he'll larn you, Andy, chile.' Wal, I reckon I went. He'd nothin' but a Bible and Watts' Hymns; but we used to stay thar all the long winter evenin's, and by the light o' the fire—we war both so durned pore we couldn't raise a candle atween us—wal, by the light o' the fire he larned me, and fore long I could spell right smart.

"Now, jest think on that, gentlemen. I, a white boy, and, 'cordin' to the Declaration of Independence, with jest as good blood in me as the old Cunnel had in him, bein' larned to read by an old slave, and that old slave a'most worked to death, and takin' his nights, when he orter hev been a restin' his old bones, to larn me! I'm d——d if he don't get to heaven for that one thing, if for nothin' else.

"Wal, you all know the rest—how, when I'd grow'd up, I settled har, in the old North State, and how the young Cunnel backed my paper, and set me a runnin' at turpentining. P'raps you don't think this has much to do with the Yankees, but it has a durned sight, as ye'll see rather sudden. Wal, arter a while, when I'd got a little forehanded, I begun shipping my truck to York and Bostin'; and at last my Yankee factor, he come out har, inter the back woods, to see me, and says he, 'Jones, come North and take a look at us.' I'd sort o' took to him. I'd lots o' dealin's with him afore ever I seed him, and I allers found him straight as a shingle. Wal, I went North, and he took me round, and showed me how the Yankees does things. Afore I know'd him, I allers thought—as p'raps most on you do—that the Yankees war a sort o' cross atween the devil and a Jew; but how do you s'pose I found 'em? I found that they *sent the pore man's children to schule,* FREE—and that the schule-houses war a d——d sight thicker than the bugs in Miles Privett's beds! and that's sayin' a heap, for ef eny on you kin sleep in his house, excep' he takes to the soft side of the floor, I'm d——d. Yas, the pore man's children are larned thar, FREE!—all on 'em—and they've jest so good a chance as the sons of the rich man! Now, arter that, do you think that I—as got all my schulein, from an old slave, by the light of a borrored pine-knot—der you think that *I* kin say any thing agin the Yankees? P'r'aps they *do* steal—though I doant know it—p'r'aps they *do* debauch thar wives and darters, and sell thar mothers' vartue for dollars—but, ef they do, I'm d——d if they doant send pore children to schule—and that's more'n we do—and let me tell you, until we do thet, we must expec' they'll be cuter and smarter nor we are.

"This gentleman, too, my friends, who's been a givin' sech a hard settin' down ter his own relation, arter they've broughten him up, and given him sech a schulein for nuthin', he says the Yankees want to interfere with our niggers. Now, thet haint so, and they couldn't ef they would, 'case it's agin the Constertution. And they stand on the Constertution a durned sight solider nor we do. Didn't thar big gun—Daniel Webster—didn't he make mince-meat of South Car'lina Hayne on thet ar' subjec'? But I tell you they haint a mind ter meddle with the niggers; they're a goin' to let us go ter h—l our own way, and we're goin' thar mighty fast, or I haint read the last census."

"P'r'aps you haint heerd on the ab'lish'ners, Andy?" cried a voice from among the audience.

"Wal, I reckon I hev," responded the orator. "I've heerd on 'em, and seed 'em, too. When I was North I went to one on thar conventions, and I'll tell you how they look. They've all long, wimmin's har, and thin, shet lips, with big, bawlin' mouths, and long, lean, tommerhawk faces, as white as vargin dip—and they all talk through the nose (giving a specimen), and they all look for all the world jest like the South Car'lina fire-eaters—and they *are* as near like 'em as two peas, excep' they don't swar quite so bad, but they make up for thet in prayin'—and prayin' too much, I reckon, when a man's a d——d hippercrit, is 'bout as bad as swearin'. But, I tell you, the decent folks up North haint ablisheners. They look on 'em jest as we do on mad dogs, the itch, or the nigger traders.

"Now, 'bout this secession bis'ness—though 'taint no use to talk on that subjec', 'case this state never'll secede—South Car'lina has done it, and I'm raather glad she has, for though I was born thar—and say it as hadn't orter say it—she orter hev gone to h—l long ago, and now she's got thar, why—*let her stay!* But, 'bout thet bis'ness, I'll tell you a story.

"I know'd an old gentleman once by the name of Uncle Sam, and he'd a heap of sons. They war all likely boys—but strange ter tell, though they'd all the same mother, and she was a white woman, 'bout half on 'em war colored—not black, but sorter half-and-half. Now, the white sons war well-behaved, industrious, hardworkin' boys, who got 'long well, edicated thar children, and allers treated the old man decently; but the mulatter fellers war a pesky set—though some on 'em war better nor others. They wouldn't work, but set up for airystocracy—rode in kerriges, kept fast horses, bet high, and chawed tobaccer like the devil. Wal, the result was, *they* got out at the elbows, and 'case they warn't gettin' 'long quite so fast as the white 'uns—

11*

though that war all thar own fault—they got jealous, and one on 'em who was blacker nor all the rest—a little feller, but terrible big on braggin'—he packed up his truck one night, and left the old man's house, and swore he'd never come back. He tried to make the other mulatters go with him, but they put thar fingers to thar nose, and says they, 'No you doant.' I was in favor of lettin' on him stay out in the cold, but the old man was a bernevolent old critter, and so *he* says: 'Now, sonny, you jest come back and behave yourself, and I'll forgive you all your old pranks, and treat you jest as I allers used ter; but, ef you wont, why—I'll make you, thet's all!'

"Now, gentlemen, thet quarrelsome, oneasy, ongrateful, tobaccer-chawin', hoss-racin', high-bettin', big-braggin', nigger-stealin', wimmin-whippin', yaller son of the devil, is South Car'lina, and ef she doant come back and behave herself in futur', I'm d——d ef she wont be ploughed with fire, and sowed with salt, and Andy Jones will help ter do it."

The speaker was frequently interrupted in the course of his remarks by uproarious applause—but as he closed and descended from the platform, the crowd sent up cheer after cheer, and a dozen strong men, making a seat of their arms, lifted him from the ground and bore him off to the head of the table, where dinner was in waiting.

The whole of the large assemblage then fell to eating. The dinner was made up of the barbacued beef and the usual mixture of viands found on a planter's table, with water from the little brook hard by, and a plentiful supply of corn-whiskey. (The latter beverage had, I thought, been subjected to the rite of immersion, for it tasted wonderfully of water.)

Songs and speeches were intermingled with the masticating exercises, and the whole company was soon in the best of humor.

During the meal I was introduced by Andy to a large number of the "natives," he taking special pains to tell each one that I was a Yankee, and a Union man, but always adding, as if to conciliate all parties, that I also was a guest and a friend of *his* very particular friend, "thet d——d seceshener, Cunnel J——."

Before we left the table, the secession orator happening near where we were seated, Andy rose from his seat, and, extending his hand to him, said: "Tom, you think I 'sulted you; p'r'aps I did, but you 'sulted my Yankee friend har, and your own relation, and I hed to take it up, jest for the looks o' the thing. Come, there's my hand; I'll fight you ef you want ter, or we'll say no more 'bout it—jest as you like."

"Say no more about it, Andy," said the gentleman, very cordially; "let's drink and be friends."

They drank a glass of whiskey together, and then leaving the table, proceeded to where the ox had been barbacued, to show me how cooking on a large scale is done at the South.

In a pit about eight feet deep, twenty feet long, and ten feet wide, laid up on the sides with stones, a fire of hickory had been made, over which, after the wood had burned down to coals, a whole ox, divested of its hide and entrails, had been suspended on an enormous spit. Being turned often in the process of cooking, the beef had finally been "done brown." It was then cut up and served on the table, and I must say, for the credit of Southern cookery, that it made as delicious eating as any meat I ever tasted.

I had then been away from my charge—the Colonel's horses—as long as seemed to be prudent. I said as much to Andy, when he proposed to return with me, and, turning good-humoredly to his reconciled friend, he said: "Now, Tom, no secession talk while I'm off."

"Nary a word," said "Tom," and we left.

The horses had been well fed by the negro whom I had left in charge of them, but had not been groomed. Seeing that, Andy stripped off his coat, and setting the black at work on one, with a handful of straw and pine leaves, commenced operations on the other, whose hair was soon as smooth and glossy as if it had been rubbed by an English groom.

The remainder of the day passed without incident till eleven at night, when the Colonel returned from Wilmington.

CHAPTER XV.

THE RETURN.

MOYE had not been seen or heard of, and the Colonel's trip was fruitless. While at Wilmington he sent telegrams, directing the overseer's arrest, to the various large cities of the South, and then decided to return home, make arrangements preliminary to a protracted absence from the plantation, and proceed at once to Charleston, where he would await replies to his dispatches. Andy agreed with him in the opinion that Moye, in his weak state of health, would not take an overland route to the free states, but would endeavor to reach some town on the Mississippi, where he might dispose of the horse, and secure a passage up the river.

As no time was to be lost, we decided to return to the plantation on the following morning. Accordingly, with the first streak of day we bade "good-bye" to our Union friend, and started homeward.

No incident worthy of mention occurred on the way, till about ten o'clock, when we arrived at the house of the Yankee schoolmistress, where we had been so hospitably entertained two days before. The lady received us with great cordiality, forced upon us a lunch to serve our hunger on the road, and when we parted, enjoined on me to leave the South at the earliest possible moment. She was satisfied it would not for a much longer time be safe quarters for a man professing Union sentiments. Notwithstanding the strong manifestations of loyalty I had observed among the people, I was convinced the advice of my pretty "countrywoman" was judicious, and I determined to be governed by it.

Our horses, unaccustomed to lengthy journeys, had not entirely recovered from the fatigues of their previous travel, and we did not reach our destination till an hour after dark. We were most cordially welcomed by Madam P——, who soon set before us a hot supper, which, as we were jaded by the long ride, and had fasted for twelve hours, on bacon-sandwiches and cold hoe-cake, was the one thing needful to us.

While seated at the table the Colonel asked:

"Has every thing gone right, Alice, since we left home?"

"Every thing," replied the lady, "except"—and she hesitated, as if she dreaded the effect of the news; "except that Julie and her child have gone."

"Gone!" exclaimed my host; "gone where?"

"I don't know. We have searched everywhere, but have found no clue to them. The morning you left Sam set Jule at work among the pines; she tried hard, but could not do a full task, and at night was taken to the cabin to be whipped. I heard of it, and forbade it. It did not seem to me that she ought to be punished for not doing what she had not strength to do. When released from the cabin, she came and thanked me for having interfered for her, and talked with me awhile. She cried and took on fearfully about Sam, and was afraid you would punish her when you returned. I promised you would not, and she left me seeming more cheerful. I supposed she would go directly home after getting her child from the nurse's quarters; but it appears she went to Pompey's, where she staid till after ten o'clock. Neither she nor the child have been seen since."

"Did you get no trace of her in the morning?"

"Yes, but soon lost it. When she did not appear at work, Sam went to her cabin to learn the cause, and found the door open, and her bed undisturbed. She had not slept there. Knowing that Sandy had returned, I sent for him, and, with Jim and his dog, he commenced a search. The dog tracked her directly from Pompey's cabin to the bank of the run near the lower still. There all trace of her disappeared. We dragged the stream, but discovered nothing. Jim and Sandy then scoured the woods for miles in all directions, but the hound could not recover the trail. I hope otherwise, but I fear some evil has befallen her."

"Oh, no! there's no fear of that," said the Colonel: "she is smart: she waded up the run far enough to baffle the dog, and then made for the swamp. That is why you lost her tracks at the stream. Rely upon it, I am right: but she shall not escape me."

We shortly afterward adjourned to the library. After being seated there a while the Colonel, rising quickly, as if a sudden thought had struck him, sent for the old preacher.

The old negro soon appeared, hat in hand, and taking a stand near the door, made a respectful bow to each one of us.

"Take a chair, Pompey," said Madam P——, kindly.

The black meekly seated himself, when the Colonel asked: "Well, Pomp, what do you know about Jule's going off?"

"Nuffin', massa—I shures you, nuffin'. De pore chile say nuffin to ole Pomp 'bout dat."

"What did she say?"

"Wal, you see, massa, de night arter you gwo 'way, and arter she'd worked hard in de brush all de day, and been a strung up in de ole cabin fur to be whipped, she come ter me wid har baby in har arms, all a-faint and a-tired, and har pore heart clean broke, and she say dat she'm jess ready ter drop down and die. Den I tries ter comfut har, massa; I takes har up from de floor, and I say ter har dat de good Lord He pity har—dat He woant bruise de broken reed, and woant put no more on her dan she kin b'ar—dat He'd touch you, heart, and I toled har you'se a good, kine heart at de bottom, massa —and I knows it, 'case I toted you 'fore you could gwo, and when you's a bery little chile, not no great sight bigger'n har'n, you'd put your little arms round ole Pomp's neck, and say dat when you war grow'd up you'd be bery kine ter de pore brack folks, and not leff 'em be 'bused like dey war in dem days."

"Never mind what *you* said," interrupted the Colonel, a little impatiently, but showing no displeasure; "what did *she* say?"

"Wal, massa, she tuk on bery hard 'bout Sam, and axed me ef I raaily reckoned de Lord had forgib'n him, and took'n him ter Heself, and gibin' him one o' dem hous'n up dar, in de sky. I toled her dat I *know'd* it; but she say it didn't 'pear so ter har, 'case Sam had a been wid har out dar in de woods, all fru de day; dat she'd a *seed* him, massa, and dough he handn't a said nuffin', he'd lukd at har wid sech a sorry, grebed luk, dat it gwo clean fru har heart, till she'd no strength leff, and fall down on de ground a'most dead. Den she say big Sam come 'long and fine har dar, and struck har great, heaby blows wid de big whip!"

"The brute!" exclaimed the Colonel, rising from his chair, and pacing rapidly up and down the room.

"But p'r'aps he warn't so much ter blame, massa," continued the old negro, in a deprecatory tone; "maybe he 'spose she war shirkin' de work. Wal, den she say she know'd nuffin' more, till byme-by, when she come to, and fine big Sam dar, and he struck har agin, and make har gwo ter de work; and she did gwo, but she feel like as ef she'd die.' I toled har de good ma'am wudn't leff big Sam 'buse har no more 'fore you cum hum, and dat you'd hab 'passion on har, and not leff har gwo out in de woods, but put har 'mong de nusses, like as afore.

"Den she say it 'twarn't de work dat trubble har—

dat she orter work, and orter be 'bused, 'case she'd been bad, bery bad. All she axed war dat Sam would forgib har, and cum to har in de oder worle, and tell har so. Den she cried, and tuk on awful; but de good Lord, massa, dat am so bery kine ter de bery wuss sinners, He put de words inter my mouf, and I tink dey gib har comfut, fur she say dat it sort o' 'peared to har den dat Sam *would* forgib har, and take har inter his house up dar, and she warn't afeard ter die no more.

"Den she takes up de chile and gwo 'way, 'pearin' sort o' happy, and more cheerful like dan I'd a seed har eber sense pore Sam war shot."

My host was sensibly affected by the old man's simple tale, but continued pacing up and down the room, and said nothing.

"It's plain to me, Colonel," I remarked, as Pompey concluded, "she has drowned herself and the child—the dog lost the scent at the creek."

"Oh, no!" he replied; "I think not. I never heard of a negro committing suicide—they've not the courage to do it."

"I fear she *has*, David," said the lady. "The thought of going to Sam has led her to it; yet, we dragged the run, and found nothing. What do you think about it, Pompey?"

"I dunno, ma'am, but I'se afeard of dat; and now dat I tinks ob it, I'se afeard dat what I tole har put har up ter it," replied the old preacher, bursting into tears. "She 'peared so happy like, when I say she'd be 'long wid Sam in de oder worle, dat I'se afeard she's a gone and done it wid har own hands. I tole har, too, dat de Lord would oberlook good many tings dat pore sinners do when dey can't help 'emselfs—and it make har do it! Oh! it make har do it!" and the old black buried his face in his hands, and wept bitterly.

"Don't feel so, Pomp," said his master, *very* kindly. "You did the best you could; no one blames you."

"I knows *you* doant, massa—I knows you doant, and you'se bery good nottur—but oh! massa, de Lord!" and his body swayed to and fro with the great grief; "I fears de Lord do, massa, for I'se sent har ter Him wid har own blood, and de blood of dat pore innercent chile, on har hands. Oh, I fears de Lord neber'll forgib me— neber'll forgib me for *dat*."

"He will, my good Pomp—He will!" said the Colonel, laying his hand tenderly on the old man's shoulder. "The Lord will forgive you, for the sake of the Christian example you've set your master, if for nothing else;" and here the proud, strong man's feelings overpowering him, his tears fell in great drops on the breast of the old slave, as they had fallen there in his childhood.

Such scenes are not for the eye of a stranger, and turning away, I left the room.

CHAPTER XVI.

"ONE MORE UNFORTUNATE."

The family met at the breakfast-table at the usual hour on the following morning; but I noticed that Jim was not in his accustomed place behind the Colonel's chair. That gentleman exhibited his usual good spirits, but Madam P—— looked sad and anxious, and *I* had not forgotten the scene of the previous evening.

While we were seated at the meal, the negro Junius hastily entered the room, and in an excited manner exclaimed:

"Oh, massa, massa, you muss cum ter de cabin—Jim hab draw'd his knife, and he swar he'll kill de fuss 'un dat touch him!"

"He does, does he!" said his master, springing from his seat, and abruptly leaving the apartment.

Remembering the fierce burst of passion I had seen in the negro, and fearing there was danger a-foot, I rose to follow, saying, as I did so:

"Madam, cannot you prevent this?"

"I cannot, sir; I have already done all I can. Go and try to pacify the Colonel—Jim will die before he'll be whipped."

Jim was standing at the farther end of the old cabin, with his back to the wall, and the large spring knife in his hand. Some half-dozen negroes were in the centre of the room, apparently cowed by his fierce and desperate looks, and his master was within a few feet of him.

"I tell you, Cunnel," cried the negro, as I entered, "you touch me at your peril!"

"You d——d nigger, do you dare to speak so to me?" said his master, taking a step toward him.

The knife rose in the air, and the black, in a cool, sneering tone, replied: "Say your prayers 'fore you come nigher, for, so help me God, you'm a dead man!"

I laid my hand on the Colonel's arm, to draw him back, saying, as I did so: "There's danger in him! I *know* it. Let him go, and he shall ask your pardon."

"I shan't ax his pardon," cried the black; "leff him an' me be, sir; we'll fix dis ourselfs."

"Don't interfere, Mr. K——," said my host, with perfect coolness, but with a face pallid with rage. "Let me govern my own plantation."

"As you say, sir," I replied, stepping back a few paces; "but I warn you—there is danger in him!"

Taking no notice of my remark, the Colonel turning to the trembling negroes, said: "One of you go to the house and bring my pistols."

"You kin shoot me, ef you likes," said Jim, with a fierce, grim smile; "but I'll take you ter h—l wid me, *shore.* You knows WE wont stand a blow!"

The Colonel, at the allusion to their relationship,

started as if shot, and turning furiously on the negro, yelled out: "I'll shoot you for that, you d——d nigger, by ——."

"It 'pears ter me, Cunnel, ye've hed 'bout nuff shootin' round har, lately; better stop thet sort o' bis'ness; it moight give ye a sore throat," said the long, lean, loose-jointed stump-speaker of the previous Sunday, as he entered the cabin and strode directly up to my host.

"What brought you here, you d——d insolent hound?" cried the Colonel, turning fiercely on the new-comer.

"Wal, I cum ter du ye a naaboorly turn—I've kotched two on yer niggers down ter my still, and I want ye ter take 'em 'way," returned the corn-cracker, with the utmost coolness.

"Two of my niggers!" exclaimed the Colonel, perceptibly moderating his tone—"which ones?"

"A yaller gal, and a chile."

"I thank you, Barnes; excuse my hard words—I was excited."

"All right, Cunnel; say no more 'bout thet. Will ye send fur 'em? I'd hev fotched 'em 'long, but my waggin's off jest now."

"Yes, I'll send at once. Have you got them safe?"

"Safe? I reckon so! Kotched 'em last night, arter dark, and they've kept right still ever sense, I 'sure ye—but th' gal holds on ter th' young 'un ter kill—we cudn't get it 'way no how."

"How did you catch them?"

"They got 'gainst my turpentime raft—the curren' driv 'em down, I s'pose."

"What! are they dead?"

"Dead? deader'n drownded rats!" replied the native,

"My God! drowned herself and her child!" exclaimed the Colonel, with deep emotion.

"It is terrible, my friend. Come, let us go to them, at once," I said, laying my hand on his arm, and drawing him unresistingly away

A pair of mules was speedily harnessed to a large turpentine wagon, and the horses we had ridden the day before were soon at the door. When the Colonel, who had been closeted for a few minutes with Madam P——, came out of the house, we mounted, and rode off with the "corn-cracker."

The native's farm was located on the stream which watered my friend's plantation, and was about ten miles distant. Taking a by-road which led to it through the woods, we rode rapidly on in advance of the wagon.

"Sort o' likely gal, thet, warn't she?" remarked the turpentine-maker, after a while.

"Yes, she was," replied the Colonel, in a half-abstracted manner; "*very* likely."

"Kill harself 'case har man war shot by thet han'som overseer uv your'n?"

"Not altogether for that, I reckon," replied my host; "I fear the main reason was her being put at field-work, and abused by the driver."

"Thet comes uv not lookin' arter things yerself, Cunnel. I tend ter my niggers parsonally, and they keer a durned sight more fur this world then fur kingdom-cum. Ye cudn't hire 'em ter kill 'emselves fur no price."

"Well," replied the Colonel, in a low tone, "I *did* look after her. I put her at full field-work, myself!"

"By ——!" cried the native, reining his horse to a dead stop, and speaking in an excited manner: "I doant b'lieve it—'taint 't all like ye—yer a d——d seceshener; thet comes uv yer bringin'-up—but ye've a soul bigger'n a meetin'-house, and ye cudn't hev put thet slim, weakly gal inter th' woods, no how!"

The Colonel and I instinctively halted our horses, as the "corn-cracker" stopped his, and were then standing abreast of him in the road.

"It's true, Barnes," said my host, in a voice that showed deep dejection; "I *did* do it!"

"May God Almighty furgive ye, Cunnel," said the native, starting his horse forward; "*I* wudn't hev dun it fur all yer niggers, by ——."

The Colonel made no reply, and we rode on the rest of the way in silence.

The road was a mere wagon-track through the trees, and it being but little travelled, and encumbered with the roots and stumps of the pine, our progress was slow, and we were nearly two hours in reaching the plantation of the native.

The corn-cracker's house—a low, unpainted wooden building—stood near the little stream, and in the centre of a cleared plot of some ten acres. This plot was surrounded by a post-and-rail fence, and in its front portion was a garden, which grew a sufficient supply of vegetables to serve a family of twenty persons. In the rear, and at the sides of the dwelling, were about seven acres, devoted mainly to corn and potatoes. In one corner of the lot were three tidy-looking negro-houses, and close beside them I noticed a low shed, near which a large quantity of the stalks of the tall, white corn, common to that section, was stacked in the New England fashion. Browsing on the corn-stalks were three sleek, well-kept milch cows, and a goat.

About four hundred yards from the farmer's house, and on the bank of the little run, which there was quite wide and deep, stood a turpentine distillery; and around it were scattered a large number of rosin and turpentine barrels, some filled and some empty. A short distance higher up, and far enough from the "still" to be safe in the event of a fire, was a long, low, wooden shed, covered with rough, unjointed boards, placed upright, and unbattened. This was the "spirit-house," used for the storage of the spirits of turpentine when barrelled for market, and awaiting shipment. In the creek, and filling nearly one-half of the channel in front of the spirit-shed, was a raft of pine timber, on which were laden some two hundred barrels of rosin. On such rude conveyances the turpentine-maker sent his produce to Conwayboro'. There the timber-raft was sold to my wayside friend, Captain B——, and its freight shipped on board vessel for New York.

Two "prime" negro men, dressed in the usual costume, were "tending the still;" and a negro woman, as stout and strong as the men, and clad in a short, loose, linsey gown, from beneath which peeped out a pair of coarse leggins, was adjusting a long wooden trough, which conveyed the liquid rosin from the "still" to a deep excavation in the earth, at a short distance. In the pit was a quantity of rosin sufficient to fill a thousand barrels.

"Here, Bill," said Barnes to one of the negro men, as we pulled up at the distillery, "put these critters up, and give 'em sum oats, and when they've cooled off a bit, water 'em."

"Yas, yas, massa," replied the negro, springing nimbly forward, and taking the horses by the bridles, "an' rub 'em down, massa?"

"Yas, rub 'em down right smart," replied the corn-cracker; then turning to me, as we dismounted, he said: "Stranger, thet's th' sort o' niggers fur ye; all uv mine ar' jess like him—smart and lively as kittens."

"He does seem to go about his work cheerfully," I replied.

"Cheerfully! d——d ef he doant—all on 'em du! They like me better'n thar own young 'uns, an' it's 'cause I use 'em like human bein's;" and he looked slyly toward the Colonel, who just then was walking silently away, in the direction of the run, as if in search of the rowned "chattels."

"Not thar, Cunnel," cried the native; "they're inter

th' shed;" and he started to lead the way to the "spirit-house."

"Not now, Barnes," I said, putting my hand on his arm: "leave him alone for a little while. He is feeling badly, and we'd better not disturb him just yet."

The native motioned me to a seat on a rosin-barrel, as he replied:

"Wal, he 'pears ter—thet's a fact, and he orter. D——d ef it arn't wicked to use niggers like cattle, as he do."

"I don't think he means to ill-treat them—he's a kind-hearted man."

"Wal, he ar sort o' so; but he's left ev'ry thing ter thet d——d overseer uv his'n. I wudn't ha' trusted him to feed my hogs."

"Hogs!" I exclaimed, laughing; "I supposed you didn't *feed* hogs in these diggins. I supposed you 'let 'em run.'"

"*I* doant; an' I've got th' tallest porkys round har."

"I've been told that they get a good living in the woods."

"Wal, p'r'aps the' du jest make eout ter live thar; but my ole 'oman likes 'em ter hum—they clean up a place like—eat up all th' leavin's, an' give th' young nigs suthin' ter du."

"It seems to me," I said, resuming the previous thread of the conversation; "that overseers are a necessity on a large plantation."

"Wal, the' ar', an' thet's why thar ortent ter be no big plantations; God Almighty didn't make human bein's ter be herded togethar in th' woods like hogs. No man orter ter hev more'n twenty on 'em—he can't look arter no more himself, an' its agin natur ter set a feller over 'em what hain't no int'rest in 'em, an' no feelin' fur 'em, an' who'll drive 'em round like brutes. I never struck one on 'em in my life, an' my ten du more'n ony fifteen th' Cunnel's got."

"I thought they needed occasional correction. How do you manage them without whipping?"

"Manage them! why 'cordin' ter scriptur—do ter 'em as I'd like ter be dun ter, ef I war a nigger. Every one on 'em knows I'd part with my last shirt, an' live on taters an' cow-fodder, fore I'd sell em; an' then I give 'em Saturdays for 'emselfs—but thet's cute dealin' in me (tho' th' pore, simple souls doant see it), fur ye knows the' work thet day for 'emselfs, an' raise nigh all thar own feed, 'cept th' beef and whiskey—an' it sort o' makes 'em feel like folks, too, more like as ef the' war *free*—the' work th' better fur it all th' week."

"Then you think the blacks would work better if free?"

"In *course* I does—its agin man's natur to be a slave. Thet lousy parson ye herd ter meetin, a Sunday, makes slavery cout a divine institooshun, but my wife's a Bible 'oman, and she says 'taint so; an' I'm d——d ef she arn't right."

"Is your wife a South Carolina women?"

"No, she an' me's from th' old North—old Car'tret, nigh on ter Newbern; an' we doant take nat'rally to these fire-eaters."

"Have you been here long?"

"Wal, nigh on ter six yar. I cum har with nuthin' but a thousan' ter my back—slapped thet inter fifteen hun'red acres—paid it down—and then hired ten likely, North Car'lina niggers—hired 'em with th' chance uv buyin' ef the' liked cout har. Wal, th' nigs all know'd me, and the' sprung ter it like blazes; so every yar I've managed ter buy two on 'em, and now I've ten grow'd up, and thar young 'uns; th' still and all th' traps paid fur, an' ef this d——d secesh bis'ness hadn't a come 'long, I'd hev hed a right smart chance o' doin' well."

"I'm satisfied secession will ruin the turpentine business; you'll be shut up here, unable to sell your produce, and it will go to waste."

"Thet's my 'pinion; but I reckon I kin' manage now witheout turpentime. I've talked it over 'long with my nigs, and we kalkerlate, ef these ar doin's go eny furder, ter tap no more trees, but clar land an' go ter raisin' craps."

"What! do you talk politics with your negroes?"

"Nary a politic—but I'm d——d ef th' critters doan't larn 'em sumhow; the' knows 'bout as much uv what's goin' on as I du—but plantin arn't politics; its bisness, an' they've more int'rest in it nor I hev, 'cause they've sixteen mouths ter feed agin my four."

"I'm glad, my friend, that you treat them like men:

but I have supposed they were not well enough informed to have intelligent opinions on such subjects."

"Informed! wal, I reckon the' is; all uv mine kin read, an' sum on 'em kin write, too. D'ye see thet little nig thar?" pointing to a juvenile coal-black darky of about six years, who was standing before the "still" fire; "thet ar little devil kin read an' speak like a parson. He's got hold, sumhow, uv my little gal's book o' pieces, an' larned a dozen on 'em. I make him cum inter th' house, once in a while uv an evenin', an' speechify, an' 'twould do yer soul good ter har him, in his shirt tail, with a old sheet wound round him fur a toger (I've told him th' play-acters du it so down ter Charles'on), an' spoutin' out: 'My name am Norval; on de Gruntin' hills my fader feed him hogs!' The little coon never seed a sheep, an' my wife's told him a flock's a herd, an' he thinks 'hog' *sounds* better'n 'flock,' so, contra'y ter th' book, he puts in 'hogs,' and hogs, you knows, hev ter grunt, so he gits 'em on th' 'Gruntin hills;" and here the kind-hearted native burst into a fit of uproarious laughter, in which, in spite of myself, I had to join.

When the merriment had somewhat subsided, the turpentine-maker called out to the little darky:

"Come here, Jim."

The young chattel ran to him with alacrity, and wedging in between his legs, placed his little black hands, in a free-and-easy way, on his master's knees, and, looking up trustfully in his face, said:

"Wal, massa?"

"What's yer name?"

"Dandy Jim, massa."

"Thet arn't all—what's th' rest?"

"Dandy Jim of ole Car'lina."

"Who made ye?"

"De good God, massa."

"No, He didn't: God doant make little nigs. He makes none but white folks;" said the master, laughing.

"Yas He'm do; Missus say He'm do; dat He make dis nig jess like He done little Totty."

"Wal, He did, Jim. I'm d——d ef *He* didn't, fur nobody else cud make *ye!*" replied the man, patting the little woolly head with undisguised affection.

"Now, Jim, say th' creed fur 'de gemman.' "

The young darky then repeated the Apostle's Creed and the Ten Commandments.

"Is thet all ye knows?"

"No, massa, I knows a heap 'sides dat."

"Wal, say suthin' more—sum on 'em pieces thet jingle."

The little fellow then repeated with entire correctness, and with appropriate gestures, and emphasis, though in the genuine darky dialect—which seems to be inborn with the pure-Southern black—Mrs. Hemans' poem:

"The boy stood on the burning deck."

"Mrs. Hemans draped in black!" I exclaimed, laughing heartily: "How would the good lady feel, could she look down from where she is, and hear a little darky doing up her poetry in that style?"

"D——d ef I doant b'lieve 'twud make her love th' little nig like I do;" replied the corn-cracker, taking him up on his knee as tenderly as he would have taken up his own child.

"Tell me, my little man," I said: "who taught you all these things?"

"I larned 'em, myseff, sar," was the prompt reply.

"You learned them, yourself! but who taught you to read?"

"I larned 'em myseff, sar!"

"You couldn't have learned *that* yourself; didn't your 'massa' teach you?"

"No, sar."

"Oh! your 'missus' did."

"No, sar."

"No, sar!" I repeated; then suspecting the real state of the case, I looked him sternly in the eye, and said: "My little man, it's wrong to tell lies—you must *always* speak the truth; now, tell me truly, did not your 'missus' teach you these things?"

"No, sar, I larned 'em myseff."

"Ye can't cum it, Stranger; ye moight roast him over a slow fire, an' not git nary a thing eout on him but thet," said the corn-cracker, leaning forward, and breaking into a boisterous fit of laughter. "It's agin th' law, an' I'm d——d ef I teached him. Reckon he *did* larn himself!"

"I must know your wife, my friend. She's a good woman."

"Good! ye kin bet high on thet; she's uv th' stuff th' Lord makes angels eout on."

I had no doubt of it, and was about to say so, when the Colonel's turpentine wagon drove up, and I remembered I had left him too long alone.

The coachman was driving, and Jim sat on the wagon beside him.

"Massa K——," said the latter, getting down and coming to me: "Whar am dey?"

"In the spirit-shed."

He was turning to go there, when I called him back, saying: "Jim, you must not see your master now; you'd better keep out of sight for the present."

"No, massa; de ma'am say de Cunnel take dis bery hard, and dat I orter tell him I'se sorry for what I'se done."

"Well, wait a while. Let me go in first."

Accompanied by the corn-cracker, I entered the turpentine-shed. A row of spirit-barrels were ranged along each of its sides, and two tiers occupied the centre of the building. On these a number of loose planks were placed, and on the planks lay the bodies of the metif woman and her child. The Colonel was seated on a barrel near them, with his head resting on his hands, and his eyes fixed on the ground. He did not seem to notice our entrance, and, passing him without speaking, I stepped to the side of the dead.

The woman's dress, the common linsey gown worn by her class, was still wet, and her short, kinky, brown hair fell in matted folds around her face. One arm hung loosely by her side; the other was clasped tightly around her child, which lay as if asleep on her bosom. One of its small hands clung to its mother's breast, and around its little lips played a smile. But how shall I describe the pale, sweet beauty of the face of the drowned girl, as she lay there, her eyes closed, and her lips parted, as in prayer? Never but once have I seen on human features the strange radiance that shone upon it, or the mingled expression of hope, and peace, and resignation that rested there—and that was in the long-gone time, when, standing by her bedside, I watched the passing away of one who is now an angel in heaven!

"Come, my dear friend, let us go," I said, turning and gently taking the Colonel by the arm, "the negroes are here, and will take charge of the dead."

"No, no!" he replied, rising, and looking around, as if aroused from a troubled dream; "that is for *me* to do!" Then he added, after a moment's pause, "Will you help me to get them into the wagon?"

"Yes, I will, certainly."

He made one step toward the body of the dead girl, then sinking down again on the barrel, covered his face with his hands, and cried out: "My God! this is terrible! Did you ever see such a look as that? It will haunt me forever!"

"Come, my friend, rouse yourself—this is weakness;

you are tired with the long ride and excitement of the past few days. Come, go home—I will look after them."

"No, no! I must do it. I will be a man again;" and he rose and walked steadily to the dead bodies. "Is there any one here to help?" he asked.

Jim was standing in the door-way, and I motioned to him to come forward. The great tears were streaming down his face as he stepped timidly towards his master, and said: "I'll do dis, massa, don't you trubble yerself no more."

"It's good of you, Jim. You'll forgive me for being so cruel to you, wont you?" said the Colonel, taking the black by the hand.

"Forgib ye, massa! *I* war all ter blame—but ye'll forgib me, massa—ye'll forgib me!" cried the black, with strong emotion.

"Yes, yes; but say no more about it. Come, let us get Julie home."

But the poor girl was already *home*—home where her sufferings and her sorrows were over, and all her tears were wiped away forever!

We four bore away the mother and the child. A number of blankets were in the bottom of the wagon, and we laid the bodies carefully upon them. When all seemed ready, the Colonel, who was still standing by the side of the dead, turned to my new friend, and said: "Barnes, will you loan me a pillow? I will send it back to-night."

"Sartin, Cunnel;" and the farmer soon brought one

from the house. Lifting tenderly the head of the drowned girl, the Colonel placed it beneath her, and smoothing back her tangled hair, he gently covered her face with his handkerchief, as if she could still feel his kindness, or longer cared for the pity or the love of mortal. Yet, who knows but that her parted soul, from the high realm to which it had soared, may not then have looked down, have seen that act, and have forgiven him!

CHAPTER XVII.

THE SMALL PLANTER.

In the first moments of grief the sympathy of friends, and the words of consolation bring no relief. How much more harshly do such words grate on the ear when the soul is bowed down by remorse and unavailing regret! Then the wounded spirit finds peace nowhere but with God.

I saw that the Colonel would be alone, and turning to him, as he prepared to follow the strange vehicle, which, with its load of death, was already jolting its way over the rough forest road, I said,

"Will you pardon me, if I remain with your friend here for awhile? I will be at the mansion before dark."

"Oh, certainly, my friend, come when you feel disposed," he replied, and mounting his horse he was soon out of sight among the trees.

"Now, Barnes," I said, shaking off the gloomy feelings that had oppressed me: "come, I must see that wife of yours, and get a glimpse of how you live?"

"Sartin, stranger; come in; I'll give ye th' tallest dinner my 'oman can scare up, an' she's sum pumkins in th' cookin' line;" and he led the way to the farmhouse.

As I turned to follow, I slipped a half-dollar into the

hand of the darky who was holding my horse, and asked him to put her again into the stable.

"I'll do dat, sar, but I karn't take dis; massa doant 'low it nohow;" he replied, tendering me back the money.

"Barnes, your negroes have strange ways; I never met one before who'd refuse money."

"Wal, stranger, 'taint hosspetality to take money on yer friends, and Bill gets all he wants from me."

I took the silver and gave it to the first darky I met, who happened to be an old centenarian belonging to the Colonel. As I tossed it to him, he grinned out: "Ah, massa, I'll git sum 'backer wid dis; 'pears like I hadn't nary a chaw in furty yar." With more than one leg in the grave the old negro had not lost his appetite for the weed—in fact, that and whiskey are the only "luxuries" ever known to the plantation black.

As we went nearer, I took a closer survey of the farm-house. It was, as I have said, a low, unpainted wooden building, located in the middle of a ten acre lot. It was approached by a straight walk, paved with a mixture of sand and tar, similar to that which the reader may have seen in the Champs Elysees. I do not know whether my back-woods friend, or the Parisian pavior, was the first inventor of this composition, but I am satisfied the corn-cracker had not stolen it from the stone-cracker. The walk was lined with fruit-bearing shrubs, and directly in front of the house, were two small flower-beds.

The dwelling itself, though of a dingy brown wood-color, was neat and inviting. It may have been forty feet square on the ground, and was only a story and a half high, but a projecting roof, and a front dormer-window, relieved it from the appearance of disproportion. Its gable ends were surmounted by two enormous brick chimneys, carried up on the outside, in the fashion of the South, and its high, broad windows were ornamented with Venetian blinds. Its front door opened directly into the "living-room," and at the threshold we met its mistress.

As the image of that lady has still a warm place in a pleasant corner of my memory, I will describe her. She was about thirty years of age, and had a fresh, cheerful face. To say that she was handsome, would not be strictly true; though she had that pleasant, gentle, kindly expression that sometimes makes even a homely person seem beautiful. But she was not homely. Her features were regular, her hair, glossy and brown, and her eyes, black and brilliant, and, for their color, the mildest and softest I had ever seen. Her figure was tall, and in its outline somewhat sharp and angular, but she had an ease and grace about her that made one forget she was not moulded as softly and roundly as others. She seemed just the woman on whose bosom a tired, worn, over-burdened man might lay his weary head, and find rest and forgetfulness.

She wore a neat calico dress, fitting closely to the neck, and an apron of spotless white muslin. A little lace cap perched cosily on the back of her head, hiding a portion of her wavy, dark hair, and on her feet—a miracle, reader, in one of her class—were stockings and shoes! Giving me her hand—which, at the risk of making her husband jealous, I held for a moment—she said, making a gentle courtesy:

"Ye ar welcome, stranger."

"I sincerely thank you, madam; I *am* a stranger in these parts."

She tendered me a chair, while her husband opened a sideboard, and brought forth a box of Havanas, and a decanter of Scuppernong. As I took the proffered seat, he offered me the refreshments. I drank the lady's health in the wine, but declined the cigars. Seeing this, she remarked:

"Yer from th' North, sir; arn't ye?"

"Yes, madam, I live in New York, but I was born in New-England."

"I reckoned so; I knew ye didn't belong in Car'-lina."

"How did you know that, madam?" I asked, laughing.

"I seed ye doan't smoke 'fore wimmin. But ye musn't mind me; I sort o' likes it; its a great comfut to John, and may be it ar to ye."

"Well, I do relish a good cigar, but I never smoke before any lady except my wife, and though she's only 'a little lower than the angels,' she *does*, once in a while, say it's a shame to make the *house* smell like a tobacco factory."

Barnes handed me the box again, and I took one. As I was lighting it, he said:

"Ye've got a good 'oman, hev ye?"

"There's none better; at least, I think so."

"Wal, I'm 'zactly uv thet 'pinion 'bout mine: I wouldn't trade her fur all this worle, an' th' best half uv 'tother."

"Don't ye talk so, John," said the lady; then addressing me, she added: "It's a good husband thet makes a good wife, sir."

"Sometimes, madam, but not always. I've known some of the best of wives who had miserable husbands."

"An' I'm d——d ef I made my wife th' 'oman she ar'," said the corn-cracker.

"Hush, John; ye musn't sw'ar so; ye knows how often ye've said ye wouldn't."

"Wal, I du, an' I wont agin, by ——. But Sukey, whar's th' young 'uns?"

"Out in the lot, I reckon; but ye musn't holler'm in—they'r all dirt."

"No matter for that, madam," I said; "dirt is healthy for little ones; rolling in the mud makes them grow."

"Then our'n orter grow right smart, fur they'r in it allers."

"How many have you, madam?"

"Two; a little boy, four, and a little gal, six."

"They're of interesting ages."

"Yas, the' is int'restin'; ev'ry 'uns own chil'ren is smart; but the' does know a heap. John was off ter

Charl'ston no great while back, an' the little boy used ter pray ev'ry mornin' an' ev'nin' fur his fader ter cum hum. I larned 'em thet jest so soon as the' talked, 'cause thar's no tellin' how quick the' moight be tooken 'way. Wal, the little feller prayed ev'ry mornin' an' ev'nin' fur his fader ter cum back; an' John didn't cum; so finarly he got sort o' provoked with th' Lord; an' he said God war aither deaf, an' couldn't har, or he war naughty, an' wouldn't tell fader thet little Johnny wanted to seed 'im 'werry mooch' "—and here the good lady laughed pleasantly, and I joined in most heartily.

Blessed are the children that have such a mother.

Soon the husband returned with the little girl and boy, and four young ebonies, all bare-headed, and dressed alike, in thick trousers, and a loose linsey shirt. Among them was my new acquaintance, "Dandy Jim, of ole Car'lina."

The little girl came to me, and soon I had two white children on one knee, and two black on the other, and Dandy Jim between my legs, playing with my watch-chain. The family made no distinction between the colors, and as the children were all equally clean I did not see why *I* should do so.

The lady renewed the conversation by remarking: "P'raps ye reckon it's quar, sir, that we 'low our'n to 'sociate 'long with th' black chil'ren; but we karn't help it. On big plantations it works sorry bad, fur th' white young 'uns larn all manner of evil from the black 'uns; but I've laboored ter teach our'n so one wont do no harm ter 'tother."

"I suppose, madam, that is one of the greatest evils of slavery. The low black poisons the mind of the white child, and the bad influence lasts through life."

"Yas, it's so, stranger; an' it's the biggest keer I hev. It often 'pears strange ter me thet our grow'd up men arn't no wuss then the' is."

In those few words that unlettered woman had said, what would—if men were but wise enough to hear and heed the great truth which she spoke—banish slavery from this continent forever!

After awhile the farmer told the juvenile delineator of Mrs. Hemans, and the other poets, to give us a song; and planting himself in the middle of the floor, the little darky sang "Dixie," and several other negro songs, which his master had taught him, but into which he had introduced some amusing variations of his own. The other children joined in the choruses; and then Jim danced breakdowns, "walk-along-Joes," and other darky dances, his master accompanying him on a cracked fiddle, till my sides were sore with laughter, and the hostess begged them to stop. Finally the clock struck twelve, and the farmer, going to the door, gave a long, loud blast on a cow's horn. In about five minutes one after another of the field hands came in, till the whole ten had seated themselves on the verandah. Each carried a bowl, a tin-cup, or a gourd, into which my host—who soon emerged from a back room* with a pail of whiskey in his hand—

---

* The whiskey was kept in a back room, above ground, because the dwelling had no cellar. The fluid was kept safely, under lock and key, and the farmer ac

poured a gill of the beverage. This was the day's allowance, and the farmer, in answer to a question of mine, told me he thought negroes were healthier, and worked better for a small quantity of alcohol daily. "The' work hard, and salt feed doant set 'em up 'nough," was his remark.

Meanwhile the hostess busied herself with preparations for dinner, and it was soon spread on a bright cherry table, covered by a spotless white cloth. The little darkies had scattered to the several cabins, and we soon sat down to as good a meal as I ever ate at the South.

We were waited on by a tidy negro woman, neatly clad in a calico gown, with shoes on her feet, and a flaming red and yellow 'kerchief on her head. This last was worn in the form of a turban, and one end escaping from behind, and hanging down her back, it looked for all the world like a flag hung out from a top turret. Observing it, my host said:

"Aggy—showin' yer colors? Ye'r Union gal—hey?"

"Yas, I is dat, massa; Union ter de back bone;" responded the negress, grinning widely.

"All th' Union *ye* knows on," replied the master, winking slyly at me, "is th' union yer goin' ter hitch up 'long with black Cale over ter Squire Taylor's."

"No, 'taint, massa; takes more'n tu ter make de Union."

counted for that, by saying that his negroes would steal nothing but whiskey. Few country houses at the South have a cellar—that apartment deemed so essential by Northern housekeepers. The intervening space between the ground and the floor is there left open, to allow of a free circulation of air.

"Yas, I knows—it gin'rally takes ten or a dozen: reckon it'll take a dozen with ye."

"John, ye musn't talk so ter th' sarvents; it spiles 'em," said his wife.

"No it doant—do it, Aggy?"

"Lor', missus, I doant keer what massa say; but I doant leff no oder man run on so ter me!"

"No more'n ye doant, gal! only Cale."

"Nor him, massa; I makes him stan' roun', *I* reckon."

"I reckon ye du; ye wudn't be yer massa's gal ef ye didn't."

When the meal was over, I visited, with my host, the negro houses. The hour allowed for dinner* was about expiring, and the darkies were preparing to return to the field. Entering one of the cabins, where were two stout negro men and a woman, my host said to them, with a perfectly serious face:

"Har, boys, I've fotched ye a live Yankee ab'lishener; now, luk at 'im all roun'. Did ye ever see sech a critter?"

"Doant see nuffin' quar in dat gemman, massa," replied one of the blacks. "Him 'pears like bery nice gemman; doant 'pear like ab'lishener;" and he laughed, and scraped his head in the manner peculiar to the negro, as he added: "kinder reckon he wudn't be har ef he war one of *dem*."

"What der *ye* knows 'bout th' ab'lisheners? Ye never seed one—what d'ye 'spose the' luk like?"

---

* No regular dinner-hour is allowed the blacks on most turpentine plantations. Their food is usually either taken with them to the woods, or carried there by house servants, at stated times.

"Dey say dey luk likes de bery ole debil, massa, but reckon taint so."

"Wal, the' doant; the' luk wuss then thet: they'm bottled up thunder an' lightnin', an' ef the' cum down har, they'll chaw ye all ter hash."

"I reckon!" replied the darky, manipulating his wool, and distending his face into a decidedly incredulous grin.

"What do you tell them such things for?" I asked, good-humoredly.

"Lor, bless ye, stranger, the' knows th' ab'lisheners ar thar friends, jest so well as ye du; and so fur as thet goes, d——d ef the' doan't know I'm one on 'em myseff, fur I tells 'em, ef the' want to put, the' kin put, an' I'll throw thar trav'lin 'spences inter th' bargin. Doan't I tell ye thet, Lazarus."

"Yas, massa, but none ob massa's nigs am gwine ter put—lesswise, not so long as you an' de good missus, am 'bove groun'."

The darky's name struck me as peculiar, and I asked him where he got it.

"'*Tain't* my name, sar; but you see, sar, w'en massa fuss hire me ob ole Capt'in ——, up dar ter Newbern-way, I war sort o' sorry like—hadn't no bery good cloes—an' massa, he den call me Lazarus, 'case he say I war all ober rags and holes, an' it hab sort o' stuck ter me eber sense. I war a'mighty bad off 'fore dat, but w'en I cum down har I gets inter Abr'am's buzzum, I does;" and here the darky actually reeled on his seat with laughter.

"Is this woman your wife?" I asked.

"No, sar; my wife 'longs to Cunnel J——; dat am my new wife—my ole wife am up dar whar I cum from!"

"What! have you two wives?"

"Yas, massa, I'se two."

"But that's contrary to Scripture."

"No, sar; de Cunnel say 'tain't. He say in Scriptur' dey hab a heap ob' 'em, and dat niggers kin hab jess so many as dey likes—a hun'red ef dey want ter."

"Does the Colonel teach that to his negroes?" I asked, turning to the native.

"Yas, I reckon he do—an' sits 'em th' 'zample, too," he replied, laughing; "but th' old sinner knows better'n thet; he kin read."

"Do you find that in the Bible, Lazarus?"

"Yas, massa; whar I reads it. Dat's whar it tell 'bout David and Sol'mon and all dem—dey hab a heap ob wives. A pore ole darky karn't hab 'nuffin 'sides dem, an' he *orter* be 'low'd jess so many as he likes."

Laughing at the reasoning of the negro, I asked:

"How would *you* like it, if your wife over at Colonel J——'s, had as many husbands as *she* liked?"

"Wal, I couldn't fine no fault, massa: an' I s'pose she do; dough I doan't knows it, 'case I'se dar only Sundays."

"Have you any children?"

"Yas, sar; I'se free 'longin' ter de Cunnel, an' four or five—I doant 'zactly know—up ter hum; but *dey'se* grow'd up."

"Is your wife, up there, married again?"

"Yas, massa, she got anoder man jess w'en I cum 'way; har ole massa make har do it."

We then left the cabin, and when out of hearing of the blacks, I said to the corn-cracker: "That *may be* Scripture doctrine, but *I* have not been taught so!"

"Scriptur or no Scriptur, stranger, it's d———d heathenism," replied the farmer, who, take him all in all, is a superior specimen of the class of small-planters at the South; and yet, seeing polygamy practised by his own slaves, he made no effort to prevent it. He told me that if he should object to his darky cohabiting with the Colonel's negress, it would be regarded as unneighborly, and secure him the enmity of the whole district! And still we are told that slavery is a *Divine* institution!

After this, we strolled off into the woods, where the hands were at work. They were all stout, healthy and happy-looking, and in answer to my comments on their appearance, the native said that the negroes on the turpentine farms are always stronger and longer-lived, than those on the rice and cotton-fields. Unless carried off by the fevers incident to the climate, they generally reach a good old age, while the rice-negro seldom lives to be over forty, and the cotton-slave very rarely attains sixty. Cotton-growing, however, my host thought, is not, in itself, much more unhealthy than turpentine-gathering, though cotton-hands work in the sun, while the turpentine slaves labor altogether in the shade.

"But," he said, "the' work 'em harder nor we does, an' doan't feed 'em so well. We give our'n meat and whiskey ev'ry day, but them articles is skarse 'mong th' cotton blacks, an' th' rice niggers never get 'em excep' ter Chris'mas time, an' thet cums but onst a yar."

"Do you think the white could labor as well as the black, on the rice and cotton-fields?" I asked.

"Yas, an' better—better onywhar; but, in coorse, 'tain't natur' fur black nor white ter stand long a workin' in th' mud and water up ter thar knees; sech work wud kill off th' very devil arter a while. But th' white kin stand it longer nor the black, and its' 'cordin' ter reason that he shud; fur, I reckon, stranger, that the sperit and pluck uv a man hev a durned sight ter du with work. They'll hole a man up when he's clean down, an' how kin we expec' thet the pore nig', who's nary a thing ter work fur, an' who's been kept under an' 'bused ever sense Adam was a young un'—how kin we expec' he'll work like men thet own 'emselfs, an' whose faders hev been free ever sense creation? I reckon that the parient has a heap ter du with makin' th' chile. He puts the sperit inter 'im: doan't we see it in hosses an' critters an' sech like? It mayn't crap eout ter onst, but it's shore ter in th' long run, and thet's th' why th' black hain't no smarter nor he is. He's been a-ground down an' kept under fur so long thet it 'll take more'n 'un gin'ration ter bring him up. 'Tain't his fault thet he's no more sperit, an' p'raps 'tain't ourn—thet is, them on us as uses 'em right—but it war the fault uv yer fader an' mine—yer fader stole 'em, and mine bought 'em, an' the' both made cattle uv 'em."

"But I had supposed the black was better fitted by nature for hard labor, in a hot climate, than the white?"

"Wal, he arn't, an' I knows it. Th' d——d parsons an' pol'tishuns say thet, but 'tain't so. I kin do half agin more work in a day then th' best nig' I've got, an' I've dun it, tu, time an' agin, an' it didn't hurt me nuther. Ye knows ef a man hev a wife and young 'uns 'pendin' on him, an' arn't much 'forehanded, he'll work like th' devil. I've dun it, and ye hev ef ye war ever put ter it; but th' nig's, why the' hain't got no wives and young 'uns ter work fur—the law doan't 'low 'em ter hev any—the' hain't nary a thing but thar carcasses, an' them's thar masters'."

"You say a man works better for being free; then you must think 'twould be well to free the negroes?"

"In coorse, I does. Jest luk at them nig's o' mine; they're ter all 'tents an' purposes free, 'case I use 'em like men, an' the' knows the' kin go whenever the' d——d please. See how the' work—why, one on 'em does half as much agin as ony hard-driv' nigger in creation."

"What would you do with them, if they were *really* free?"

"Du with 'em? why, hire 'em, an' make twice as much cout on 'em as I does now."

"But I don't think the two races were meant to live together."

"No more'n the' warn't. But 'tain't thar fault thet they's har. We hain't no right ter send 'em off. We orter stand by our'n an' our faders' doin's. The nig' keers more fur his hum, so durned pore as it ar', then ye or I does fur our'n. I'd pack sech off ter Libraria or th' devil, as wanted ter go, but I'd hev no 'pulsion 'bout it."

"Why, my good friend, you're half-brother to Garrison. You don't talk to your neighbors in this way?"

"Wal, I doan't;" he replied, laughing. "Ef I dun it, they'd treat me to a coat uv tar, and ride me out uv th' deestrict raather sudden, I reckon; but yer a Nuthener, an' the' all take nat'rally ter freedum, excep' th' d——d dough-faces, an' ye aren't one on 'em, I'll swar."

"Well, I'm not. Do many of your neighbors think as you do?"

"Reckon not many round har; but up in Cart'ret, whar I cum from, heaps on 'em do, though the' darn't say so."

By this time we had reached the still, and, directing his attention to the enormous quantity of rosin that had been run into the pit which I have spoken of, I asked him why he threw so much valuable material away.

"Wal, 'tain't wuth nothin' har. Thet's th' common, an' it won't bring in York, now, more'n a dollar forty-five. It costs a dollar an' two bits ter get it thar, and pay fur sellin' on it, an' th' barr'l's wuth th' diff'rence. I doan't ship nuthin wuss nor No. 2."

"What is No. 2?"

He took the head from one of the barrels, and with an adze cut out a small piece, then handing me the specimen, replied:

"Now hole thet up ter th' sun. Ye'll see though its yaller, it's clean and clar. Thet's good No. 2, what brings now two dollars and two bits, in York, an' pays me 'bout a dollar a barr'l, its got eout o' second yar dip, an' as it comes eout uv th' still, is run through thet ar strainer,' pointing to a coarse wire seive that lay near. "Th' common rosum, thet th' still's runnin' on now, is made eout on th' yaller dip—thet's th' kine o' turpentine thet runs from th' tree arter two yars' tappin'—we call it yallar dip ca'se it's allers dark. We doant strain common 't all, an' it's full uv chips and dirt. It's low now, but ef it shud ever git up, I'd tap thet ar' heap, barr'l it up, run a little fresh stilled inter it, an' 'twould be a'most so good as new."

"Then it is injured by being in the ground."

"Not much; it's jest as good fur ev'rything but makin' ile, puttin it in the 'arth sort o' takes th' sap eout on it, an' th' sap's th' ile. Natur' sucks thet eout, I s'pose, ter make th' trees grow—I expec' my bones 'ill fodder 'em one on these days."

"Rosin is put to very many uses?"

"Yes, but common's used mainly for ile and soap, th' Yankees put it inter hard yaller soap, 'case it makes it weigh, an' yer folks is up ter them doin's," and he looked at me and gave a sly laugh. I could not deny the "hard" impeachment, and said nothing. Taking a specimen of very clear light-colored rosin from a shelf in the stillhouse, I asked him what that quality was worth.

"Thet ar brought seven dollars, for two hundred an' eighty pounds, in York, airly this yar. It's th' very best No. 1; an' its hard ter make, 'case ef th' still gets overhet it turns it a tinge. Thet sort is run through two sieves, the coarse 'un, an' thet ar," pointing to another wire strainer, the meshes of which were as fine as those of the flour sieve used by housewives.

"Do your seven field hands produce enough 'dip' to keep your still a running?"

"No, I buys th' rest uv my naboors who haint no stills; an' th' Cunnel's down on me 'case I pay 'em more'n he will; but I go on Franklin's princerpel: 'a nimble sixpence's better'n a slow shillin.' A great ole feller thet, warn't he? I've got his life."

"And you practice on his precepts; that's the reason you've got on so well."

"Yas, thet, an' hard knocks. The best o' doctrin's arn't wuth a d——n ef ye doan't work on 'em."

"That is true."

. We shortly afterward went to the house, and there I passed several hours in conversation with my new friend and his excellent wife. The lady, after a while, showed me over the building. It was well-built, well-arranged, and had many conveniences I did not expect to find in a back-woods dwelling. She told me its timbers and covering were of well-seasoned yellow pine—which will last for centuries—and that it was built by a Yankee carpenter, whom they had " 'ported" from Charleston, paying his fare, and giving him his living, and two dollars and a half a day. It had cost as near as she "cud reckon, 'bout two thousan' dollars."

It was five o'clock, when, shaking them warmly by the hand, I bade my pleasant friends " good-bye," and mounting my horse rode off to the Colonel's.

CHAPTER XVIII.

THE BURIAL OF "JULE."

THE family were at supper when I returned to the mansion, and, entering the room, I took my accustomed place at the table. None present seemed disposed to conversation. The little that was said was spoken in a low, subdued tone, and no allusion was made to the startling event of the day. At last the octoroon woman asked me if I had met Mrs. Barnes at the farmer's.

"Yes," I replied, "and I was greatly pleased with her. She seems one of those rare women who would lend grace to even the lowest station."

"She *is* a rare woman; a true, sincere Christian. Every one loves her; but few know all her worth; only those do who have gone to her in sorrow and trial, as—" and her voice trembled, and her eyes moistened—"as I have."

And so that poor, outcast, despised, dishonored woman, scorned and cast-off by all the world, had found one sympathizing, pitying friend. Truly, "He tempers the wind to the shorn lamb."

When the meal was over, all but Madam P—— retired to the library. Tommy and I fell to reading, but the Colonel shortly rose and continued pacing up and down the apartment till the clock sounded eight. The lady then entered, and said to him.

"The negroes are ready, David; will *you* go, Mr. K——?"

"I think not, madam," I replied; "at least not now."

I continued reading, for a time, when, tiring of the book, I laid it down, and followed them to the little burial-ground.

The grave of Sam was open, and the plantation blacks were gathered around it. In the centre of the group, and at the head of the rude coffin, the Colonel was seated, and near him the octoroon woman and her son. The old preacher was speaking.

"My chil'ren," he said: "she hab gone ter Him, wid har chile: gone up dar, whar dey doan't sorrer no more, whar dey doan't weep no more, whar all tears am wiped from dar eyes foreber. I knows she lay han's on har-seff, and dat, my chil'ren, am whot none ob us shud do, 'case we'm de Lord's; He put us har, an' he'll take us 'way when we's fru wid our work, not afore. We hab no right ter gwo afore. Pore Juley did—but p'raps she cudn't help it. P'raps de great sorrer war so big in har heart, dat she cudn't fine rest nowhar but in de cole, dark riber. P'raps she warn't ter blame—p'raps," and here his eyes filled: " p'raps ole Pomp war all ter blame, fur I tole har, my chil'ren"—he could say no more, and sinking down on a rude seat, he covered his face, and sobbed audibly. Even the Colonel's strong frame heaved with emotion, and not a dry eye was near. After a time the old man rose again, and with streaming eyes, and upturned face, continued:

"Dars One up dar, my chil'ren, dat say: 'Come unter Me, all ye dat am a weary an' a heaby laden, an' I will gib you ress.' He, de good Lord, He say dat; and p'raps Juley hard Him say it, an' dat make har gwo." Again his voice failed, and he sank down, weeping and moaning as if his heart would break.

A pause followed, when the Colonel rose, and aided by Jim and two other blacks, with his own hands nailed down the lid, and lowered the rude coffin into the ground. Then the earth was thrown upon it, and then the long, low chant which the negroes raise over the dead, mingling now with sobs and moans, and breaking into a strange wild wail, went up among the pines, and floating off on the still night air, echoed through the dark woods, till it sounded like music from the grave. I have been in the chamber of the dying; I have seen the young and the beautiful laid away in the earth; but I never felt the solemn awfulness of death, as I did, when, in the stillness and darkness of night, I listened to the wild grief of that negro group, and saw the bodies of that slave mother and her child, lowered to their everlasting rest by the side of Sam.

CHAPTER XIX.

HOMEWARD.

THE morning broke bright and mellow with the rays of the winter sun, which in Carolina lends the warmth of October to the chills of January, when, with my portmanteau strapped, and my thin overcoat on my arm, I gave my last "God bless you" to the octoroon woman, and turned my face toward home.

Jim shouted "all ready," the driver cracked his whip, and we were on our way to Georgetown.

The recent rains had hardened the roads, the bridges were repaired, and we were whirled rapidly forward, and, at one o'clock, reached Bucksville. There we met a cordial welcome, and remained to dinner. Our host pressed us to pass the night at his house, but the Colonel had business with one of his secession friends residing down the road — my wayside acquaintance, Colonel A——, and desired to stay overnight with him. At three o'clock, bidding a kindly farewell to Captain B—— and his excellent family, we were again on our way.

The sun was just sinking among the western pines, when we turned into a broad avenue, lined with stately old trees, and rode up to the door-way of the rice-planter. It was a large, square, dingy old house, seated on a gentle knoll, a short half-mile from the river, along whose banks stretched the rice-fields. We entered, and were soon welcomed by its proprietor.

He received my friend warmly, and gave me a courteous greeting, remarking, when I mentioned that I was homeward bound, that it was wise to go. "Things are very unsettled; there's no telling what a day may bring forth; feeling is running very high, and a Northern man, whatever his principles, is not safe here. By-the-way," he added, "did you not meet with some little obstruction at Conwayboro', on your way up?"

"Yes, I did; a person there ordered me back, but when things began to look serious, Scipio, the negro whom you saw with me, got me out of the hobble."

"Didn't he tell the gentleman that you were a particular friend of mine, and had met me by appointment at Captain B——'s?" he asked, smiling.

"I believe he did, sir; but I assure you, *I* said nothing of the kind, and I think the black should not be blamed, under the circumstances."

"Oh, no; I don't blame him. I think he did a smart thing. He might have said you were my grandmother, if it would have served you, for that low fellow is as fractious as the devil, and dead sure on the trigger."

"You are very good, sir," I replied: "how did you hear of it?"

"A day or two afterward, B—— passed here on his way to Georgetown. I had been riding out, and happened to be at the head of my avenue when he was going by. He stopped, and asked if I knew you. Not knowing, then, the circumstances, I said that I had met you casually at Bucksville, but had no particular acquaintance with you. He rode on, saying nothing further. The next morning, I had occasion to go to Georgetown, and at Mr. Fraser's office, accidentally heard that Scip—who is well-known and universally liked there—was to have a public whipping that evening. Something prompted me to inquire into it, and I was told that he had been charged by B—— with shielding a well-known abolitionist at Conwayboro'—a man who was going through the up-country, distributing such damnable publications as the New York *Independent* and *Tribune*. I knew, of course, it referred to you, and that it wasn't true. I went to Scip and got the facts, and by stretching the truth a little, finally got him off. There was a slight discrepancy between my two accounts of you" (and here he laughed heartily), "and B——, when we were before the Justice, remarked on it, and came d——d near calling me a liar. It was lucky he didn't, for if he had, he'd have gone to h—l before the place was hot enough for him."

"I cannot tell you, my dear sir, how grateful I am to you for this. It would have pained me more than I can express, if Scip had suffered for doing a disinterested kindness to me."

Early in the morning we were again on our way, and twelve o'clock found us seated at a dinner of bacon, corn-bread, and waffles, in the "first hotel" of Georgetown. The Charleston boat was to leave at three o'clock; and, as soon as dinner was over, I sallied out to find Scip. After a half-hour's search I found him on "Shackelford's wharf," engaged in loading a schooner bound for New York with a cargo of cotton and turpentine.

He was delighted to see me, and when I had told him I was going home, and might never see him again, I took his hand warmly in mine, and said:

"Scip, I have heard of the disgrace that was near being put upon you on my account, and I feel deeply the disinterested service you did to me; now, I *can not* go away without doing *something* for you—showing you in *some* way that I appreciate and *like* you."

"I like's *you*, massa," he replied, the tears coming to his eyes: "I tuk ter you de bery fuss day I seed you, 'case, I s'pose," and he wrung my hand till it ached: "you pitied de pore brack man. But you karnt do nuffin fur *me*, massa; I doant want nuffin; I doant want ter leab har, 'case de Lord dat put me har, arn't willin' I shud gwo. But you kin do suffin, massa, fur de pore brack man,—an' dat 'll be doin' it fur *me*, 'case my heart am all in dat. You kin tell dem folks up dar, whar you lib, massa, dat we'm not like de brutes, as dey tink we is. Dat we's got souls, an' telligence, an' feelin's, an' am men like demselfs. You kin tell 'em, too, massa,—'case you's edication, and kin talk—how de pore wite man 'am kep' down har; how he'm ragged, an' starvin', an' ob no account, 'case de brack man am a slave. How der chil'ren can't get no schulein', how eben de grow'd up ones doan't know nuffin—not eben so much as de pore brack slave, 'case de 'stockracy wan't dar votes, an cudn't get 'em ef dey 'low'd 'em larning. Ef your folks know'd all de trufh—ef dey know'd how both de brack an' de pore w'ite man, am on de groun', and can't git up, ob demselfs—dey'd do suffin'—dey'd break de Constertution—dey'd do *suffin'* ter help us. I doant want no one hurted, I doant want no one wronged; but jess tink ob it, massa, four million ob bracks, and nigh so many pore wites, wid de bressed gospil shinin' down on 'em, an' dey not knowin' on it. All dem—ebry one of 'em—made in de image ob de great God, an' dey driven roun', an' 'bused wuss dan de brutes. You's seed dis, massa, wid your own eyes, an' you kin tell 'em on it; an' you *will* tell 'em on it, massa;" and again he took my hand while the tears rolled down his cheeks; "an' Scip will bress you fur it, massa; wid his bery lass breaf he'll bress you; an' de good Lord will bress you, too, massa; He will foreber bress you, fur He'm on de side ob de pore, an' de 'flicted : His own book say dat, an' it am true, I knows it, fur I feels it *har;*" and he laid his hand on his heart, and was silent.

I could not speak for a moment. When I mastered my feelings, I said, "I *will* do it Scip ; as God gives me strength, I *will.*"

Reader, I am keeping my word.

CHAPTER XX.

CONCLUSION.

This is not a work of fiction. It is a record of facts, and therefore the reader will not expect me to dispose of its various characters on artistic principles—that is, lay them away in one of those final receptacles for the creations of the romancer—the grave and matrimony. Death has been among them, but nearly all are yet doing their work in this breathing, busy world.

The characters I have introduced are real. They are not drawn with the pencil of fancy, nor, I trust, colored with the tints of prejudice. The scenes I have described are true. I have taken some liberties with the names of persons and places, and, in a few instances, altered dates; but the events themselves occurred under my own observation. No one acquainted with the section of country I have described, or familiar with the characters I have delineated, will question this statement. Lest some one who has not seen the slave and the poor white man of the South, as he actually is, should deem my picture overdrawn, I will say that "the half has not been told!" If the whole were related—if the Southern system, in all its naked ugliness, were fully exposed—the truth would read like fiction, and the baldest relation of fact like the wildest dream of romance.

* * * * * * *

The overseer was never taken. A letter which I received from Colonel J———, shortly prior to the stoppage of the mails, informed me that Moye had succeeded in crossing the mountains into Tennessee, where, in an interior town, he disposed of the horse, and then made his way by an inland route to the free states. The horse the Colonel had recovered, but the overseer he never expected to see. Moye is now, no doubt, somewhere in the North, and is probably at this present writing a zealous Union man, of somewhat the same "stripe" as the conductors of the New York *Herald* and the Boston *Courier*.

I have not heard directly from Scipio, but one day last July, after a long search, I found on one of the wharves of South Street, a coasting captain, who knew him well, and who had seen him the month previous at Georgetown. He was at that time pursuing his usual avocations, and was as much respected and trusted, as when I met him.

A few days after the tidings of the fall of Sumter were received in New York, and when I had witnessed the spontaneous and universal uprising of the North, which followed that event, I dispatched letters to several of my Southern friends, giving them as near as I could an account of the true state of feeling here, and representing the utter madness of the course the South was pursuing. One of these letters went to my Union acquaintance whom I have called, in the preceding pages, "Andy Jones."

He promptly replied, and a pretty regular correspondence ensued between us, which has continued, at intervals, even since the suspension of intercourse between the North and the South.

Andy has stood firmly and nobly by the old flag. At the risk of every thing, he has boldly expressed his sentiments everywhere. With his life in his hand, and—a revolver in each of his breeches-pockets, he walked the streets of Wilmington when the secession fever was at its height, openly proclaiming his undying loyalty to the Union, and "no man dared gainsay him."

But with all his patriotism, Andy keeps a bright eye on the "main chance." Like his brother, the Northern Yankee, whom he somewhat resembles and greatly admires, he never omits an opportunity of "turning an honest penny." In defiance of custom-house regulations, and of our strict blockade, he has carried on a more or less regular traffic with New York and Boston (*via* Halifax and other neutral ports), ever since North Carolina seceded. His turpentine—while it was still his property—has been sold in the New York market, under the very eyes of the government officials—and, honest reader, *I* have known of it.

By various roundabout means, I have recently received letters from him. His last, dated in April, and brought to a neutral port by a shipmaster whom he implicitly trusts, has reached me since the previous chapters were written. It covers six pages of foolscap, and is written in defiance of all grammatical and orthographical principles; but as it conveys important intelligence, in regard to some of the persons mentioned in this narrative, I will transcribe a portion of it.

It gave me the melancholy tidings of the death of Colonel J——. He had joined the Confederate army, and fell, bravely meeting a charge of the Massachusetts troops, at Roanoke.

On receiving the news of his friend's death, Andy rode over to the plantation, and found Madam P—— plunged in the deepest grief. While he was there a letter arrived from Charleston, with intelligence of the dangerous illness of her son. This second blow crushed her. For several days she was delirious, and her life despaired of; but throughout the whole the noble corn-cracker, neglecting every thing, remained beside her.

When she returned to herself, and had in a measure recovered her strength, she learned that the Colonel had left no will; that she was still a slave; and soon to be sold, with the rest of the Colonel's *personal property*, according to law.

This is what Andy writes about the affair. I give the letter as he wrote it, merely correcting the punctuation, and enough of the spelling, to make it intelligible.

"W'en I hard thet th' Cunel hadent leff no wil, I was hard put what ter dew; but arter thinkin' on it over a spell, I knowed shede har on it sumhow; so I 'cluded to tel har miseff. She tuk on d——d hard at fust, but arter a bit, grew more calm like, and then she sed it war God's wil, an' she wudent komplane. Ye nows I've got a wife, but wen the ma'am sed thet, she luk'd so like an angel, thet d——d eff I cud help puttin' my arms round har, an' hugin' on har, till she a'moste screeched. Wal, I toled har, Id stan' by har eff evrithing went ter h—l— an I wil, by ——.

"I made up mi minde to onst, what ter dew. It war darned harde work tur bee 'way from hum jess then, but I war in fur it; soe I put ter Charleston, ter see th' Cunel's 'oman. Wal, I seed har, an' I toled har how th' ma'am felte, an' how mutch shede dun at makein' th' Cunel's money—(she made nigh th' hul on it, 'case he war alers keerles, an' tuk no 'count uv things; eff tadent ben fur thet, hede made a wil,) an' I axed har ter see thet the ma'am had free papers ter onst. An' whot der ye 'spoze she sed? Nuthin, by —— 'cept she dident no nuthin' 'bout bisniss, an' leff all uv sech things ter har loryer. Wal, then I went ter him—he ar one on them slick, ily, seceshun houn's, who'd sell thar soles fur a kountterfit dollar—an' he toled me, th' 'ministratur hadent sot yit, an' he cudent dew nuthin til he hed. Ses I: 'ye mean th' 'ooman's got ter gwo ter th' hi'est bider?' 'Yas,' he sed, 'the Cunel's got dets, an' the've got ter bee pade, an' th' persoonel prop'ty muste bee sold ter dew it.' Then I sed, 'twud bee sum time fore thet war dun, an' the 'ooman's 'most ded an' uv no use now; 'what'll ye *hire* har tur me fur.' He sed a hun'red for sicks months. I planked down the money ter onst, an' put off.

"I war bilin' over, but it sumhow cum inter my hed thet the Cunnel's 'ooman cudn't bee *all* stun; so I gose thar agin; an' I toled har what the loryer sed, an' made a reg'lar stump-'peal tew har bettar natur. I axed har ef she'd leff the 'ooman who'd made har husban's fortun, who war the muther ov his chil'ren, who fur twenty yar, hed nussed him in sickness, an' cheered him in healtf; ef shede let *thet 'ooman*, bee auckyund off ter th' hi'est bider. I axed al thet, an' what der ye think she sed, Why jest this. '*I* doant no nuthin' bout it, Mister Jones. Ye raily must talke ter mi loryer; them maters I leaves 'tirely ter him.' Then, I sed, I 'spozed the niggers war ter bee advertist. 'O, yas!' she sed, (an' ye see, she know'd a d——d site 'bout *thet*), 'all on 'em muss be solde, 'case, ye knows, I never did luv the kuntry,—'sides *I* cud'ent karry on the plantashun, no how.' Then, sed I: 'the Orlean's traders 'ill be thar—an' she wunt sell fur but one use, fur she's hansum yit; an' ma'am, ye wunt leff a 'ooman as white as you is, who fur twenty yar, hes ben a tru an' fatheful *wife* tar yer own ded husban,' (I shudn't hev put thet in, but d——d ef I cud help it,) ye wunt put *har* up on the block, an' hev har struck down ter the hi'est bider, ter bee made a d——d —— on?'

"Wal, I s'pose she hadent forgot thet, fur more'n twelve yar, the Cunnel hed *luv'd* t'other 'ooman, an' onely *liked* har; fur w'en I sed thet, har ize snapped like h——l, an' she screetched eout thet she dident 'low no sech wurds in har hous', an' ordurd me ter leave. Mi'tey sqeemish thet, warn't it? bein' as shede ben fur so mony yar the Cunnel's ———, an' th' tuther one his raal wife.

"Wal, I *did* leav'; but I left a piece of mi mind a-hind. I toled har I'de buy that ar 'ooman ef she cost all I war wuth and I had ter pawne my sole ter git the money; an' I added, jess by way ov sweet'nin' the pill, thet I ow'd all I hed ter har husband, an' dident furget *my* debts ef she did *her'n*, an' ef his own wife disgraced him, I'd be d——d ef *I* wud.

"Wal, I've got th' ma'am an' har boy ter hum, an' my 'ooman hes tuk ter har a heep. I doant no w'en the sale's ter cum off, but ye may bet hi' on my bein' thar; an' I'll buy har ef I hev ter go my hull pile on har, an' borrer th' money fur ole Pomp. But *he'll* go cheap, 'case the Cunnel's deth nigh dun him up. It clean killed Ante Lucey. She never held her hed up arter she hoerd 'Masser Davy' war dead, fur she sot har vary life on him. Don't ye fele consarned 'bout the ma'am—I knows ye sot hi' on har—*I'll buy har*, shore. Thet an' deth ar th' onely things thet I knows on, in this wurld, jess now, that ar SARTIN."

Such is Andy's letter. Mis-spelled and profane though it be, I would not alter a word or a syllable of it. It deserves to be written in characters of gold, and hung up in the sky, where it might be read by all the world. And it *is* written in the sky—in the great record-book—

and it will be read when you and I, reader, meet the assembled universe, to give account of what *we* have done and written. God grant that our record may show some such deed as that!

THE END.

www.ingramcontent.com/pod-product-compliance
Lightning Source LLC
Chambersburg PA
CBHW022051230426
43672CB00008B/1137